D1348438

STEPHEN
HENDRY

STEPHEN
HENDRY

ME AND THE TABLE

MY AUTOBIOGRAPHY

JOHN BLAKE

First published in Great Britain by John Blake Publishing,
an Imprint of Kings Road Publishing
Suite 2.25 The Plaza
535 Kings Road
London SW10 0SZ

www.johnblakebooks.com

www.facebook.com/johnblakebooks
twitter.com/jblakebooks

First published in paperback in 2018

Hardback ISBN: 978 1 78606 568 1
Trade Paperback ISBN: 978 1 78606 871 2
Ebook: 978 1 78606 904 7

British Library Cataloguing-in-Publication Data:
A catalogue record for this book is available from the British Library.

Design by www.envydesign.co.uk

Printed and bound in Great Britain by Clays Ltd, Elcograf S p. A

1 3 5 7 9 10 8 6 4 2

Papers used by John Blake Publishing are natural, recyclable products made from
wood grown in sustainable forests. The manufacturing processes conform to the
environmental regulations of the country of origin.

Every attempt has been made to contact the relevant copyright-holders, but some
were unobtainable. We would be grateful if the appropriate people could contact us.

John Blake Publishing is an imprint of Bonnier Books UK
www.bonnierbooks.co.uk

CONTENTS

PROLOGUE

May 2012, Sheffield, UK – World Snooker Championship
(quarter-final)

'm sitting – actually, I'm almost sagging – in my dressing room backstage at the Crucible Theatre as I reflect on the missed pink that has allowed my opponent to snatch the fourth frame. I guess I'm embarrassed, though in truth I'm past crucifying myself for stupid mistakes like the one I've just made. The collective intake of breath from the audience at the miss only confirms in my mind what I already know; that after seven World Championship wins, five UK Championships, six Masters wins and a whole bunch of other triumphs and records broken, my game is gone. Now it's time for me to go with it.

Why, after a run of poor performances following my last World Championship win more than ten years previously, am I still here? I'm now out of the top sixteen in the rankings; this season's championship is the first one I've had to qualify for since I was a teenager. After everything I've achieved, to have to do this feels beneath me. The qualifiers are not played at the Crucible but at Sheffield's Institute of Sport, in a hall with around six tables and only a small audience attending. I don't mean to take anything away from those I'm playing against in these preliminary rounds, but this isn't what I'm used to. When you've beaten almost every record in the game, knocking balls around a table in an uninspiring hall is a humiliating and depressing experience. At this stage I just want to qualify, saving what's left of my snooker for the main event. I'm up against the Chinese player Yu Delu. It's not pretty snooker. My only thought is about getting to the ten frames. I play solidly, aiming to win as quickly as I can, just to make it to the Crucible.

I'm glad I'm through, and for this reason: I have already made the decision that this will be my last World Championship. In fact, it will be my last tournament ever in professional snooker. I've decided to retire. I've talked to Mandy, my wife, about it and she agrees that I'm not playing as well as I used to.

'If you're not winning or enjoying it any more,' she says, 'what's the point of carrying on?'

I don't disagree. Neither am I sorry. In fact, I'm relieved – relieved that I will no longer have to play in public the kind of snooker I've been playing. I won't have to go through the tedious motions of practice day in, day out, which I haven't really been doing anyway. Since turning professional I'd always practised in the same club, the John Spencer's, in Stirling, but when this was sold I needed somewhere else to go. The solution seemed obvious: to convert the triple-garage adjacent to my house into a practice room. This was done, and the space was made as comfortable as possible. Too comfortable, in fact. I'll set off to practice at about 11am – the time I've always stuck to – and do an hour before it's tea-break time. The radio or TV hums away nicely in the background, and what is meant to be a quick break becomes fifteen minutes, thirty minutes, an hour and sometimes an entire afternoon. Then I'll say to myself, 'Ach, no worries – I'll just do it again tomorrow.' All my discipline, intensity and focus has gone in one easy move. I've always thought of practice as going to work – now it is something I do if I feel like it.

Also, I won't have to play in a series of smaller tournaments I'm not interested in, just to keep in the rankings. I've convinced myself that I can no longer play as well as I used to, and it has become a self-fulfilling prophecy. Every time I miss a ball or lose a match I think, 'There you go . . . told you so. You're not up to it. Your game's gone.' And it has. It truly has.

Back in the auditorium, as I sit in my chair, enviously watching my opponent at the table, the surroundings of the Crucible Theatre disappear, to be replaced by a TV studio in Birmingham. The year is 1983, and a small-for-his-age fourteen-year-old Scottish boy is about to make his screen debut playing snooker. It's the quarter-final of *Junior Pot Black*, the under-sixteens version of the hugely popular BBC snooker knockout series. This kid has made it to the quarter-finals through sheer determination. He's only been playing the game for about eighteen months, but already he's won the Pontins 'Star of the Future' snooker tournament and the Scottish and British Under-16s Championships. He has natural talent, sure, but there is something else at work here – the will to win, and win well. No prizes for guessing who this wee boy is.

At the age of fourteen I'm playing for the sheer love of the game and the fun of it. Everything about my playing style is totally natural. My stance, the way I cue, the determination to clear up as quickly as possible, never giving my opponent a second chance – it's all intuition and learning from watching snooker on TV. I need to use the rest often because of my size (as commentator Ted Lowe helpfully points out) but even as a raw kid I'm aggressively break-building, going for everything with a fearlessness that doesn't quite sit right on an awkward teenager who looks about ten.

My dad, Gordon, is at Pebble Mill to see my first appearance on TV. He watches all my early games. Dad is my kind-of manager and driver and, with my mum Irene and brother Keith, my biggest supporter.

'Our Stephen's gonna be World Champion one day,' he'll say to anyone who cares to listen.

Both he and my mum are innocently confident this will happen. They aren't pushy – they know that at my age anything can change, and that one morning I might wake up and totally lose interest in the whole thing. But I doubt it, and so do they.

I win the *Junior Pot Black* quarter-final convincingly, beating my opponent 70–23. But in the semi-final I go out to a cocky kid a few years older than me. I'm devastated. I'm asked a few interview questions after the game and I can barely get my words out, so choked up am I. Even so, when the experience of losing is behind me I realise that I've enjoyed every minute of that tournament and want to do it again. And again, and again.

What a contrast to now – a dejected, depressed-looking former champion trying and failing to hang on to past glories. And yet, despite myself, in the first round of this World Championship I make a maximum break during the game against Stuart Bingham. It's my eleventh professional 147, setting a personal record. Bingham misses an easy red to the left-middle pocket and in I go. For the length of this break I'm on fire again. Five or six shots in I get the feeling that I can make the maximum and the magic returns as I concentrate and stay focused. This is how I used to be for an entire tournament. Now it is for just a few minutes, but when it happens the will to win overrides everything else. I taste the anticipation as the crowd senses something major is brewing. During the break there are flashes of the old me – keen to quickly pot again even as the referee is placing the ball back on the spot – and when I see off the final black I pump my fist in the air to the cheering crowd. And so we have a delighted audience and praise from the commentators, and I take home around £50,000 in bonus money for my efforts. Should I be overjoyed? Of course I should. Who wouldn't be? And I am – it's a 147 break that has required ten minutes or so of pure adrenalin and focus. But in my heart I know that out of the thirty-six shots it takes to make the maximum, I'm only happy with about five or six of them. When I pot the first black I barely shift the pack of reds. In years gone by I'd have sent them scattering, allowing them to be picked off easily. Nonetheless, I'm celebrating with uncharacteristic emotion – it's because I know I will never repeat such a feat at this venue.

'Who says he's not the player he was!?' shouts TV commentator John Virgo.

Me – I say it.

I win the match 10–4 and in the second round I'm facing John Higgins. John is a one of the game's greats and I worry that he'll humiliate me. I'd have never let such a thing trouble me in the past, but even as I reach the table I'm fretting about my concentration and my courage. Luckily, John is having a real off-day. The game is scrappy for both of us, although we both make century breaks. If anything, John is under more pressure than I am because he's the defending World Champion, and perhaps because he and I have never played each other at the Crucible. This is – or was – my turf. It has been the setting for my greatest games and the place that sealed my reputation. So for various reasons John has something to prove, whereas I'm not certain I do any more. Later, John says it's the worst he's ever played at the Crucible and I believe him. I beat him 13–4 and to my astonishment I'm into the quarter-final against Stephen Maguire.

With no disrespect to my opponent, I could be playing anybody, from the greatest to the lowest, because the fire and flair with which I played more than a decade previously has disappeared. Yet I know that with determination, I can win.

With a renewed dose of the courage and concentration I once took for granted, I could get into the semis and, yes, I could win the whole tournament. The Stephen Hendry of old would know this instinctively; the new one, however, is nowhere near as certain, and as the game begins it's clear that my opponent has the hunger and the will to win that I lack. Maguire takes the first three frames and in the fourth I'm clearing up to win the frame, but I get on the wrong side of the blue. I pot that, but when I get down to the pink I have only 20 per cent confidence that I'm going to pot it. I butcher it and lose the frame. I'm disgusted with myself. The fourteen-year-old who practically jogged around the table in Birmingham the best part of thirty years ago would never have messed up so badly.

There is a short interval, and as I head back to the dressing room I realise that any last hopes of a miracle happening and me winning this year's championship are gone, leaving me feeling embarrassed and dejected.

By my dressing-room door I see Chris Henry, my snooker coach.

'It's over, mate,' I say to him.

'Ah, come on, Stephen,' he says. 'It's still early. You can't give in yet. Just focus.'

But I tell myself that I'll not come back from this. In my mind, the game is over. I've mentally conceded it, even before I go back out there. As Maguire continues his onslaught I can only watch and brood. I'm jealous that he's on the table, racking up the points, locking into the zone that comes with the will to win. And in a strange way I'm willing him on – simply because I can no longer be bothered. All I'm thinking about is how bad my game is, what I will say at the post-match press conference, how I will spend my retirement. My focus is completely, utterly gone and I look as miserable as sin – even more miserable than they normally say I look. My body language gives it away; slumped, dejected, down-in-the-mouth.

At one point I even say, 'Well played,' to Maguire. When I win a second frame, I tell him, 'It's just delaying the inevitable.' What am I saying? I'm actually being a good sport – something I'd never have done when I was playing to win, and win well. I wouldn't give an inch back then. And now?

I play the occasional decent shot – every twenty shots or so – and when I do I think, 'Oh, that wasn't so bad . . . maybe I'm in this game after all.' Then the demon pops back in and tells me 'no' – and sure enough, the next nineteen shots are terrible. Finally, it's over. I lose the match 13–2 and during the press conference I announce my retirement from the game. 'It's time to move on,' I say, 'to spend less time on the road, to be at home more,' blah, blah – the kind of things you feel you should say on these occasions. Normally when I've lost badly, my answers to journalists' questions aren't much more illuminating than 'yes' or 'no'. Now, in my defeat, I'm being gracious and courteous because I know it's all over – game, set, match and career. The applause from the gathered reporters as the press conference finishes is perhaps testament to that. The truth is, my game's dreadful and it's making me feel that way about myself. I pack away my cue and sign a few autographs as I leave via the stage door and head straight back up to Scotland. The King of the Crucible has well and truly lost his crown – and he couldn't be more relieved.

CHAPTER 1

My parents are young – just teenagers – when they meet at work. Irene is a secretary, working at a woollen merchant's in Edinburgh that supplies high-class Savile Row tailors such as Gieves & Hawkes. She is from Kirkliston, a small town in West Lothian where everyone knows each other, and each other's business. They certainly know Irene's mother's business, because she has left her husband for another man and has had a baby by him, and in 1960s small-town Scotland that is big news indeed. Irene leaves school at fifteen, without qualifications, but like many working-class people is far from stupid, as she'll prove in later life. She becomes a secretary and is working hard to earn money for her family when she meets Gordon Hendry. He's a tall, gap-toothed young guy, the well-dressed son of a bookmaker whose background is a cut above Mum's. Despite being shy and reserved, Gordon is attracted to the outgoing, chatty girl behind the typewriter. They begin courting, the inevitable happens and she is pregnant. There is more scandal about Mum's family to tut over behind the curtains of respectable Kirkliston. Mum leaves home under a cloud and moves to Edinburgh, hoping never to have to return to the town she calls 'Peyton Place'.

At first, Mum and Dad live in one room of his grandmother's apartment in St Leonards, just below Arthur's Seat. They must share an outside bathroom with another couple and, at eighteen, Mum is now preparing for life as a full-time mother. There will be no possibility of her going back to work now – in this era, women who have babies don't do that sort of thing. And in January 1969 I come along – blond and (according to my mother) beautiful. Three is more than a crowd in an already cramped apartment and so my parents move to Robertson Avenue, Gorgie, which is where I spend my early years.

What do I inherit from my parents? Looks-wise, I'm like my dad, and in personality too. He's a quiet guy, not given to a huge amount of conversation and not one for having masses of friends. So it's appropriate that I'm given his first name as my middle name. From my mother? Skinny ankles and, more importantly, her drive and determination; I'm nothing if not a determined kid, despite the shyness. When I'm first up and walking I take a ramble down the stairs of the apartment and out on to the busy Edinburgh street. My mother is pegging out washing in the back yard and hasn't noticed I've gone until a passing stranger kindly returns me, having spotted me out on the road. There are tears and slapped legs in equal measure. My determination not to be fazed by much is put to good use when my mother finds herself reluctant to overcome her fear of mice and sends me toddling into the living room before her, so that the little creatures will scuttle out of sight before she arrives.

It's obvious we're not living in the best of circumstances and by 1972, when my brother Keith has arrived, Mum and Dad decide to move out of the city. New estates are being built in Baberton, south-west of Edinburgh, and it's to Baberton Mains that the Hendry family decamp. My dad is now working in the fruit-and-vegetable wholesale business and still needs to be close to the city's fruit market in Gorgie, where he's spending long hours learning the trade. Another kind of education is going on at my new primary school, Juniper Green, but right from day one it's obvious I'm no scholar. I enjoy learning to write but other subjects, particularly maths, are beyond me and will continue to be so right through my school career. I make efforts to keep up but, to put it mildly, I'm just not that interested. I like lunchtimes – even if the thick skin on the custard that smothers the treacle tart makes me feel slightly weird – and I also like sports, but I have an aversion to swimming. I'm aware that as a very small child I fell into a stream and remained under the water for a few seconds before being hauled out, screaming at the top of my lungs. Though the details of this incident have long since been buried, the feelings of suffocation and panic persist and I'm very reluctant to join the crowd of excited kids heading to the local pool. If I can get out of it, I will.

I'm small for my age, so although I appear to have good coordination and movement I'm none too keen to get involved in sports that involve a degree of contact. I hate rugby and, although I will play it, football can be intimidating too because I don't like being tackled. I have a low threshold for pain and would rather avoid confrontation than get into the thick of the action. This is a pity, as I love football. Gorgie's boundaries include Tynecastle Park, home of Heart of Midlothian Football Club, the team my dad supports. From an early age I'm taken to home games by Dad and his brother George, inevitably known as 'Dod' (a nickname for George peculiar to Scotland). Before kick-off we make a pilgrimage to a nearby social club, smoke-filled and packed with men who are full of beer and chat. I sit on a tatty plastic chair and swing my legs a foot from the floor while munching a huge Wagon Wheel biscuit bought from the paper shop. Dad, Dod and their pals seemingly talk endlessly about

Hearts, accompanied by pint after pint of McEwan's Export or Tartan bitter. I'm bored out of my mind and I hate the smell of smoky clubs – ironic, really, when so much of my future will be lived out in them.

'Stop the chatting,' I think, 'let's just get to the game.'

Eventually we're there, pushing our way through the turnstiles and up on to the terrace, where the sound of the crowd is like the crashing of ocean waves. At the top of the steps the atmosphere really hits; all these people, pushing and shoving, bawling and bantering, singing their hearts out, just waiting for Jim Brown, Drew Busby, Jim Cruickshank and the rest to emerge from the tunnel. When they do, I swear the roar can be heard right across Edinburgh.

Winger Bobby Prentice is my favourite. Very often we're standing up close to him, as he's playing at number eleven, and right from a young age I notice the flair with which he sweeps and dribbles through the opposition. No messing around or safety play here: Bobby is heading for the goalmouth, to score or to set one up, and the home crowd is pushing him on. Dad and Dod are roaring, jumping up and down when Hearts score and bawling their 'advice' when they don't. I see the contrast between my dad's quiet demeanour at home and his animated personality in the ground. This is the way he lets off steam – during the week he's incredibly hard-working and he's almost always late in at night.

Back at school on a Monday I'm keen to copy what I've seen on the pitch the previous weekend. I'm small but I'm quick, and I earn a place in the football team. We play on Saturday mornings, and on Friday nights I'm beside myself with excitement, cleaning my boots, laying out my kit and just preparing for the match ahead. Like Bobby, I play on the left wing as I can kind-of kick with both feet, but I'm still not confident up against the bigger guys who want to send me sprawling across the pitch. As I say, I'm not into pain.

We play badminton at school and I work my way into that team too. I like the competitive element and that it's a non-contact sport. We play various tournaments against other schools around Edinburgh, including at the Meadowbank Stadium, which hosted the Commonwealth Games in 1970. At one such tournament there I'm the only player in my team not to win a game. I'm gutted. The fact that people are watching me crash to defeat makes it worse. My parents try to console me.

'It's just a game, Stephen.'

'It's the taking part that counts, not the winning.'

'Sometimes you win, sometimes you lose.'

But I don't want to lose. I want to win, and not just that – I want to win well. I want to beat everyone else. I hate losing.

I also hate tartan. One summer, when I'm about eight or nine, my dad's sister gets married and Keith and I are employed as pageboys, in matching kilts and jackets. We've probably had our hair cut into the same style too. I feel like the biggest idiot and I swear that from this day forward I will never wear a kilt again. Mum seems to enjoy dressing Keith and me up in similar clothes, and at another family wedding we're kitted out in matching dark-brown velvet jumpers and flared cream trousers. I might look back now and cringe, but my parents are snappy, stylish dressers and I'm inheriting that. I'm starting to learn what I like and don't like.

Maybe the desire of my parents for us all to look well dressed comes from an upturn in their fortunes. By the end of the 1970s Dad is out of the wholesale side of the fruit-and-veg business and, with a partner, has obtained the lease of three greengrocers' shops; one in Inverkeithing, one in Dalgety Bay and the third (and largest) in Dunfermline. He's working harder than ever, and as a family we're seeing even less of him. We're a happy family, I think, but there's not much sitting round the dinner table discussing things the way families on TV seem to do. More often than not it's our dinner on our knee and *Crackerjack* or *Top of the Pops*. Dad comes in late, having gone for a pint on the way home from work, and goes to bed. I don't see much closeness between him and Mum; no hugging or kissing, or much affection of any kind. Being young, I think nothing of this. Later, the gap between them will widen more obviously.

Dad's work gives the Hendry family little time for holidays and often Keith and I – sometimes just I – go off with Mum's mum, whom we call 'Granville'. She and her second husband Dod take us and their son George (who is just a few years older than me) away in their caravan into Ayrshire or around northern Scotland. The scenery is spectacular, of course, but often the weather is less than kind and we spend days looking out of the caravan's plastic windows into the wind and rain. I'm badly travel-sick too, which doesn't add much to the holiday atmosphere, but despite all this we always manage to have a good time and a laugh. George and I get on particularly well and we snigger uncontrollably when Dod farts loudly as he wakes up in the morning.

Occasionally on summer mornings Dad will take me to the fruit market in Gorgie to buy the produce for the shops. I'm usually not one for an early start, particularly in the holidays, but now and then I'll make up my mind to go with him. I like travelling in the van, and the feeling of going to work. At 5am the market is packed full of traders inspecting the goods and haggling for deals. The air is thick with the smell of ripe fruit, and the vivid colours are a wake-up call for tired eyes. Dad goes from dealer to dealer, finding the best prices for his customers. When he's done, and the van is loaded up, we head for Dunfermline, Inverkeithing and Dalgety Bay, always stopping off at the same paper shop for breakfast – which for me is a can of juice and a Topic. Dad buys fags and we set off again, not saying much but not uncomfortable in our mutual silence.

Dad is spending more and more time in Fife, just across the Firth of Forth, where the shops are located. Eventually it is decided that it makes sense for us to move over the water and, conveniently, we have a house to move into. My Auntie Christine's husband has a job in Egypt, so their bungalow is vacant. Dalgety Bay has seen a lot of house-building since the 1960s and its status as a commuter town near Edinburgh gives me the idea that it is a bit 'posh'. The house is detached and has a garage and a garden – ideal for a family with two growing boys who need to run off their energy somehow. There are great views of the Forth Bridge across the bay and, although I must leave my school in Baberton Mains and finish my primary education in a new place, I'm not at all unhappy about the move. Within a year I'm a new pupil at Inverkeithing High School, a couple of miles up the road from where we're living. It's a standard school of the period, educating about 1,300 kids of varying degrees of ability.

My contribution to school life is unremarkable. Each day I go through the motions of turning up, attending classes, hanging around with the friends I'm making and going home. Aside from sport and English there is not a lesson being taught that holds the slightest bit of interest for me. I'm not stupid; I'm just not really 'there'. My reports say things like, 'Needs to concentrate more' or 'Is a bit of a dreamer'. I don't hate school and I don't particularly like it. I just take the attitude that it's something you need to get through, day-by-day, until it's finished. My chattering in class earns me the belt two or three times. In Scotland this is known as the 'tawse', a stiff leather strap a couple of inches wide, its end divided into two 'tails' like the forked tongue of a snake. These tails are the source of all the pain as they catch the palm of your hand. One time I'm belted by a science teacher for messing around with a Bunsen burner in class. The sting of it remains in the mind long after the physical pain has gone away. I feel it's unfair, but I don't complain – that's not the sort of thing pupils do in the early 1980s.

Besides, it can be a rough school. Playground fights are frequent and because I'm still small I shy away from confrontation with bigger, older boys. And I'm not as keen on playing football as I was. Everyone appears to be growing apart from me, and they all seem interested in throwing their newly gained muscle around, particularly on the sports field. Small kids like me are useful targets and before long I'm forging my mum's handwriting to get out of rugby and the dreaded swimming. I particularly hate having to get undressed for that – it's all so embarrassing, and a drag.

But all told, Keith and I are lucky kids. At this time, Scotland is going through the recession which is hitting the rest of the UK, particularly in industrial and manufacturing towns and cities. But Dad's business is doing well, and we want for nothing. We're not spoiled by any means, but when Christmas or birthdays come around we always get the presents we want – golf clubs, bikes, sports stuff, Subbuteo. Christmases are fun times; the family are around, and Mum and Dad seem happy with life. As I head towards my teens my parents find it more and more difficult to buy me presents I haven't already had. Which is why, in the run-up to Christmas 1981, Mum and I are trailing up the main shopping street in Dunfermline, the nearest large town, and she's scratching her head as she looks in various toy-shop windows.

'I just don't know what to get you,' she says. 'You two have everything you'd ever want or need. What *do* you want, Stephen?'

Unhelpfully, I reply that I don't know. And I don't. I can't think of a single thing. For my parents, the post-Christmas period always involves the headache of having to go back to the shops each January to seek out my birthday presents. In January 1982 I'll turn thirteen and, like most young people on the cusp of teenagehood, I'm not the most communicative person in the world. I don't know what I want out of life, never mind Christmas.

Eventually we come to John Menzies, the newsagent and general retailer. Mum looks in the window, then points to the biggest thing on display.

'What do you think of that?'

I shrug my shoulders. 'Sure,' I reply, 'it looks fun. Yeah, that would be great, thanks.'

There is a sigh of relief from Mum.

'I'll have a word with your dad,' she says, 'but I'm sure it'll be OK. I wonder how much it is.'

She cranes her neck to look at the price: £117. 'Maybe I'll put a deposit on it,' she says. 'Just in case it goes.'

Mum roots in her purse for a tenner and gestures me to the doorway of the shop. I follow her inside, wondering what it will be like to have a snooker table in the house.

Top 5 MEMORIES OF CHILDHOOD

1. Getting a Grifter bike for Christmas
2. Playing Subbuteo
3. Reading Famous Five books
4. Receiving The Broons and Oor Wullie Christmas annuals
5. Wearing a new Hearts strip

CHAPTER 2

My dad is beginning to lose his temper now. Three times he's asked me if I'm ready to go. We're due at Nana's – my dad's mum – in Musselburgh at 3pm for Christmas dinner and I haven't even got changed out of my pyjamas.

'Stephen,' he says, his voice infused with irritation, 'if you don't go down the corridor and sort yourself out now you'll make us late!'

I hear him, but barely react. I need to pot the blue, then the pink and, finally, the black. Then I'll have won. I have no opponent but that doesn't matter; I'll have potted every ball, taken the trophy. It's been this way since my brother Keith and I stumbled out of our beds at 6am, keen to see what 'Santa' had delivered for us.

Of course, I already knew what mine would be and in the weeks between the chance encounter with the snooker table in John Menzies' window and Christmas Day I've been taking an ever-increasing interest in the game and its stars. The UK Championship, played at Preston's Guild Hall, has just finished and I've watched it on TV every moment I can. I need to know the rules of the game, how the table is set up, what the players are wearing, how they hold the cue, how they pot the balls, how they look when they're not at the table, what the referee's job is – I need to find out everything about this game, because I want to get up on Christmas morning and be able to play snooker.

This year, the only true winner in professional snooker is Steve Davis. He's just twenty-four, but to me he looks every inch the grown-up sportsman that he is. This year, Steve has won the World Championship, the English Professional title, the Classic and International Masters titles and now the UK Championship. Steve is suddenly everywhere and, while he's not giving much away off the table, he plays like a machine. I think of him as almost robotic in the coolly deliberate way he destroys his opponents.

And then there's Jimmy White; Jimmy the Londoner who really grabs my attention. Jimmy is still a teenager and in less than a month I will be one too. The 'Whirlwind' has more than a whiff of danger about him as he circles the table like a shark, snapping at everything in sight. He smashes open the reds and effortlessly slots them away into the pockets, preparing the next shot even as the ref is placing a colour back on the table. There is no hesitancy, only speed; Jimmy plays like a man who needs to be somewhere else, and in a hurry. I love how quickly he finishes his frames, and how he controls the cue ball. The fluency of his game has, in 1981, earned him the Northern Ireland Classic and Scottish Masters titles, and it's reckoned that one day he'll be World Champion too if he can find a chink in Davis's armour.

Jimmy is cool. Jimmy looks like he was born under a green baize table. He's a left-hander, which makes him stand out, and I admire the way he runs rings round the older guys on the circuit. Jimmy is already my hero. And now, as I pot ball after ball, I think only of Jimmy and the flowing, easy way he demonstrates the naturalness of his cue action.

'Stephen!'

Reluctantly, I lay my cue on the table and go to find my best clothes.

'How long are we gonna be?' I ask. 'Can we just have the food and come home?'

'You have all your holidays to play with your table,' Mum replies.

She's right, and I spend the next two weeks at my table, day in, day out. Keith plays me a time or two, but I dispatch him quickly and think nothing of it. He's younger than me, and that's what you do to younger brothers. Besides, he's got his own Christmas presents to play with. He's not really interested in mine. I continue playing imaginary games against Steve Davis or Alex 'Hurricane' Higgins or Tony Meo; all these players are now very familiar to me as if they're standing in the room. From the corner of my eye I catch my dad watching me closely as I pot a red and line up perfectly on the next colour. I like it that I seem to be in full control of the cue, and that my feet have found a natural, comfortable stance.

'You're getting good at that, Stephen,' he says. 'You're enjoying it, right?'

'It's fantastic,' I say. 'Best present ever.'

'Good. Well, let's have a game on Sunday, when I'm not working. What d'you reckon?'

'I reckon I'll beat you, Dad,' I say.

Dad smiles confidently. Although he only plays the occasional game in the pub, he thinks he has snooker in him. Dad's bookmaker father, now deceased, was by all accounts a very good player indeed. He played around Edinburgh's snooker clubs and had enough about him to turn pro. Why he didn't is a mystery, but I'm guessing being a bookie was a far more lucrative occupation than playing snooker back then.

Sunday comes, and after dinner I take Dad up on his challenge. He breaks first, pots a couple of reds early, taking the brown and yellow with them. Then he misses and it's my turn. I make a break of about twenty or so and, although Dad tries, he's unable to catch up. The frame is mine.

'Best of three?'

Fine by me. He wins the next frame, but only just, and I take the deciding frame very quickly.

'Well played,' he says.

'It feels easy,' I reply.

'Oh, thanks a lot! I'm not that bad . . .'

'No, I didn't mean that.' Now I'm embarrassed. 'I just mean . . . it seems to come easily to me. I don't find it hard, that's all.'

Christmas and Hogmanay slide by, the table's celebrity billing as the star of our living room is over and it is reassembled in my bedroom. This is a problem in some ways, because the room is small and the space around the table so narrow that only a kid of my dimensions can squeeze around it and play the shots he needs to play. Despite some discomfort I keep up the practising, hours at a time. I know what's on the horizon, and that before long my beloved table and I will be parted – for a few hours a day, at least. It's now early January 1982 and, for me, it's back to school.

If I was uninterested before, now I'm almost completely disengaged from the education process. I go through the motions, as I've always done, and cause very little trouble, but it's just not happening. All I want to do is get through the day as quickly as possible, so I can go home and practise snooker in my bedroom. I might squeeze in a cursory twenty minutes or so of homework, just to keep on the right side of the teachers. Even now, on the cusp of teenagehood, all I can think, eat, drink, breathe and sleep is snooker.

Ten reds (it's a quarter-sized table), six colours. Red-colour, red-colour, red-colour, red-colour, red-colour, red-colour, red-colour, red-colour, red-colour, red-colour. Yellow-green-brown-blue-pink-black. And repeat. You miss? Set the table up, start again, from the top. Red-colour, red-colour, red-colour, red-colour, red-colour, red-colour, red-colour, red-colour, red-colour, red-colour. Yellow-green-brown-blue-pink-black. And repeat. I swear that my dreams are punctuated by reds, greens, pinks, blues and more reds, swirling all over the baize, bouncing off the cushions, dropping into the pockets.

Within a few weeks I'm making forty- or fifty-point breaks easily. Keith isn't interested in playing against me and even Dad is wary. No one likes to lose, and he does lose – often. A couple of weeks after my thirteenth birthday, on 13 January, he wonders if I want to go to the local snooker club, Maloco's in Dunfermline, for a game on a full-sized table?

Yes, I do want to go, badly. I want to stride around a 'proper' table, just like Jimmy White, with a light suspended above it, blocking out any distractions. I want to hear the slapback 'clack!' of a full-sized cue ball as it clatters into a red or a colour.

Maloco's is just off the High Street. It's been there for many years and has seen better days. The emerging snooker boom which is forcing other clubs, particularly in England, to smarten up their act, appears to have bypassed Maloco's completely. Quite frankly, it's a bit of a dive, even down to the balls we're given; each red is a different shade and one or two even have tiny chips out of them. There is one table where all the reds match and the baize remains untorn. This, we're told, is reserved for the 'best players', not for the likes of me or Dad. I don't care. I'm just so delighted to be here, with my dad and his brother Dod, in this fuggy, old-school snooker hall with its high, arched ceiling, rows of tables and men – always men; contrary to what my dad expects, there are no boys here,

STEPHEN HENDRY

and certainly no females – lurking in the shadows, cue in one hand, cigarette in the other. Smoke drifts up past the canopy lights and hangs in the air like a cloud. There is very little conversation; only the 'tcchh-ka!' of cue against ball disturbs the silence. Straight away, I love it.

The tables themselves seem huge, four times the size of mine. But, to my joy, I recognise that I'll be able to walk easily around them, unlike the one squashed against the wall in my bedroom. Dad and Dod select a table and begin to set up the balls. I'm suddenly aware that I'm not going to stand a cat in hell's chance of playing on this table the way I'd like – it's too big, and I'm too small. I'll have to use the rests – the spider, the extended spider and the swan-neck – to be within a fighting chance of potting anything. Dad catches me looking at the table and seems to know what I'm thinking. But I'm here now, and I've no intention of sitting quietly in the corner with a Coke and a bag of crisps while he and Dod enjoy frame after frame.

Dad breaks, and he and Dod knock balls around for five minutes or so. Then Dad nods to me, gesturing me over.

'Go on, son,' he says, 'give it a knock.'

With my Christmas cue I aim to put a red into the left middle. On my table it would've been an easy pot. Here, the cue ball dribbles towards its target and gently taps it. Dad and Dod laugh, and Dad hands me a full-sized cue.

'You're going to need to give it some welly with this, Stephen,' Dod says, 'else you'll never pot a thing.'

I take the advice, discovering that I need to hit the cue ball nearly twice as hard as I have been doing, particularly over the longer shots. After a while I settle into the rhythm that the longer cue and bigger table require and, although everything is a stretch, eventually I manage to put a red away and set myself up for a decent knock on a brown, which I also pot. A feeling

24

comes over me; the same feeling I've been experiencing when I've been making good breaks on the small table at home. It's the sensation that, somehow, you're unstoppable. At this age, of course, I'm very stoppable, but already I know that I have confidence in the way I play. Dad and Dod stand aside as I clear two more reds and colours. A guy playing at the next table looks up for a moment.

'The wee man's no' bad,' he says. 'What age is he?'

'Just turned thirteen,' says my dad. 'He got a little table for Christmas.'

'Guid on him,' says the man, resuming his game.

I'm silent, of course, and blushing deeper than any faded red on the table. 'Wee man' indeed. Cheeky sod! My height is a bone of contention and regularly I wonder why I'm not growing like a lot of the other kids in my class. No matter. I'll just have to get used to using the rests.

We play for an hour or so, bashing the balls around, until Dad looks at his watch. 'Home time, Stephen,' he says. 'You've school tomorrow.'

I shake my head in frustration. I don't want to leave this place, ever. And I certainly don't want to swap it for boring school. I ask if we can come back again soon. Dad nods in affirmation. I smile. This place feels like home and I can't wait to return.

Within a couple of days Dad and I are back again. As soon as I walk through the door I'm hooked again by the atmosphere of this place, faded pink balls and all. Dad sets up and I break impatiently, wanting to get the game under way. This time, I'm a little more confident and when the initial excitement of being there has settled I find my feet and get down to the job of building a break.

Soon I'm something of a regular at Maloco's, shyly acknowledging the nods and winks of the older guys at the tables as I slip past them. Dad is still accompanying me, and occasionally I catch a look of pride steal across his face as he notices the club's elder statesmen watching me. Snooker is becoming ever more popular, and the youthfulness and skill of players like Steve and Jimmy are drawing in big TV audiences. I get the occasional comment about winning this or that championship one day, but I don't take any of it seriously. At this stage, I'm just enjoying potting balls and soaking up the vibe of the club.

After a month or two of visits to Maloco's, Dad arrives home one day clutching the local newspaper. 'Look at this,' he says to me. 'A new snooker club is opening in the town next week. We should give it a whirl.'

Wide-eyed, I read the article. The new club – called the Classic Snooker Centre – sounds amazing and when, in a week's time, we make it through the doors my heart leaps. This place is a world away from smoky old Maloco's; the tables are brand new, the fresh-smelling carpets are free of cigarette burns and chewing gum and – best of all – the balls are the colours they should be. This is like stepping into a five-star hotel after a dingy seaside B&B. I'm in seventh heaven and can't believe such a cool club has arrived in Dunfermline. I vow that from this moment every school-free minute I have will be spent in here.

Dad's impressed too, not least because the Classic Snooker Centre also has a little bar – something Maloco's was short of – and now he can have a pint while he's playing. Then we meet Bill Fletcher, the club's owner and a miserable sod to boot. He obviously isn't keen that youngsters like me will be messing up his shiny new club and as time goes on he makes very little effort to hide his annoyance at the noisy young rabble who come in on Saturday afternoons and hog all the tables.

But even Bill's attitude isn't going to put me off. True to my word, I spend hours in this place and when everyone piles out of school and heads home, I make for the stop next to the council estate and wait for the red-and-cream Alexander bus to take me into Dunfermline. I'm the only person at the stop, and sometimes the bus is late, but that doesn't bother me. If I can get a few frames in before teatime, I'm happy.

My parents see that in the space of a few months I've gone from being a kid with a Christmas present to one completely obsessed by everything snooker. They know my schoolwork is taking a knock, and occasionally I'm reminded that homework needs to come before my hobby. Generally, though, they're encouraging – albeit that if I want to continue playing at the Classic Snooker Centre I need to find a way of paying my entry fee. They can't subsidise me forever, so Dad suggests that I do a few hours in the fruit-and-veg shop in Dunfermline on a Saturday morning to earn some pocket money.

I agree – anything to keep me on the table – and Dad gets me packing potatoes. In the back of the shop the tatties are emptied from a big 56lb sack into a bucket and it's my task to sort them into 3lb, 5lb and 10lb bags. It's mind-numbing stuff all right, but I get through it and within three hours I have my table money, plus a bit more for an iced cube of gingerbread and a little bottle of cold milk, both of which I buy from a bakery on the high street. I love the icing when it's soft. If it's hard, I don't. I'm becoming fussy that way. I'm also a bit obsessed about setting the potatoes into piles, depending on their weight, and I'll get a touch annoyed if a customer comes in and disturbs my nicely crafted pile by daring to buy a bag. I build these piles if I'm in the mood and can be bothered. It's a bit like my snooker practice; if I'm in the zone I can do it for hours without thinking. I don't know it now, of course, but the job in my dad's shop is the only one not related to snooker that I will ever have in my life. If I can't do it for some reason, Dad will pay for me to attend the club.

'Tell Bill I'll square up with him later,' he says as I'm leaving. And so I must inform grumpy Bill that he won't be getting his money until Dad arrives after work and has a pint while watching me play.

Sometimes I practise alone, sometimes I play against other kids who are hanging around the place. One of these is Conrad Whitelaw, a rough-and-ready but nice lad from Kelty, who also works in my dad's shop. Conrad loves snooker almost as much as me and worships Alex Higgins the same way I admire Jimmy White. When we play, we play as Alex and Jimmy, the bad boys who keep the audience on the edge of their seats with their freewheeling style. It's kids' stuff, sure, but if I really am going to be Jimmy White I might as well play as hard as he does. And play to win. Grumpy Bill can see how passionate we are about the game, but not once does he ever offer to give us even a second of free table time, even though we're only young lads. In fact, the only time he shows us a bit of generosity is when his wife gives birth to their first child and, to celebrate, Bill allows Conrad and I to play that day with a new set of balls.

I still enjoy a game against Dad, and it is during a match with him at the Classic Snooker Centre, a few months after my thirteenth birthday, that I make my first century break. It's a quiet afternoon, not many people in the club, and following the break-off we're evenly matched. Then I open the bunch of reds and start to pick them off. That feeling creeps over me again; the tingling sensation which tells me this is going to be good. Without hesitation or fear I pot and pot again. Dad scribbles down the score as it mounts with each ball that tumbles into the pocket. Even though I'm thrashing him I can feel him quietly urging me on. And then I pot the final black and he looks at me in astonishment.

'You made a hundred and two,' he says. 'You've done it, Stephen. Your first century break!'

He rushes off to tell Bill Fletcher, who is also amazed. Grumpy Bill wonders whether there were any witnesses. Apparently, it's hard to believe that someone so young, and so wee, could do this. Sadly, there are no witnesses. But judging by the open-mouthed looks on our faces, we aren't making this up.

Dad is bursting with pride. Even before he's through the front door of our bungalow he is shouting to Mum, 'Guess what Stephen's done!'

'What?' she says, looking shocked. 'What's he done? Surely not got into trouble?'

'He's made a century break, Irene!' Dad shouts. 'Can you believe that? He scored a hundred and two. He's amazing!'

Mum's delighted. She kisses me on the head. 'Well done, son,' she says.

'You know, I reckon Stephen might be World Champion one day,' Dad says. 'I can just feel it.'

'I think you're right, Gordon,' Mum says. 'He has a talent there.'

I stand there, puzzled, not quite knowing how to react. Are they right? And how do they know? And what do I need to do to be the best in the world?

Top

5 FAVOURITE CHILDHOOD FOODS
1. Mince and tatties
2. Macaroni cheese
3. Fish and chips
4. Haggis supper (deep fried from chip shop)
5. My granny's homemade soups

CHAPTER 3

Almost everything else in my life appears to be falling away now. Whatever interests I had previously – setting up my Subbuteo collection, playing a bit of golf – are discarded in favour of snooker. Outside of the club, I've no real enthusiasm for hanging around with boys of my own age, doing the things thirteen-year-olds are supposed to be doing. I just want to get down and play.

Schoolwork is suffering, too. Try as I might – and in truth, I barely try at all – I can't find much enthusiasm for the curriculum we're meant to be studying. This has always been the way, but it is even more pronounced now. I'm behind in everything.

'Stephen is a dreamer.'

'Stephen is a nice boy but lacks focus.'

'Stephen is not giving of his best in this subject.'

The twice-yearly reports all have the same theme running through them; I'm there in body, but not in mind. If I could leave now and spend all day in the Classic Snooker Centre, I would. The only significant progress in my life is being made with a cue in my right hand. To their credit, my mum and dad understand this has become a passion and a way of life for me and if they have concerns over my schoolwork they keep them largely to themselves. It's at the Classic that I buy my first 'proper' snooker cue. There is a cabinet of cues for sale and for a while I've admired a Rex Williams signature cue, for no other reason than because I like how it's designed. It's £40 so I save up and buy it, and immediately it feels like a natural extension of my right arm. True to form, Bill offers no discount on it!

For my dad, this obsession with snooker is rubbing off. He's seen something in my dedication, and the speedy, efficient way I seem to be able to see off all comers when I'm playing. We've ventured out to one or two other local snooker clubs; nothing major, just places similar to the Classic and Maloco's, where guys hang out, pot balls and enjoy a few pints. I'm watched closely as I win, and win again, and far from feeling shy and unconfident, as I usually do away from the table, I enjoy the attention I'm getting. Dad listens to various suggestions about how I should progress my 'career' – even though it's not even approaching a career yet. The idea that I should join a team and play league matches is a good one, though there is the problem of my age, and the fact that technically I'm not allowed into many licensed premises, to contend with. The British Legion clubs, big promoters of amateur league snooker, are particularly tough on this and in time I will learn how to slip quietly through the back door into such places, avoiding the bar area.

For now, though, Dad has his eye on a snooker tournament to be held in the summer at the Pontins holiday camp in Prestatyn, North Wales. The competition is called 'Star of the Future' and it goes hand in hand with a professional tournament that has been running at Pontins since 1974. This competition serves the twin purposes of giving the top players something to do once the World Championship has finished (and in an era where professional tournaments are few and far between) and providing entertainment for the camp's guests. In the 1970s and early 80s the British holiday camp experience is still a popular one among working-class people and the snooker-related events are a big draw.

Dad is keen to enter me into the Under-16s event and, while I'm somewhat daunted, never having played anyone other than from my local area, or even been out of Scotland much, I agree to give it a go. Dad persuades Mum to keep an eye on the fruit-and-veg shops for a week, and he takes me down to North Wales to see how I'll get on against thirty or so under-sixteens.

And I get on well. So well, in fact, that I win the tournament. No struggle, no fight. I just pot balls, quickly and without fuss, and one by one my contenders fall by the wayside. The prize is a trophy, plus £100 in cash and £100 in Pontins holiday vouchers. When we return home I give Mum £50 to put into a bank account for me and I use £50 to buy myself a watch. As we're not much of a holidaying family, the vouchers remain unused.

Dad is so proud he could burst. He's not one for talking up a situation any more than needed, but during the week, as my opponents go down like dominoes, I hear him say, 'He's my son,' to anyone who might be watching me. He wants me to be a professional snooker player and promises to do all he can to make it happen. He's not pushing – neither he nor Mum would ever push in that way – but he's keen to be part of something he's now experienced as a real thing – that I can go into tournaments and more than hold my own against other players.

We begin to explore the local amateur circuit, spending evenings and weekends travelling from club to club, playing in leagues against young and not-so-young players. I turn out for several clubs, including the Classic, and another in Rosyth called the Dockyard Club. At these and other clubs I'm the youngest player by far, but no less deadly than anyone I face on the table. The teams are three- or four-man affairs and we play a total of two frames each. Barely enough to really get you into the flow of a game, to be honest, but more than enough to whet my appetite for winning. Every week I look forward to the Tuesday or Wednesday night jaunt around clubs that, overall, have seen better days. The condition of the tables is almost uniformly terrible. The cloth and cushions are shiny with age, and there are chips out of the faded balls. No matter. I'm just bursting to get on to those rickety old tables and give it all I have. The two frames are over in no time and when I'm done I'm straight out of the door, into Dad's car and on my way home to bed. There is no lingering at the bar for me – I'm not even supposed to be at many of these clubs anyway.

At the Dockyard Club I'm introduced to Lawrie Annandale: dockyard worker and enthusiastic snooker player, referee and cue collector. Lawrie encourages me to turn out for the club and, in time, will be the only person I trust to put new tips on the end of my cue. Most snooker players do this themselves, but I don't trust myself to do what is a precision job involving fiddly bits of toughened leather and glue. Lawrie always does this superbly and I will employ his skills right through my career – to the point where on one occasion I will fly him from Scotland to a tournament in Antwerp because I have a problem with my tip. Others will scoff, but I like the tip to be shaped in a certain way and only Lawrie can do this exactly.

At thirteen and fourteen I'm still learning, of course, and most of the time my play is all about attack. Safety shots, and the kind of strategic snooker I see the older pros playing on TV, is not my thing at all. I just want to keep potting balls. It's as simple as that. It doesn't take long for my name to be mentioned more and more frequently within the confines of these leagues, though of course the talk might be related as much to my age and size as it is to my playing ability. Dad thinks that it might be smart to aim for the Scottish Junior Championship, and maybe even the UK Championship for the same age group. These events would give me the chance to break out of the constraints of two-frame games which are, in any case, beginning to become a source of frustration for me. I want to taste victory – real victory – the way I tasted it at Pontins. If that means leaving behind the local scene and looking further afield to tougher opponents in Edinburgh and Glasgow, so be it.

In the meantime, it's time to see the real masters at work in the flesh. Dad buys tickets to an exhibition match at a local leisure centre featuring my hero, Jimmy White. With the rest of the audience I watch spellbound as Jimmy shows off his talent. The charm and skill of the man is undeniable and yet, for all my attacking play and determination to clear the table quickly, I'm beginning to realise that I don't share Jimmy's colourful personality. I'm disappointed about that, as I'd like to be laddish like he is, but I'm just not. So I accept it, and get on with being who I am.

Because of endless hours watching snooker on TV my own cue action is developing nicely. I'm still copying Jimmy's way of aiming very low at the cue ball but I'm also observing how coolly Steve Davis lines up to take his shots. In the beginning I 'pump' my arm up and down as I line up on the cue ball. It's probably a waste of energy and it doesn't make for particularly powerful shots, but no one tells me otherwise and therefore it's completely natural and unaffected. And I pot balls regularly and win games, so who's to say whether it's right or wrong? It works for me, and it shows, because not long after my fourteenth birthday I win both the Scottish and British Junior (Under-16s) Championships. The Scottish event is held in Glasgow while it is to Birmingham that I travel for the final of the British Junior event, in which I beat Martin Clark. In time, Martin will turn pro but problems with his neck will force him into early retirement, which is sad because he is a tough opponent.

The victories at both Scottish and British levels automatically qualify me for *Junior Pot Black*, the teenage version of the popular one-frame BBC TV show that has been running since the late 1960s. So in April 1983 we're summoned back to Birmingham, and Pebble Mill studios, for my first appearance on TV.

At the studios on the morning of the recording I catch my reflection in the dressing-room mirror. For a second, I don't recognise myself. Dad and I have just come from the hotel, where I've spent an hour getting used to my new look – a smart, fitted suit in blue, complete with waistcoat and dickie bow. At present I'm wearing standard black school shoes but for added flair I've chosen a pair of light-grey loafers to match the colour of my shirt. If I get through the quarter-final match that lies ahead, I will wear them with pride. Not having been on television before, I've no idea that these shoes will actually appear white on camera, and that I will bear more resemblance to a junior jazz singer than a snooker star in waiting. But at this moment, all I'm thinking about is the game.

My opponent is Nick Pearce, a couple of years older and much taller than me. I've already beaten him in the British Junior Championship, so I'm not worried about him. Neither am I bothered by the fact that there are TV cameras, an audience of around 300 people and famous commentators and players (including Willie Thorne) hanging around the studio. None of it fazes me in the slightest. I just want to get out there and win.

I get into the game early. So desperate am I to pot balls that I'm almost playing my next shot as the referee replaces the pink I've just clattered into the middle pocket. I want the old guy out of the way so I can carry on and win. My dad watches from the front row as I open with a twenty break and soon I'm thirty-five points ahead. A look of seriousness is passing beneath Nick's dark fringe. He's rattled, all right. He's missing stuff he should be slotting away easily. So am I, to be fair, but somehow I'm always back into the game far more quickly than he is. Ted Lowe, the legendary snooker commentator, makes some remark about Nick using a cue that had to be shortened when he was younger, and that I 'make no bones' about whether my cue is short or long. He's right there. Sensing Nick's discomfort I press ahead, flying around the table. Nick snookers me and I play a foul shot. Trying not to show annoyance, I shove my tongue into my cheek and battle on. Nick gifts me a yellow from right up the table and in it goes. Then I promptly snooker myself, but I'm up forty-one points with just twenty-five points left on the table. Blood is smelled.

Using the rest, I slot away the brown decisively and line up the blue for the middle pocket. 'Just able to reach it,' murmurs 'Whispering' Ted as it slides into the bag. In the rush to the finishing line I miss the pink and my face falls momentarily. Nick misses it too, then in my desperation I play a foul stroke and hand six points to him. In the audience my dad is silently urging me to slow down, evaluate and breathe. No time for that. Within two shots it's all over, 70–23, and I'm into the semi-final.

Straight after the match, presenter Alan Weeks asks me how I'm feeling.

'No' bad,' I squeak, in my best wee Scots accent. When he asks me how often I play, I tell him that I play every day, 'aboot two or three oors an' aw day at weekends'. I mention that I've learned by watching snooker on TV.

'And what programme is that?' he asks leadingly.

'*Pot Black*,' I answer, looking surprised that he even needed to ask.

In the semi-final I'm pegged against Steve Ventham, whom I regard as a bit of a poser. I've already seen him in action at Pontins and he's confident he's the next big thing in snooker. I think I can show him a thing or two and to prove it I make a comfortable break of forty-seven. Then I play a safety shot to catch the red half-ball, so it will come off the side cushion into what I hope is a safe place, the cue ball heading to the other end of the table.

Unfortunately, I've hit the red far too thinly, knocking it over the pocket instead. As soon as I've hit it I know I've made a bad shot. Ventham isn't slow to punish me for this and makes a great clearance of sixty-five to win the match. It's probably the first time in my career that I've been taught the lesson that an unforced error can put you back in your chair, and you'll suffer while your opponent clears up. I can hardly believe I've created such a commanding lead before throwing it away to a one-visit wipe-out by an opponent, and in the post-match interview I'm struggling to hold back the tears. Another lesson learned – keep your emotions well in check.

Losing leaves me devastated. I so wanted to beat Ventham, then I wanted to beat John Parrott, who is nineteen years old (and will, of course, go on to be World Champion) in the final. On the train journey home I'm pretty much mute.

'Ach, come on, Stephen,' Dad says, 'be a good loser. You were in the semi-final. And you were on telly! That's amazing, you know.'

I think about it. It is amazing, I guess. I just want to do it all over again, and this time I want to win. I'm beginning to realise, contrary to Dad's expectations, that I will never be a good loser. When the programme is broadcast a month or two later there is a little bit in the local paper but not a lot else. Word about the programme reaches school, though, and there is a bit of ribbing about the 'white' shoes.

'They're grey,' I protest, 'it's just that telly makes them look white.'

The teasers lap it up, but within hours it's forgotten. The teachers never mention either the programme or the offending shoes. Even if they've seen it, which I doubt, they're probably thinking that my time would be better spent behind a school desk than in front of a snooker table.

In the meantime, it is back to the snooker clubs, and opponents ranging from the almost semi-pro to the truly dreadful. Dad realises that if I'm really going to pursue snooker as a career I need to be moving up into higher leagues and playing matches all over the country, not just in Scotland. But still we go on, spending time shuttling between Edinburgh and Glasgow and taking in towns and cities across Scotland's central belt. One of these is Stirling, and it is at a snooker centre here, on a winter's night in 1983, that a member of the audience watches me with more than just a casual interest in a young kid who can play well.

The man, Ian Doyle, is a local businessman and owner of the club. His son, Lee, is also a player and I'm drawn against him. I win and think no more about the match than any of the many fixtures I've played in the last few months. But Lee Doyle thinks about it. On the way home from the match he turns to his father and says, 'You know, Dad, I've just played the future champion of the world . . .' To his credit, Ian Doyle doesn't disagree. Later, he will say that he was 'absolutely captivated' by what he saw as my 'arrogant and assured' style of play. As yet, he doesn't do anything about it. But an idea is planted in his head . . .

Top

5 SWEETS

1. Cherry Lips
2. Chewing Nuts
3. Jelly Tots
4. Curly Wurly
5. Fry's Chocolate Cream

CHAPTER 4

At fourteen, I'm already past playing snooker with lads my age at the Classic in Dunfermline. Now, on a Saturday Lawrie Annandale takes me into Edinburgh to play at the city's Locarno snooker club. Dad would do it, but Saturday is the busiest day of his week. I look forward to Saturdays so much that I stand in the window of our front room and watch for Lawrie's car coming up the road. When we arrive in Edinburgh I will spend the day playing older guys, individuals who've practically lived their lives at the snooker table. They're not men who take too well to losing, especially to a kid. Most times they're OK about it, but I hear a lot of 'wee man' stuff and, while it's generally good-natured, I know when I'm being patronised. I try not to give it much thought and just concentrate on my game. On the way home, Lawrie always stops at a fish and chip shop and treats me to a haggis supper.

In as much as I ever think about life, it all seems perfect. I'm not keen on school but now I have snooker and that means the world to me. Yet that world is about to change drastically. One day, Mum and Dad gather us in the living room and tell us, matter-of-factly but with obvious and huge sadness, that they are going to split up. I disappear into the bathroom and sit there in silence. I don't cry, I don't bang my fists – I'm just stunned. I haven't seen it coming. Neither has Keith, and when they announce they are separating we both go into shock. There has been no shouting and bawling, no scenes in the kitchen, nothing. We have been a close family, I thought, and a happy one. But neither have I seen much affection between the two of them, no kissing or holding hands.

There are serious money problems – my dad's gambling, to be specific. There have been unspoken tensions, silences. Things beyond my young understanding. We've been sheltered from it up to this point, but now it's out. And worst of all, our house must be sold, and we are temporarily moving to Mum's father's house. He and Nana have been good enough to take us in, but the three of us will be living in one room in a council house in Kirkliston – the town she couldn't wait to get away from. Dad, meanwhile, will be moving to a tiny little flat in Broxburn, a few miles away from us.

Our world has fallen apart. Our family is no longer together, our house is gone and we even have to move schools. I start at Queensferry High School, near to Kirkliston, and while others might worry about fitting in at a new place, or falling behind with schoolwork, my biggest concern is that I can still take occasional days off to attend matches in England. This was the arrangement at Inverkeithing High School, negotiated by Dad. He approached the headteacher, telling him that I might make a living from snooker one day, and could I leave early for practice or matches? Amazingly, the headteacher agreed, regarding it as part of my education and 'preparation for life'. I don't know if Dad makes the same arrangement at the new school but in any case, I tend to leave early (or not turn up at all) so that I can get to my games.

Now, more than ever, snooker is a fixation. I discover that the physical and emotional disturbance caused by the split can be pushed away into a corner when I'm at the table. There's no doubt I'm angry at what's happened, and I blame my dad for seemingly bringing on the trouble. I don't say anything to him outright because I don't like confrontation of any kind. But I think he knows from my silences what's going on in my head.

And the silences are often long and uncomfortable, especially when we travel to faraway places in and around London and the south-east of England. We travel with the cheapest rail tickets Dad can find and we stay in budget bed-and-breakfasts that are, frankly, nothing less than shitholes. I try not to mind; Dad has had to sell the shops to pay off debts and I know how skint he is. It's not easy, having to put up with him snoring in the other single bed when I have a match the following day, but it doesn't put me off my game. Neither do the guys I'm playing, although I'd have every reason to be intimidated. A lot of the time I'm playing 'geezers' from East London or Essex – hardened, streetwise snooker players determined not to be humiliated by some little 'Scotch' kid. I'm aware that accents and manners are different down south; where we're quiet and reserved these guys are flash and brash. Their sheer cockiness can lose you the game before you've even touched the cue ball and there are times when I let that notion in and I'm done for. Quickly, though, I learn not to let them get to me – a lesson that will hold true in the years to come.

By the end of 1984 I've won the Scottish Amateur Senior Championship, the Locarno Open Championship, the Scottish International and the Pontins Star of the Future competition (for the second time). I'm going great guns, and channelling everything I'm feeling into the game is paying off.

For the final of the Scottish Amateur I wear a new outfit

purchased at some cost. It comprises a matching maroon leather waistcoat and jacket, combined with a pair of grey trousers. I think I look the business in it, but unfortunately it comes with a hidden difficulty in that the leather of the waistcoat somehow impedes my cue action, making the cue sticky. It's a weird situation but nonetheless I go through and win the final. Unfortunately, the suit doesn't come out again.

Around this time, and in light of my Scottish national victories, I'm invited to be part of a two-man team (the other guy being George Carnegie) representing Scotland in the World Amateur Championship, to be played at the Grand Hotel in Malahide, near Dublin. I do well, winning six matches out of nine, and although I don't win the tournament there is a buzz around me as a young player with talent and potential. I'm aware that Steve Davis is around as a guest, but I don't get to meet him this time.

One person I do meet, however, is my all-time hero Jimmy White. Jimmy is over to present the prize to the winner, but Jimmy being Jimmy the focus is more on the good time he will be having around the pubs and clubs of Dublin that evening. He has a few mates in Ireland, and I'm talking to one of them when I spy him walking towards us. I've been waiting for this moment for a couple of years; the chance to say 'hello' to the great man in the flesh, and maybe tell him what an influence he is on me. Jimmy strides up to his mate and, completely ignoring me, grabs him by the shoulder.

'C'mon,' he says, 'hurry up. We're going out.'

'Hang on a minute,' replies his mate, 'I'm just talking to Stephen here.'

Jimmy looks at me for a second. 'Fuck Stephen,' he says, 'we need to get going.'

The mate shrugs an apology and the two of them disappear into the night, leaving me standing open-mouthed. But I'm not so bothered; I know Jimmy has a bad-boy reputation that I couldn't match even if I tried – and I never do try. We're just very different people so I brush off his comment and continue trying to win every game I can.

In January 1985, just before my sixteenth birthday, I win the Scottish Amateur Championship for the second time, beating Jimmy McNellan 9–6. Although I'm still young, the wins I'm notching up against much older players are pointing the way to a future as a professional snooker player. My parents realise this is now almost inevitable, and they're fully behind me, but there is a problem – money. Since the divorce, Mum and Dad are having a hard time paying for me to attend matches all over the country, and there is a need for an evening suit or two, plus accommodation which doesn't involve staying in the worst dives possible. I have a bit of my own winnings money that I spend on tapes, CDs and other bits and pieces that every teenager hankers after. But none of us have any real money of the kind needed to keep a professional sportsperson on the road, and Dad knows it.

Luckily from the shadows steps Ian Doyle, the Stirling-based businessman who saw me play a year or so ago and on whom I made a deep impression. Ian – or rather, Ian's hardware company – has sponsored some of the Scottish amateur events and our spheres are moving ever closer. He knows that I'm a young Scotsman in a game dominated by English players and he's very aware of what Barry Hearn, the sports promoter and manager, has done with Steve Davis. Ian has a snooker club of his own in Stirling and is keen to replicate Hearn's magic touch north of the border.

To this day I don't know who approached who first, but at some point Dad and Ian have a conversation that ends with Ian becoming my manager. He has the financial clout and the business expertise to take on the task and, just to be on the safe side, if my career doesn't work out he says he will offer me a job in one of his businesses. So when I leave school I'll either become a snooker player or an ironmonger. If that isn't an incentive to practise hard, I don't know what is.

Dad feels bad that someone else has stepped into his shoes. Snooker has been our bond and, although there have been difficult times recently, we've stuck together and there is no doubt that his and Mum's support has got me to this stage. But if I'm to turn professional and have any chance of real success in snooker, a professional approach must be taken both to my game and to the business of being a pro player. Ian declares himself the right man for the job. He's a gruff, confident and blunt Glaswegian, tall and well dressed with a good head of steely-grey hair and matching moustache, and he will take no nonsense from anyone. He doesn't disguise the fact that he's worked his bollocks off to be successful, and he expects those working for him to have the same attitude.

'You're good, son,' he says, 'but I won't take any messing around. You work for me, you work hard. Understand?'

I nod and smile, not knowing how to react. My dad's never done the hard-man stuff, really. The most he's ever said in terms of criticism is 'Keep your head up', whenever I let it drop during my opponent's turn at the table. We're a quiet family, not given to tough talking or flashy stuff.

'How often do you practise?' Ian asks.

'Dunno,' I reply. 'Maybe a couple of hours a day. Bit more. Not sure.'

He looks at me and curls his lip. 'We'll soon change that,' he says.

If I'm to turn professional so young, he tells me, I must take everything about that very seriously indeed. And it's clear there is no choice other than to become a professional snooker player. The combination of a lifelong lack of interest in education and the move to Kirkliston means that I'm barely attending school at all. In fact, when I'm due to attend the two terms that will lead to my final exams, I don't think I go back in once. If the school contacts Mum with their fears for my education, she doesn't pass them on to me. So between us – Mum, Dad, Ian and me – we have a decision to make. Having won the Scottish Amateur Championship twice, I think I have a good chance of winning the World Amateur Championship. But that, of course, would mean staying as an amateur. After some discussion we agree that I'm not going to learn much more from the amateur game and so the decision is taken: I will be turning professional in July 1985, when I officially leave school, and for better or worse, my whole existence will revolve around snooker.

My couple of hours' practice tends to take place at a snooker club called Millers in Broxburn, not far from Dad's flat. But it's not how you'd describe 'practice' in the professional sense. It's cups of coffee with mates, games of three-card brag, hanging out talking or watching TV. Important stuff, of course, when you're fifteen or sixteen. Who wants to take anything seriously at that age? I love playing snooker and winning, but I seem to be able to do that and joke around with the other young guys too. However, Ian Doyle has other ideas. One day he drops into the club on a spying mission to see how I'm doing and catches me messing around with my mates. I think little of it because I'm still winning so many games, but at our next meeting he makes it clear that the days of relaxed practice in Broxburn are over.

'From now on you'll practise at my club seven days a week,' he says. 'Your dad will drop you off at half-past nine and you'll be ready for practice by 10am. You'll finish at 6pm and then you will be taken home. Got that?'

'OK,' I reply uncertainly. It's dawning on me that I will have to get myself out of bed far earlier than has been the case recently, when the lack of school has meant the end of the alarm clock. Lie-ins are mandatory as far as I'm concerned.

'Dad never bothered if I didn't get up early for practice,' I add. Dad thinks talent alone is enough to take me all the way to the Crucible and the winning of the World Championship one day. He's about to be proved wrong.

'Dad's not in charge any more, Stephen. I am, and we're doing it my way. You need money to travel, to stay in decent hotels – not those shitholes you and your dad have been staying in. Right?'

'Right.'

'And you need new suits, shoes. And a car when you pass your test. Right?'

'Sure.'

'What I'm saying to you, Stephen, is that you're a lad with talent, but there'll be no more messing around from now on. You have to apply yourself to this. If I'm investing in you, which I am, we follow my rules. OK? Oh – and I'm at the club most days. It's where I have my office. So I'll be keeping an eye on you.'

It's a ticking-off, but it works. The following Monday, Dad picks me up and we drive to Stirling for 9.30am. Ian is waiting for us as we arrive and, with a nod, he gestures us to follow him into a room where there are six full-sized snooker tables. One stands out from the others. It has had new cloth fitted to it, and proper professional lights have been installed above it. This, I see, is 'my' table, in all its perfection.

'OK, son,' Ian says. 'Welcome to your new job.'

'Is there anyone to play against?' I ask hopefully.

'Nope. It's just you and the table. You know what you should be doing. Let's get on with it, eh?'

Fifteen reds (this time, it's a full-sized table), six colours. Red-colour, red-colour, red-colour, red-colour, red-colour, red-colour, red-colour, red-colour, red-colour, red-colour, red-colour, red-colour, red-colour, red-colour, red-colour. Yellow-green-brown-blue-pink-black. And repeat. You miss? Set the table up, start again, from the top. Red-colour, red-colour, red-colour, red-colour, red-colour, red-colour, red-colour, red-colour, red-colour, red-colour, red-colour, red-colour, red-colour, red-colour, red-colour. Yellow-green-brown-blue-pink-black. And repeat.

When I was doing this at home, in the days and weeks after I got my first table, it was a pleasure. I'd do an hour or so, then watch a video or listen to music. Maybe I'd have another hour later in the day, maybe not. Now, it's no pleasure at all. In fact, it's nothing short of torture. I'm almost crying with boredom as the minutes stretch slowly into hours. Worse still, Ian's office is right by and every thirty minutes or so he will pop out to check that I'm still at the table. He doesn't say much, occasionally raising his eyebrows as if to say, 'This is what it takes to be a winner. Talent alone is not enough.' And he's right: snooker is no longer a hobby. If any new player is to pose a serious threat to the likes of Steve or Jimmy or Alex, they will have to put the work in. And there is no harder taskmaster than Ian Doyle. His ambition is to have a Scottish Steve Davis, a snooker machine that keeps on winning. And to achieve that he needs a player who can be moulded into a pro, prepared to do anything to be a major success, without question. Ian is nothing if not honest about this and although I feel I'm still being dragged out of bed every morning, as time passes I notice a marked improvement in my game. No pain, no gain, as they say.

The ambitions Ian harbours for me are huge. With a bit of nudging from him, I give an interview to the *Daily Record* in which I state that I will be World Champion by the time I'm twenty-one – just six years away. I'm surprised that the journalist didn't pack away his tape recorder then, with the words 'What a load of bollocks' on his lips, and even I can't quite believe what I've just committed myself to. Once you've said something, particularly to the press, it's very hard to unsay it and so our plans for world domination are now out there for everyone to see – and to mock if they all go wrong.

And they would mock, too, especially in Scotland. At this stage, our dreams might be pie-in-the-sky, but Ian and I are aware that Scottish sportspeople rarely, if ever, talk themselves up. 'Getting a bit above yourself' is not a typical Scots trait, but he and I feel it's held Scotland back, particularly in the sporting field. We want to go against that – the attitude that says, 'Don't be too confident because if you are you'll fall down and we'll all laugh at you'. In our book, that doesn't make for winners.

To achieve any chance of major success Ian would like me to live a life without a single distraction, one completely focused on snooker. As far as I can, I oblige. I don't drink or smoke, and I barely socialise. Weekdays I practise, weekends and evenings I play. School is finished. I'm meant to be sitting four O Levels but I don't turn up for two and the other two I fail. So that's the end of that. There is no real choice other than to play snooker for a living.

And yet, there is a distraction on the horizon, one that Ian will puff and pant and fume and rant about. He will warn me that such distractions are no good for my game, and that there may be trouble, but committed as I am to snooker, in the case of this distraction I'm going to make an exception. Ian isn't happy, and will continue to be unhappy as time progresses, but at this moment there's little he can do about it. That's what happens when you fall in love . . .

Top

5 FAVOURITE
SCHOOL SUBJECTS

1. P.E. (except rugby)
2. English
3. Art
4. Woodwork
5. German

CHAPTER 5

I'd first noticed her at one of the tournaments at Pontins in Prestatyn. I could have been fourteen, perhaps. She looked a bit older, as girls do at that age. She was blonde, wore a white leather jacket and white high-heeled shoes and she looked amazing. Well, I thought so, anyway, but it was the early 1980s and fashion then could be fairly eye-watering. Naturally, I'm too shy to approach her but I swear that if I come back the following year, I will try to beat my natural reserve and at least say a mumbled 'Hello' in her direction.

A year later, and I'm back at the tournament. Having won it twelve months previously at least I have a bit more kudos to attract the young lady in white leather. She's not here for the fun of it, I know that much, but has come to support her sister, who's a pretty good player. Her looks quickly attract the attention of Nick Pearce and Greg Lawson, a couple of fellow players I've been hanging around with. They're older than me, and way more confident, so they get chatting to the girl and find out she's called Mandy. They have the eye for her, but she just doesn't appear interested. Meanwhile, I'm hanging back, saying very little and wondering how I might get the opportunity to talk to her properly.

As I'm never going to go the whole, 'Hey, baby, what's a nice girl like you doing . . .' stuff I have to think of another approach. Nick, Greg and I meet her parents and I start chatting to them. It turns out they're from Blackpool and Mandy has been brought along because her parents, who own a retirement-home business, don't think she can stay home alone. Her father is very keen on snooker, so it helps that I win the tournament again. Slowly, shyly, but surely, I get talking to Mandy and she doesn't reject me. The week progresses, we become closer and by the end of the tournament we somehow decide that we're boyfriend and girlfriend. This despite the distance involved and the fact that I have zero experience with girls.

We talk on the phone most days. Mandy would like to come up to see me and because she can't drive, Dad offers to pick her up. I want to see her too; I've fallen in love, for the first time, and the physical separation can be painful, but I'm worried about what she will think of me. Or, to be more specific, what she will think of our new accommodation. By now we've moved from Mum's parents' home to a council house of our own in Kirkliston, and the place is nothing short of a dump. It isn't anyone's fault (except for the people who'd occupied it previously) and at least it's somewhere of our own, but even after living in one room at my grandparents' it is still a shock. There is no heating, the wallpaper is hanging off, there is damp everywhere. We can hear the next-door neighbour screaming at her kids in a tone we know will never drop below that of 'bellowing'. Mum starts to cry.

'Don't worry,' I say, putting an arm round her, 'we'll fix it up.' And although I'm no DIY expert, I strip the banister of paint and give it a new coat, and we get rid of the vile, peeling wallpaper.

We obtain furniture, fixtures and fittings from friends and family and within a couple of weeks we have the place looking like new. Admittedly, it's still not a great place to be and the neighbour takes to banging on the walls whenever Keith or Mum or I have our music on, which is quite often. We're a happy household, and Mum seems more relaxed than she ever was when Dad was around. And yet, we're still very skint. Before Ian intervenes in my practice routine we are literally scraping every penny together so that I can get the bus to the snooker club in Broxburn. It isn't an easy way to live, and it's all the more difficult knowing that Mandy comes from an affluent background. I ring her and ask her what she's doing.

'I'm sitting in the living room,' she replies.

I expect she wants some privacy while we talk, and ask where her parents are.

'In the other living room,' she says.

Mandy lives in a big house with two living rooms, and we're here, in our broken-down council house with barely two pennies to rub together and a crazy woman next door. No wonder I'm nervous about her coming to visit. She does visit, though, and if she's shocked by the state of the place and the area she doesn't say. It doesn't seem to bother her that as a family, we're not in good financial shape. We're two young people in love and nothing much else matters.

It matters to Ian, though. He's terrified that Mandy's presence, even over a distance of 200 miles, will destroy my game and the plans he has for it. He insists that I ask his permission whenever I want to go to Blackpool for the weekend, and when I do, there are dark mutterings about careers going down the pan that make me scared to even broach the subject of visiting my girlfriend. Mandy, however, is made of sterner stuff and she won't be put off by threats. If she wants me to visit, I will visit, and Ian will just have to put up with it. That said, it isn't easy. If I lose a match, the previous trip to Blackpool will be trotted out as a reason. 'You'll never be a World Champion,' I'm told, 'if you don't put in one hundred per cent of your effort all the time.' I agree, but one weekend away to see my girlfriend? Really?

That said, I trust Ian wholly. He is a good manager and he alone knows what I'm capable of with the right motivation. And Ian is just Ian. I see how hard he is with his son, Lee, who works in his hardware business. If he puts a foot wrong he's on him like a ton of bricks. He's the same with me and yet I respect him for it, much as you would a stern father who's nonetheless doing the best he can for you. There are times when we have disagreements and I say, 'Hang on, I'm not your son,' but to all intents and purposes that's what I've become – a son who will do what he's told, and not question the judgement of his 'father'.

I'm not sure what Mum and Dad make of all this. They can see that Ian has my best interests at heart, but I think they worry that I'm slipping out of their grasp, especially when I finally turn professional in the summer of 1985 – at sixteen years old I'm the youngest professional snooker player in the world. As Ian promised, the days of hunting down cheap rail tickets and booking into damp B&Bs are finished. He supplies me with a driver, a friend of his by the name of Tommy McEwan, and insists that I have my own room wherever I stay. No more bunking up with my dad. Ian says it isn't what we're about now.

'If you're playing professionals and you find out they're staying somewhere nice and you're not, you're at an immediate disadvantage,' he says. 'You've turned pro, so be pro.'

He's right, and I'm hardly going to argue. He's also right not to listen to the more senior among the Scottish amateurs who claim that I'm far too young to become a professional. These are guys who've put in years at the table, working their way up through tough clubs. The way they see it, they're from the school of hard knocks and I'm just some kid who's acquired a flashy manager and has barely paid his dues. There isn't much I can say or do to make them change their opinions – except, of course, to beat them fair and square. Even then, there are mutterings of, 'Ach, he's bottled it,' should I miss a shot or lose a frame. I try to ignore it, but it's not always easy.

Ian arranges money matches for me to play, with purses of up to £1,000. Such matches take in all kinds of clubs, including some in Glasgow that are eye-openers for a young, unstreetwise kid like me. They're rough places, populated by players who make their living playing for hard cash and don't like being beaten. I've had a sheltered upbringing, and I'm distinctly uncomfortable in such places, especially when I'm surrounded by the muttering, menacing friends of my opponent. When he's at the table and I'm in the chair I can feel their heavy, intimidating presence all around me. There is a permanent stench of beer and fags, and wall-to-wall swearing and cursing. 'Miss, ya bastard!' is frequently thrown my way as I'm about to play a shot. It's an environment I find difficult to be successful in, and I develop an aversity to money matches that will last my entire career.

Ian also negotiates a contract with top snooker table manufacturer Riley, and soon I'm on the road almost every night, playing exhibition matches in clubs and promoting the Riley brand. This is a better way of making some quick money; although I'm now professional, I'm nowhere in the rankings and prize money from tournaments is nothing to write home about. Ian puts me on wages, which suits me, and sets up a limited company to manage my business affairs. I take little to no notice of any of this. Maths has never been my strong point and at sixteen it's nothing short of amazing to get any money at all for something I love doing.

And I do love doing it. The initial reluctance to put in so much practice time at the table has subsided, to be replaced with a strong drive to prove myself and win, time after time. By September 1985 I'm ready for my first ranking tournament as a professional player, the Matchroom Trophy, to be played at Trentham Gardens in Stoke-on-Trent. Right from the start, I know I've made the right choice to be a pro. The whole atmosphere of this event is a world away from the smoky, beer-soaked venues I've been used to. I love the fact that we all have to wear formal evening dress for each game, and that even the practice tables are in pristine condition. We're staying in the nearby Holiday Inn too – definitely a cut above the cheap B&Bs we've been used to. Plus, I win my first ever game as a professional, beating Barry West 5–4 in a match during which I make an eighty-eight break. I lose the next game, and so I'm out of the running, but I'm pleased to get off to a decent start, and to now understand what it is to be a full-time sportsman.

All this is in direct contrast to one of my next tournaments, the 1985 UK Championship. To qualify, I must play my opponent, Omprakesh Agrawal, from India, in a small club. There are a few seats around the table and I know that to get to the main event I have to do my best, but something about the smallness of the venue really puts me off. I've been a little bit spoilt by the conditions at Trentham Gardens and I just can't respond to these more cramped surroundings. Omprakesh won the first World Amateur Championship I played, in Ireland, but since turning pro has achieved very little. Yet he beats me 9–2 and afterwards I get a roasting from Ian which I fully deserve. He makes the point that no matter the surroundings, I need to concentrate on the game. Point taken.

Ian's approach is that I should enter each tournament with the notion that I can win it outright. There is little point going for anything less, he says, and it's with that attitude that I make my way to the 1986 Mercantile Credit Classic, to be played in Warrington. Jimmy White's there, and so too are John Parrott, Cliff Thorburn, Dennis Taylor, Ray Reardon, Tony Meo, Alex Higgins and Steve Davis, among many others. This is another opportunity to progress up the rankings and eventually fulfil the promise I made publicly when I turned professional – to be World Champion by the age of twenty-one. Now I've said it I'm determined to hold myself to it. Nothing less will do.

I enter the Classic with a mixture of apprehension and confidence. Truthfully, I don't expect to win the thing outright – I'm not so naive that I think I'll leap to the top of the mountain immediately – but I do want to get past the preliminary rounds and look like I mean what I say by the way I play. My confidence is boosted by comprehensive wins against Dessie Sheehan and Graham Miles (5–2 and 5–1 respectively), and in the next round I face Silvino Francisco, the South African player with years of experience behind him. Now forty, he's been playing longer than I've been alive and he's ranked fourteenth in the world. Getting past him will be no easy task and he proves his mettle when he wins the first frame relatively easily. I'm under pressure but, remaining calm, I even up the score and we play a battle of wills right to the end, when I squeak past him to win 5–4 and gain my first ranking point. In the next round I lose to Neal Foulds, but only just; at this stage Neal is rated as one of the world's top eight players and I watch in amazement as he makes a very high-quality break at 4–4, mostly using the blue ball. I can see why he's rated so highly, but his narrow win makes me realise that I can face the top players and feel that I can compete against them with confidence.

In April 1986, aged seventeen, I beat Matt Gibson 10–5 to win the Scottish Professional Championship and close on the heels of this tournament is the 1986 World Championship – if I qualify, it will be the first time I will set foot in the legendary Crucible Theatre, Sheffield, as a professional player. I get through the four preliminary rounds, though it feels a long slog, and in the last thirty-two I'm drawn against Willie Thorne, the player I looked up to (literally) at *Junior Pot Black* three years before.

The feeling of playing at the Crucible is almost indescribable. It's a strange place, much more suited to live theatre – with its rabbit warren of backstage corridors, dressing rooms, lighting rigs and all the rest – than to professional snooker but there is an atmosphere about the place you can taste, a sense that you're here among the greats and you must step up to the mark, otherwise failure beckons. Immediately I love everything about it, right down to watching how the TV floor managers organise the live coverage and seeing the top players as they practise and mingle before each match. I look at their fashionable clothing and admire their style. I so want to be a major part of all this but right now, I'm too tongue-tied and shy to feel that I even belong in their presence, never mind play them, and as ever I sit and observe, silently thrilled to have some involvement in everything going on here.

'One day,' I say to myself, 'I will come back here and win the whole event. And I won't take too long about it . . .'

The match against Willie is televised. It should bother me, but it doesn't. The only thing that really concerns me is not to get thrashed. I know that if I do, I'll be on the back foot, confidence-wise, for a while – I'm not a good loser. But I needn't worry. Determination (and maybe a small dose of fear about making a fool of myself) sees me secure the first two frames and, while Willie subsequently mounts a strong comeback, I hold my own almost to the end, when I go down 10–8. I'm gutted not to be able to progress any further but despite that I've loved the experience of being at the Crucible. Already, it feels a great fit. As far as snooker goes, I'm right at home here.

With the greatest respect, playing against the likes of Willie and Silvino is one thing. What I really want is to face one of the very few players whose style and approach have truly shaped my own game. As they say, be careful what you wish for . . . at the start of the 1986/87 season I find myself drawn against my hero, Jimmy White, in the quarter-final of the 1986 Scottish Masters event.

This is daunting stuff. In my wildest dreams I couldn't have imagined playing Jimmy in a professional event, watched by a live audience who've turned up to Glasgow's Hospitality Inn to watch the likes of Jimmy, Alex Higgins, Tony Knowles, Kirk Stevens etc. do their stuff. The TV is also here, and my match is broadcast on BBC Scotland – to my embarrassment, because Jimmy mercilessly thrashes me 5–1. I put the effort in, but for most of the six frames I seem to be sitting in my chair, watching Jimmy and thinking, 'I can't believe I'm playing Jimmy White.' This, of course, is a fundamental error. Even though I've played at the Crucible I'm star-struck in the presence of Jimmy, and in my mind I'm still the enthusiastic amateur, grateful for the privilege of playing one of my heroes.

After the game, Ian and my dad rightly upbraid me for my lack of professionalism. 'You've got to get rid of that attitude, Stephen,' Ian says, 'otherwise you'll just become like every other Scottish player – you'll go to pieces every time you play one of the top guys.'

Ian is nothing if not ambitious. He's a proud Scot and doesn't want to turn out yet another second- or third-rate Scots sportsman. Aside from football, of course, there have been enough of these over the years. Ian wants to produce a real winner – someone who will put Scotland on the sporting map. I'm in total agreement with his ambition.

There is another transition of sorts between amateur and professional status, which lies in the clothes I now wear for matches. Ian has paid for me to have a couple of bespoke suits made, courtesy of his tailor in Glasgow, and when I wear them I instantly feel that I'm going to work. I've always liked clothes and have never been one for dressing down when I'm playing. The 'grey shoes / white shoes' mix-up on *Junior Pot Black* and the subsequent ribbing hasn't put me off wanting to look sharp, because I discover there is a distinct psychological advantage in wearing the right gear, and so it proves when, shortly after turning pro, I play John Spencer for two consecutive nights in Edinburgh. These are money matches, with £500 at stake each night for the winner. The first night we dress formally and I beat John hands down. After the match John mentions that we needn't come suited and booted for the second night. 'It's only a money match,' he says, 'there won't be many people watching. Let's make it casual, eh?' I agree, and turn up in jeans and a T-shirt. John is in a casual polo shirt and trousers. And guess what? He thrashes me. I think John understands the power of gamesmanship, and I learn another swift lesson in professionalism.

This season Jimmy beats me again, in the quarter-final of the 1986 Rothmans Grand Prix, but I've quickly wised up to not appearing in awe of him (or anyone), and the game is far more evenly matched at 5–4. A month later I face another 'great', Alex Higgins, at the UK Championship at Preston Guild Hall. Alex has an attacking, flamboyant style that I admire, though I'm aware of his reputation off the table and his capacity for using his menace to intimidate players into losing their concentration. Towards me, though, he is never less than gentlemanly and, noticing that I'm shy about coming forward, often invites me to practise with him before events. He is charm itself, because I'm not the enemy – yet. Eventually I will be the enemy and Alex will try to throw me off my game – unsuccessfully, as it turns out. But for now, he is all sweetness and light, giving me useful tips alongside practice time, and gently mocking my cue, which isn't what you'd describe as top-of-the-range.

'That thing,' he laughs, 'is only good for holdin' up fuckin' tomatoes!'

Alex beats me at Preston but at 9–8 I've given another top player a decent scrap. He's gracious about me after the game, telling the press that he was 'under the cosh' and only experience (his, not mine) enabled him to get away without a beating. Alex points out that I go for every shot, even the ones that 'verge on madness' as he puts it. And Alex has played some mad shots himself in his time. The praise is flattering, but in my heart I know there is one outstanding player I need to face before I can consider myself truly a part of this game. It's an opponent I will relish and fear in equal measure.

Top

5 SNOOKER PLAYERS TO WATCH

1. Ronnie O'Sullivan
2. Alex Higgins
3. Jimmy White
4. Judd Trump
5. Ding Junhui

CHAPTER 6

I've mentioned that Alex Higgins has an enemy, one he snarls and snipes at the minute he enters the room. And although we don't express it in quite the same inimitable way, the rest of us on the mid-1980s professional snooker circuit understand what it is about this man that irritates Alex. This is an enemy common to us all – a snooker machine who seems to walk off mercilessly with every trophy going without even a backwards glance at his crestfallen opponent.

Since turning pro, the player I've come to respect above all others (including Jimmy White, my childhood hero) is Steve Davis. He is, of course, right at the top of his game during this era. He seems unstoppable, and he is. Everyone tries hard, but few even get close. With little ceremony but a lot of skill and tactical play, Davis systematically annihilates his opponents and, while he's doing so, shows little or no emotion. He's courteous enough off the table, but I notice that he doesn't mix much with the other players and keeps well away from players' lounge banter. I don't mix with the other players either – more because I'm shy than anything else. I'd like to be a part of the inner circle but I'm so much younger than they are. They're married, they have kids, they go to the pub, they have grown-up stuff to deal with. I just don't know what to say to them. I keep myself to myself, and perhaps my fellow players see this as a sign that I'm deliberately copying Steve Davis. He keeps away from the others because he's a winner, and winners like him are a breed apart. His separation is conscious and, to an observer like me, intriguing. I've always liked Jimmy – freewheeling, talented Jimmy, the people's choice – but Steve is the player I most admire, and most want to be: the best in the world.

Another thing I notice about Steve – which I deliberately copy – is that on the table he always looks immaculate. The other players smarten up for matches, of course, but Steve appears to have a particularly good tailor who makes everything fit perfectly. The sleeves of his jacket are just the right length, his waistcoat fits snugly, and his polished shoes are never seen with even a speck of dust on them. Being a bit of a clothes-obsessive, this impresses me deeply. Even before he's played a shot he has an advantage in that he already looks like the winner. I quickly discover that away from the table Steve has another uniform comprising of a scruffy T-shirt and jogging bottoms, but that doesn't matter. As soon as he dons his black suit he's in Snooker Terminator mode and there is no stopping him.

'Steve is the target, Stephen,' says Ian. 'Defeat him, and you're on your way to the top.'

It's easier said than done, of course. Beating Steve in a final or semi-final is nigh-on impossible because he just dominates this sport like no one else. You think you've got him under pressure, that he's on the run – then he just finds another gear and leaves you behind. My impression is that he will strangle you with safety play and when he does get in, his long potting is so good that you'll not stand a chance. Everything looks perfect; his technique, the way he stands, his cue action – everything seems flawless, every single time he plays. His game is designed to tie you up in knots, and for someone like me, who goes for everything on the table, that spells trouble. To understand Steve, to unpick his approach and find the cracks in his armour, I have to play him.

I first get my chance in early January 1987 at the Mercantile Credit Classic in Blackpool. On the way to the semi-final I beat Ray Reardon and Silvino Francisco, among others. At 5–0 the latter match is a whitewash and, as I go into the semi against Steve, my confidence is soaring. Ian chirps to the *Daily Mirror* that very soon 'we' will be able to 'buy a bigger forest than the one Steve owns'. I'm not sure I want to spend any winnings on a forest (I have my eye on a car instead, even though I can't yet drive) but nonetheless the point is made.

I should've known. In the match Steve does an effortless demolition job on me, tying me up all over the table and giving me little chance to stage any real comeback. Halfway through the match I pull back three frames, but Steve takes all this in his stride and the game ends 9–3. It isn't the worst result, but it proves that I'm still wandering the foothills as far as beating him goes. After the game Steve tells the press he considers me a 'dangerous player' (good) and that I remind him of Jimmy White (maybe not so good, especially if I keep losing). He does add that he thinks I'll be in the world's top eight by the time I'm twenty. I hope to be in the top three by then.

Although I'm disappointed not to have played better, I'm about to get another chance – six other chances, to be accurate. Ian's obsession with me getting past Steve and becoming the youngest World Champion ever (an ambition I share) has translated into a deal he has reached with Barry Hearn, Steve's manager, and the *Daily Record*. In mid-January I will play Steve in a week-long series of six 'Challenge' matches across towns and cities in Scotland: Edinburgh, Livingston, Renfrew, Inverness, Glasgow and Irvine. Essentially, these are exhibition games for the entertainment of the public but of course they are a way of testing my mettle and learning from the greatest player in the game. The theory is that if I learn how to crack open Steve now, I will remember the formula when it comes to the serious stuff later in the year.

The Challenge has all the razzmatazz you'd expect of this type of event. The prize money is £4,000 a night, plus a bonus of £6,000 for the overall winner. Not bad for six nights' work. A liveried double-decker bus is hired for Steve, and I occasionally share this when I'm not being driven to the matches from home. I soon discover that while we're on nodding terms, there is no way Steve is going to be any kind of good friend or mentor. We might play a hand of cards to pass the time but, incredibly, we never discuss snooker. I'm so in awe of him that I don't ask a single question about his game. Instead, I watch carefully at the way he conducts himself on and off the table, how he limbers up, how he deals with the fans. This isn't just a lesson in how to play Steve Davis and win; instead, it's a masterclass in how to become a World Champion, with all that that entails.

One of the first things I notice about Steve is his dedication to practice. These might 'only' be exhibition matches but he is up here to win and, as I know from my own regime, winners must put in the practice. Wherever he is, he finds himself a local snooker club and gets to work. I'm impressed and pleased that we share the same dedication to the boring stuff – the boring stuff which gets results.

I'm excited and eager to get on with the first game, at Edinburgh's Grosvenor Hotel, but I'm aware that I'll have a hell of a fight on my hands. Steve hasn't lost a game in Scotland for five years and isn't going to give me an inch. I wouldn't expect anything less. Even so, I'm on home turf and the 300 people in the audience are here to cheer on a fellow Scot against an English champion. At least I think they are – as the week progresses I'll be a little less sure of this.

As the lights go down on the opening match I'm lucky enough to make a couple of quick opening breaks – nothing major, but a confident start. My cue action is still pumping and jumpy, in contrast to Steve's smooth slide towards the white ball. Like a snake, he watches carefully as I make my opening break and when I eventually let him in he's merciless. The game finishes 6–3 to him and, although I'm disappointed not to have done better, I feel I've acquitted myself reasonably well. And, more importantly, Steve has respected me as a player by not giving me any chances. His tactical, safety-shot style of play is not mine but each moment we're at the table I'm learning something new. The following day, the *Scotsman* newspaper prints an article about the match with the headline 'The schooling of Hendry has begun'. How right they are, and how right they will be over the next five nights.

The following night Steve does it again, tying me up all over the place and taking the seventh frame 136–0. I can only sit and watch as he does a job on me. And so it goes on, night after night. He tells the press that I'm 'cannon fodder' and I can hardly argue. I try to put him under pressure but there's something about his coolness and determination not to give anything away that makes him an impossible nut to crack. As the week progresses I feel more and more demoralised, not helped by Ian's somewhat unsupportive approach to each defeat. I'm hammered 8–1 in Inverness, only managing to pull one back in the sixth frame, and after the game Ian tells the press that he 'cannot believe' I've played so badly.

'Perhaps the pressure of top-line snooker has finally got to him,' he says. 'Naturally I'm very disappointed for the fans who expected so much from him.'

Thanks, Ian, nothing like a morale boost from your manager!

Steve clobbers me again on the final night in Glasgow, taking the series 6–0 and going back down south with the £30,000. There isn't much comfort to be taken from any of this, other than it has been a total learning experience. At no point in the entire series does Steve play to the crowd and they respect him for that. In fact, as the week goes on I think they take a perverse delight in seeing one of the greats crush a relative newcomer, even if the newcomer happens to be one of their own. They want to see a real winner, and they certainly get that. Steve remains aloof from it all; happy to sign autographs and stop for a word here and there, but never showboating or even demonstrating how he is feeling during the matches themselves.

And, as a player, he never gives me a chance. From this moment on, I vow to do the same to anyone and everyone I play. During the week I hear murmurs of, 'Ach, but he's only a bairn. Give him a break . . .' Steve, however, has played fair; he's tested me to the limits and given me plenty to think about. He's intimidated me, rattled me and given me an inferiority complex. If I'm ever to beat him I need to work much harder and, in some ways, become a much smarter player than I am presently. I've been Steve's support act, and I haven't played with the ruthlessness required to put him in his place. There are times on the tour that I've thought, 'I'll never be as good as him,' and for good reason. Steve has demonstrated what it takes to be a champion and I know I have a long way to go.

Criticism in the press aside, Ian's decision to put me up against Steve has been a masterstroke. When I arrive for practice in Stirling the following Monday, I have a new determination to take on board every lesson I've been taught so painfully. In a nutshell, Steve Davis has shown me how used he is to winning, and how rarely defeat comes into the equation. That's what I want for myself.

Also, and perhaps less consciously, I've learned from Steve the ways in which a champion conducts himself. I know I'm not one of 'snooker's bad boys' as the press like to portray Jimmy and Alex, among others. I don't go out drinking, I'm not into chasing women. And I'm still living at home! All that, ironically, goes in my favour, because I'm seen as a kind of 'boy next door' snooker player. Increasingly, there is attention if I walk down the street or visit the shops, but it's very much of the 'my mum's your biggest fan' sort of thing. Which, when you've just turned eighteen, isn't necessarily what you want to hear, but I really am as innocent and naive as I look – off the table, at least. I'm also very shy, and Ian arranges for me to have some media training so that I can answer questions in words of more than one syllable.

And, contrary to expectations, I quite enjoy media interviews. My appearances in the press tend to be confined to the back pages, and the questions are directed towards snooker so I'm well within my comfort zone. However, there are an increasing number of 'profile' pieces appearing further up the paper, or in magazines, and these focus on other areas of my life that I'm not as eager to talk about. Like how much I'm earning, what I'm spending my money on and how will I feel when I'm a millionaire within a couple of years? The money question is one that pops up time and time again; I always seem to be 'pocketing' a big cheque or 'swelling my bank balance' with yet another large sum. The truth is that while I'm earning very decent money from tournaments and exhibitions, my pockets aren't being filled with much of it. Ian pays me a wage suitable for my age, and a large proportion of the rest goes on travel, accommodation, clothing, tax, etc. Ian takes his cut, of course, and some of the money is invested.

Hands up, though – when I decide to spend, I spend. Without first passing my test, I decide to splash out on a £17,000 Mercedes 190. It's not what you might describe as the average seventeen-year-old's first car, and when I finally pass my test, at the age of eighteen and drive solo in it for the first time, I get looks of both admiration and sheer envy. During the test itself I'm too nervous to put it into fourth gear because I know that its powerful engine will take it over the 30mph speed limit and into the examiner's bad books. Once the test is out of the way I'm taking to the road with my mix tapes playing through the sound system and feeling every inch the lucky lad. And it is Ian who recommends the Mercedes brand, because he has one. I even get mine from the same garage.

Some of the 'profile' type interviews I do around this time are telling, not least because the interviewer spots clues to my personality, and my relationship with Ian, that at this moment I'm just not sophisticated enough to see. Like the way Ian decides who I will be in the future ('a clean-cut entertainer') and how he views my time off with Mandy ('that week cost £11,000 in lost earnings'). He has comments on my off-table social life ('His face is getting so well known he must be patrolled') and my table manners in restaurants ('I've noticed tremendous changes already'). Interviewers also pick up on non-verbal clues; how I look at Ian for reassurance when I answer a question and how on edge I sometimes seem in his presence. One interviewer tells the story of how I accidentally rested the toe of my shoe on a table while I was in a meeting with Ian and a business contact.

'Without breaking his sentence he (Ian) snapped his fingers quietly and Hendry's foot was on the floor.'

Meanwhile, I'm telling another interviewer that for Christmas

I've bought my mum a coat, some perfume for my granny and a furry gorilla toy for Mandy. I also disclose that I still live at home, and that my mum gives me a talking-to if I refuse to do the dishes for the reason that 'I'm a superstar now!' Talk about a boy in a man's world . . .

Still, I know I must act like a man, not a boy, if I'm ever to beat Steve Davis. During the Challenge week I've been far too caught up in the emotion of it all to really study Steve at work, so Ian insists that we sit down in his office and watch back-to-back videos of Steve playing. We study every move he makes at the table, every calculated shot, every inch of his safety play.

'We're gonna learn about this guy inside out,' says Ian. 'Knowing your enemy is the best way of finding out how to beat him.'

I see from the videos, and from experience gained during the Challenge week, that Steve is not invincible after all. He does make mistakes and doesn't always play perfect snooker – who does? What he rarely does is make unforced errors, and he makes far fewer mistakes than anyone else in snooker. Even when he does, he remains so implacable that you hardly notice he's done it. Learning how to read the man and his game is, I realise, a good percentage of the fight needed to defeat him. And not to be in awe of him, either. He's a tough nut, but beatable. And not everybody is Steve Davis. There are many other players I can beat on the way. He's the benchmark, but I won't be playing him every match.

I study his cue action and understand that I need to calm down my own natural pumping action. I must make it more deliberate, more calculated and technical. To some extent, this goes against my instincts. The up-and-down action of my right arm has so far served me well and I'm somewhat reluctant to change. But change needs to happen if I'm to stand a fighting chance of winning a match against Steve. One aspect I won't compromise on, however, is my dedication to attacking play. I can't think of anything more boring than to keep strangling my opponents with safety shots. I like to break open the pack early and make big breaks, whereas Steve likes to pick off the stray reds before going into the pack. Our game is utterly different in this respect and I have no desire to change it in favour of Steve's style. I might be raw, comparatively speaking, but I know the kind of snooker I want to play. Even when the shots I go for are deemed to be crazy, the fact that I'm going for them at all puts my opponents on the back foot, keeping the pressure on them.

The rest of the 86/87 season yields patchy results. I win the Scottish Professional Championship again, beating Jim Donnelly 10–7, but come nowhere in the British Open, losing 5–2 to Eddie Sinclair in the first round. I do much better at the 1987 World Championship in Sheffield, beating Willie Thorne 10–7 on the way to a quarter-final appearance against current World Champion Joe Johnson. Willie acknowledges that my safety play has improved massively in a year (the result of all those Steve Davis videos, no doubt, though Willie adds that 'professionals don't attempt' the more challenging shots that I'm always up for) and while Joe Johnson batters me to 8–1 in the first session, I manage to pull it back to 12–12. The final frame is a nail-biter, but Joe has the edge of experience and wins it 67–6 with a forty-six break. I'm gutted to have lost so narrowly, particularly at the Crucible. The atmosphere here is electric and I want to stay for as long as possible.

After the match, the former snooker player turned commentator John Spencer comes into my dressing room. Normally, after such a disappointing defeat I'd rather sit and sulk alone, but John has consoling words for me.

'That was really some performance, Stephen,' he says. 'I just wanted to tell you that. You were beaten by a brilliant player, but you were amazing out there.'

John's words cheer me up no end. He's a real authority on the game and he didn't have to say what he said, but I'm delighted he did. And in the following day's press coverage of the match, the headline above the article is 'Kid Courage'.

Top 5 CARS I'VE OWNED

1. Audi A8 4.2 turbo diesel
2. Ferrari F355
3. Range Rover
4. BMW M5
5. Mercedes 2.5–16v

CHAPTER 7

The summer of 1987 includes my first major trips abroad. I haven't been very far in the world, both professionally and personally, and I will be making appearances at the Australian Masters, the Tokyo Masters and the Hong Kong Masters. I'm excited to go, but also apprehensive. Ian will accompany me, and he's adamant that I will not be joining the other players for any post-dinner drinks, visits to nightclubs or anything else that tends to go alongside a snooker tour abroad.

Admittedly, the thing I'm most nervous about is the food. At this point I'm very much a meat 'n' tatties type of guy and even when we're in restaurants I don't vary much from a few basic dishes. Australia should be OK, but I'm anxious about what will be served up to me in Tokyo. Before we leave, I'm pictured in the papers posing with a bowl of stir-fry. There's no way I will be eating this. I'm told that burger and chips should be available, and I'm happy to stick to that.

I discover that Australians enjoy snooker, largely thanks to the efforts of Aussie player Eddie Charlton who is promoting this event, and the matches at the 300-seater ANZAC Memorial Club in Sydney are sold out. I beat a local guy, John Campbell, and Cliff Thorburn, and in the semis I face Alex Higgins. At this point Alex has been banned from all other tournaments for headbutting a referee and suffice to say he's not in the best of moods during this tournament. He tries to rattle me by referring to me as 'Stan Laurel' – a reference to my very new, very 1987, spiky hairdo – and says that he'll teach me 'a thing or two'. Unfortunately for Alex I have the last laugh by beating him on aggregate over five frames. He's not at all happy, and the kindness he's previously shown to me in practice, and off the table generally, turns into snarls and snipes.

In the final I beat Mike Hallett to win my first ever major title, and the first of the 1987/88 season. From the beginning I go out to attack my opponent and within the hour the five-frame game is mine. The audience responds with a standing ovation and Mike throws a white handkerchief on the table in a gesture of surrender. During the tournament we've been sharing a room, and after his defeat he tells me he might as well not have bothered changing into his dinner suit. It's a gentlemanly thing to say, especially when, having seen my domestic incompetence, he has been kindly ironing my shirts for me!

After a few weeks at home we're off again to Tokyo and then on to Hong Kong for the Masters events. In the company of Barry Hearn's Matchroom team we board a 31-hour Cathay Pacific flight from Heathrow to the Japanese capital. We're travelling first class and I can barely believe the luxury on offer, right down to the trolley bearing a joint of beef, which is sliced at your seat. I sit with Jimmy White, who endears himself to Willie Thorne by placing a hot towel on his bald head. Then he falls asleep, and a team of us (including cabin crew) is needed to wake him up when we arrive in Tokyo, which he does to much grumbling on his part.

We stay in the deluxe Tokyo Prince Hotel and, true to my

pre-tournament concerns, it serves predominantly Far Eastern food. At this stage in my unsophisticated youth I just can't face it, so I stick to a Western diet. One night I ordered spaghetti bolognese, priced at £37. Alistair Ross, a sports writer for the *Sun*, is with us in the hotel and has a pizza – at a handsome £29. We look at each other in horror.

Fortunately, I'm not paying the bill. Someone else is, and he's not at all happy when, having spent an hour or so on the phone each night to Mandy from my hotel room, the bill we are presented with when we check out of the place amounts to some £2,500. Ian is fuming. I can see why. In my innocence, I have no idea that phone calls from abroad could cost so much. Ian Not Happy, Part One. Ian's also displeased with the way I've played – Dennis beats me in the quarter-final of the tournament and my manager is annoyed because by this stage I really should be leaping ahead of the proponents of the old-school, defensive style of play.

From there we go to Hong Kong and from the minute we land I know I'm in love with this place. The unrelenting nature of the city, the restless to-ing and fro-ing of its people, the skyscrapers, the way Kowloon Harbour is lit up at night – I'm in awe of Hong Kong and for many years to come it will be one of my favourite places to visit.

The players are invited to practise at the Royal Hong Kong Club, a very exclusive expats' enclave. They have what can only be described as a magnificent snooker room, the likes of which I've never seen before. It is here that to liven up one particular practice session, Jimmy and Willie invite me to play 'points' with them. This is a game in which you allocate a pound to every point scored, and you pay whoever follows you. If, for example, you make a mistake and your opponent gets on and scores a hundred break, you owe him £100. This is an incentive, of course, to stay on for as long as possible, and if you play for an hour or two the gains and losses tend to even out between the players. Sadly for me, my attacking style of play meant that every time I missed a shot, Willie and Jimmy would be rubbing their hands with glee and at the end of the practice I had to ask Ian for the £600 I owed them. Ian Not Happy, Part Two.

A few days later, we're all invited to an honorary lunch at the Royal Hong Kong Club. The night before, Jimmy invites me to play golf with him and I leap at the chance. Ian gets wind of the fact that I'm planning an outing with Jimmy, even though it's only a morning event, and says that I can go along, 'as long as you're back for the lunch'.

The golf goes well until we meet a couple of Jimmy's Hong Kong-based friends and, inevitably, we're more than late for the lunch. So late, in fact, that by the time we arrive back at our hotel it's over. And to make matters worse, as we reach the lift, who should step out of the doors but Ian. His face is the only thundercloud on this sunny island, particularly when Jimmy says, 'Awright, Ian?' in his breezy south London way. Ian is very far from all right, and I get a huge bollocking, to Jimmy's amusement.

As punishment for this (and probably for the phone bill and the game of 'points' too) Ian informs me that, contrary to what he said previously, Mandy will now NOT be allowed to join me when I play at the Carling Championship in Dublin this coming September. I'm furious, but he's adamant. No Mandy. Ian Not Happy, Part Three.

Despite this, and being in a real huff with Ian, I get to the final of the Hong Kong Masters, in which I'm beaten 9–3 by Steve Davis. Again, I feel I have very little chance of winning once Steve starts notching up the points with all the skill and cunning he can muster. I know I can beat him. I just know it. But something is holding me back. Will I ever conquer this demon with the flaming hair?

Ian senses I'm despondent, not just at losing to Steve (again) but also because Mandy has been banned from Dublin. In a rare moment of sympathy he relents and says that she can come to Ireland after all. He also releases me for a night out following the final and, along with Jimmy White and a few of the others, we hit the bars. Uncharacteristically, I get pissed and I'm not in great shape the following morning for the planned boat trip to a nearby island, which has been organised by Jimmy's mates.

Even before I step on board I feel rough, and the undulations of the boat as it crosses Kowloon Harbour and out to the island really doesn't help matters. I'm as sick as a dog the whole way there and it doesn't stop when the boat finally anchors off what looks to be an idyllic tropical beach, complete with inviting white sand. In fact, being moored only makes the seasickness worse. A speedboat has been towed alongside the main vessel and Jimmy and friends intend to have some fun for the afternoon. There's no way I'm going to last a speedboat ride, so someone suggests I jump overboard and swim to the island, where I can take a lie-down on the beach.

It's a great idea – the only difficulty being that I can barely swim, and certainly not in a current. So Barry Hearn and Robbo (Steve Davis's driver-cum-minder) offer to take me on their shoulders and kind of float me across. Realising I have no choice, I take up the offer and I'm deposited on the beach, where I promptly fall asleep for two hours. At one point I wake up to see a hollering Jimmy driving the speedboat, with a white-faced Steve Davis in the passenger seat. Later, Jimmy somehow manages to sink the speedboat in shallow water. When the fun is over I'm hoisted once again on to Barry and Robbo's shoulders and taken back to the boat for the trip home.

Jimmy and I sit in the front and watch the scenery go by.

'That was a laugh, eh?' he says, as we watch some poor guy bailing out the speedboat as it's towed along behind us.

'Yeah, it was all right,' I say, 'apart from the sickness.'

'Yeah, well, I thought you was brave getting in that water,' Jimmy says, 'especially when it's full of sharks . . .'

When we arrive at the hotel I go up to my room to pack for the flight, and it's there I discover that half my face is bright-red with sunburn. Cue constant piss-taking the whole flight home.

From starting out as a player very much on the sidelines of the game, there seems to be a respect for me among the top-rankers as the season progresses. I'm disappointed not to have made it any further than the quarter-final of the Scottish Masters – I don't like losing anywhere but being beaten on home turf is a particularly unpleasant experience – and although I get to the semis of the 1987 International Open, Cliff Thorburn gives me a 9–1 pasting which barely sees me out of my chair. Still, in professional terms I've 'arrived' and there are plenty of tournaments for the taking. What I really want is a decisive win in the UK.

My chance comes at the 1987 Rothmans Grand Prix, played at the Hexagon Theatre in Reading. Specifically, it comes during the last-sixteen match against none other than our friend Steve Davis. Steve, as ever, is his usual calm, collected self. We've played each other nine times now and there is no reason why he won't do his usual and send me home disappointed. But between our last encounter and this one, there has been a quantum leap in terms of my game, and my attitude to playing Steve. Watching the videos and understanding that playing the occasional safety shot isn't a crime (and may actually benefit my game, especially against him) has led me to the conclusion that I'm no longer scared of him, nor should I be. He's an incredible player but he's not invincible, and when I go 1–0, then 2–0 up, I sense a tiny little crack opening in that famously superior confidence.

Steve fights hard, trouncing me in the third frame. But as ever, the ebb and flow of a determined battle comes into play and in the fourth frame he can only muster one point. A break of seventy in the next frame really puts me into the 'I-can-win-this' zone. It's a place that is hard to describe. Everything else seems to fall away and suddenly you're faced with a kind of tunnel vision in which you can almost see events happening even before you've set them in motion. It's just you and the table. Anything could be happening around you; there could be a murder in the auditorium and you wouldn't notice. You're there solely to win, and that knowledge somehow makes you unstoppable. I'm telling myself, 'You can't afford to miss anything, because to do so will put Steve back on the table and he'll go all-out to regain the advantage.' You compose yourself and focus. Then everything starts to flow and before you know it, you're doing what you set out to do.

And, with a break of seventy-two in the seventh frame, I've done it. I've played out of my skin and broken the spell. Steve, the favourite for the tournament, has been beaten, and the demon is banished. Ian is struck dumb – a rare thing. As I enter the dressing room immediately after the game, all he can do is clench his fist in triumph and wave it in my direction. Although I've not hesitated to employ my usual attacking approach I have been more careful than usual not to make daft mistakes, and it's paid off. Although Steve concedes nothing – not even a 'well played' – he does acknowledge to a post-match interviewer that if I keep playing the same way, he and I will 'have a few battles in the future'.

Steve and I are interviewed together by David Vine, one of

Steve's most enduring supporters. David takes the piss a bit over the fact that I've been watching videos of Steve in action (something Ian has dutifully leaked to the press). Steve smiles as I reluctantly acknowledge the rumour to be true, and when David Vine asks Steve if he's been watching videos of me he replies in the negative, saying that he'd 'been watching *Coronation Street* instead'. I feel a bit stupid, but in any case I've beaten him and watching the footage has helped. Steve, like me, isn't a great loser and isn't likely to give me any credit for winning.

For myself, I'm delighted to fulfil an ambition, but I'm determined not to go out in the next round. That, in my opinion, would be a waste of the win. As it turns out, it provides the hope and confidence needed to see me all the way to the final of this tournament, beating Tony Knowles and John Parrott along the way. I'm particularly pleased to beat John, because alongside Steve and Jimmy, I see him as a major rival.

Off the table, Ian takes care of everything for me so that all I need to focus on are the games. However, he isn't around to get involved when an incident involving my driver, Tommy, threatens to disturb my concentration. Tommy and I are sharing a room and I'm already in bed and asleep when he comes in late from a night out. This isn't unusual and under normal circumstances I wouldn't pay any attention to it. However, this evening he appears not to be alone. A female voice is to be heard and within a few seconds they're on the bed and hard at it. I pretend to be asleep as the noises and squeaks intensify. Finally, they subside and I'm able to drift off. In the morning, with the lucky lady long gone, I confront Tommy.

'For fuck's sake, Tommy,' I shout, 'I've got a tournament going on here! What were you thinking about?'

'I'm really sorry,' he replies, 'I just got carried away. You won't tell Ian, will you?'

I know what will happen to Tommy if I do, so I promise that I won't. With hindsight, I should've spilled the beans there and then . . .

The final will be against Dennis Taylor. On his day he can be a dangerous player, but I'm on a roll now and feel that I can overcome him without too much difficulty if I stick to what I've been doing throughout this tournament – employing attacking yet concentrated and focused play. Albeit that he's a former World Champion, I've never quite put Dennis in the 'big threat' category, feeling that although he's a great player, he's not a consistent winner. Through safety play he'll try to force mistakes from me but I'm aware of that and just want to get in there early, blowing his confidence before he's barely into the game. Before I leave for the auditorium Mum gives me a big kiss, leaving lipstick on the collar of my shirt. Maybe it's a good omen. Possibly it's just embarrassing.

At first, Dennis's cautious, unflashy but canny approach appears to be paying off. I'm really going for it, splitting the reds early and trying to pot as much as I can to build good breaks and a decent lead. But Dennis is measured and methodical and holds me off for the first three frames, nudging ahead to establish a close but reasonably comfortable lead. He knows that I'm inclined to take risks, especially unnecessary ones, in the quest to clear the table.

Then, in the fourth frame Dennis misses an easy red. Almost out of nowhere, I snatch a seventy-nine break and deny him a single point. In the first three frames he's been walking around the table in something of a superior manner, but now he's in his chair I see his face reddening slightly behind his trademark massive clown glasses. Building the break puts me into the zone and, as ever, I'm eager that referee Len Ganley puts the potted colours back on the table as soon as possible so that my flow is uninterrupted. At seventy-nine I fail to pot a red and Dennis concedes the frame. Somewhere in the darkness of the commentary box, Ted Lowe calls me 'the young prince of potting'.

Even at this early stage I sense a hint of the winning line in sight. Yet at one stage, when I miss an easy black, I display a rare loss of temper and tap another ball with the end of my cue. I can almost taste the pressure now but if I focus on that, instead of what's happening next, the game will be up. And I know that somewhere in the auditorium, Ian will be seething that I've allowed my emotions to show. If I lose now because of it, he will be furious. The audience feels the pressure too; my parents are among the crowd and at one point – probably backstage during the break between sessions – my mum makes the comment that 'Stephen's gonna win it,' delivered in a stage-whisper. Passing by, Dennis catches it and throws back the opinion that 'He's not won yet.' And although I'm holding Dennis at 9–5 midway through the evening session, victory is not yet mine. There is still a feeling of this game being one of a man versus a boy. Dennis throws in all his years of experience and tactical play, and pulls back two frames to make it 9–7.

Sitting by my parents, Ian offers the opinion that my bottle's going. But the final frame goes my way, leaving Dennis needing snookers to get back in the game. Manfully he tries, but within a minute or so I'm back on the table to sink the pink and it's all over. I've won my first major title and, at eighteen, I'm the youngest ever winner of a ranking tournament. As I lift the trophy, a small grin on my face, my mum is in tears. Ian is smoking furiously, clapping his hands and biting his lip with the tension of it all. 'What can I say, son?' he says. 'I'm stunned.' Then he slaps both my cheeks, nearly knocking me off my feet.

As usual, winner and loser are interviewed together by David

Vine. Dennis is gracious in defeat. He says he 'couldn't believe' some of the shots I've played 'from ridiculous positions'. Dennis admits he was all-out to knock me out of my rhythm, causing me to miss easy pots. 'Which is only natural,' he adds. 'He's only eighteen, after all . . .' True enough. But young as I am, I'm the one taking home the trophy and the cheque for £60,000. Not that the money will be going straight into my account, of course, though try telling that to the papers. The following day they're full of 'facts' about how much I've earned, how much I'm likely to earn, how much my suits cost, how many houses I now own. Like I've just put my card into a cash machine, checked the balance and seen a six-figure sum sitting in there!

The reality is much different and I'm still on a wage. But it is true that I've bought expensive suits – from Robert Dick Tailors in Glasgow, where Ian gets his suits. And I have purchased property. Finally, my mum, Keith and I have been able to leave the council house we all hate and move into a semi-detached that we now own. It's a relief for all of us, though it must be said that getting us out of that place hasn't been a prime motivator in my determination to win a major tournament. We're a happy trio at home and Mum always keeps things positive and upbeat. Keith and I like to tease her by jumping out at her in the dark from behind the curtains in her bedroom. 'It'll serve you right one day if I've already taken off my clothes!' she laughs.

I also help Dad out with a house, enabling him to move out of the tiny flat he's been living in. So money is spent, though judging by the newspaper pictures of me holding the Grand Prix trophy, no amount of cash seems to be able to cure my teenage acne, which in time I will become infamous for. At my age, this is a hard thing to cope with, particularly when the spots are shown in all their gory glory close-up on TV. I have a particularly bad dose of it, and I try various remedies, including medication and even a sunbed. Some of the treatments suggested have nasty side effects, including reduced vision and depression, so I avoid those and try to ignore the sniggers. At one stage, Steve Davis will joke to audiences during exhibition matches that he went into a nightclub with me where admission was £10 a head. 'And it cost Stephen two hundred quid!' he laughs. I can't be seen to be rattled by it, but it does get me down at times. It also makes me feel even younger than I am – a kid in a man's world.

Tournaments sponsored by the cigarette companies – Rothmans, Benson & Hedges and Embassy – are always the best financed, both in terms of the prize money and the facilities the players and supporting cast enjoy. The party following the final is a lavish affair featuring gallons of champagne, though me being me I'm not much of a drinker and, after hands are shaken and autographs signed, I leave early. I need to be in bed on time because tomorrow I will play an exhibition match, and my career path will continue upwards.

Exhibitions can take place anywhere there is an appetite for snooker; even places you wouldn't choose to visit in most other circumstances. A guy called Paul Mulligan gets in touch from Ireland and asks if we'll visit a few clubs along the border with the North. Although Paul lives in the Republic his work is cross-border and so I play exhibitions in Crossmaglen – at the heart of what at the time is known as 'Bandit Country'. During this period the area is crawling with soldiers and it is an unnerving experience to cross through border checkpoints, very slowly and with the car's headlights off. The soldiers take a good look at us and I know cars are routinely stopped and searched. In my dinner suit, however, I look somewhat respectable and so we're waved on through. Even so, there are times when Paul feels we might be being followed along the winding border roads and this is very unsettling for us all. We also travel to Belfast, where I play an exhibition match on the Shankill Road. For these engagements Paul must borrow a car with a Northern Ireland registration plate; arriving in a car which would identify him as living in the Republic would be a very bad idea in this hardline Loyalist area.

The season continues as many snooker seasons do, with good wins and bad moments you'd rather forget about. One of these comes immediately after the Rothmans, when I'm knocked out in the early stages of the 1987 UK Championship by Canadian Jim Wych. It's 9–7, so it's a close-run thing, but perhaps I'm still in a bit of shock from my big win. Whatever, I'm taught a lesson by a relative outsider – though it hasn't quite sunk in by the time I meet Steve Davis in the Mercantile Credit Classic in Blackpool, played over the first couple of weeks of January 1988. Steve exacts a cool revenge for the Rothmans by beating me 5–3 in the quarter-final, leaving me wondering whether my defeat of him was a fluke. Happily, in February 1988 I retake the Scottish Professional Championship title that I'd lost the previous year, beating Murdo MacLeod 10–4.

With my winning head back on I venture into the 1988 British Open, played at the Assembly Rooms in Derby. Victory here will hoist me a bit further up the rankings and might set me up nicely for the World Championship. Received wisdom is that I'm not quite ready for the big one yet. I beg to differ and play as though that prize will be rightfully mine in a few short weeks. I'm up against some big hitters, including Terry Griffiths, Jimmy White and Cliff Thorburn. Jimmy in particular gives me a tough game in the quarter-final, battling me all the way in my 5–4 win and once I'm past Cliff in the semis I face Mike Hallett in the final. The game is later described as 'ruthless', and I'm not going to argue with the press's verdict. Mike is a nice guy and is also being managed by Ian so we're stablemates, but from the off I don't give him a moment of mercy. He takes the fourth frame, and another later, but that's really the extent of his fight. At 13–2 it's finished and for the second time this season I lift a major ranking tournament trophy. Buoyed with confidence, I tell the press after the game that I'm thinking of quitting professional snooker within five years – once I've won the World Championship at least twice. Where this career plan comes from I'm not sure, but I emphasise it by stating that if I don't win the world title I will see myself as 'a total failure'. At nineteen, and on a winning streak, this could be put down to youthful black-and-white thinking. But I'm deadly serious; I want that title very badly indeed. Ian backs me up, saying I'll go to the Crucible as 'the man to fear', though adding that he thinks Steve Davis will be this year's champion. Ian knows exactly which buttons to press as far as my ambitions are concerned!

Unfortunately for me, this year Ian is on the money. In Sheffield I make it through to the last sixteen, where Jimmy turns the tables on his British Open defeat and in a truly gripping match beats me 13–12 in the deciding frame. It's the first time we've played each other at the Crucible and throughout I make no fewer than three century breaks – my best tally in professional snooker so far. Jimmy keeps his cool and, as the more experienced player, rarely eases up on the pressure he puts me under. There are moments, particularly at the start of the match, when I almost have to pinch myself – I'm here, at the Crucible, playing Jimmy White, my all-time hero. But painful experience has taught me what that kind of thinking can lead to and I remind myself to focus, and focus some more. By the middle of the first session I've settled down and we slug it out, frame after frame, neither of us yielding an inch. Jimmy's noisy fan club are on the edge of their seats as we reach the final frame and all I can do is watch gloomily as he makes a break of eighty-six to secure the victory. It's been a great game and I'm gutted to lose it. As expected, Steve Davis is this year's champion and as he lifts the trophy, a small smile of triumph on his face, I wonder whether my retirement will be a little further away than I've predicted.

Top 5 FAVOURITE ALBUMS

1. U2: Achtung Baby
2. Pink Floyd: The Wall
3. Neil Finn: One Nil
4. Morrissey: Vauxhall and I
5. Neutral Milk Hotel: In the Aeroplane Over the Sea

CHAPTER 8

Not so long after I turned pro, and around the time Ian was lining me up as a potential successor to Steve Davis, I decided that my game needed tweaking. Not by a lot, because at that point, and for a good few years afterwards, what counts is my natural way of playing. It's winning me plaudits and pulling me up the rankings. So no dramatic changes, just some low-level tinkering, particularly around my long potting. In a nutshell, I'm not potting long shots as consistently as I should be. Sometimes it can be as high as 90 per cent, sometimes as low as 30 per cent. When I tell Ian he makes enquiries and decides that I should spend a bit of time with Frank Callan. In fact, this 'bit of time' turns into a few years.

Frank is in his late sixties. He's a blunt, no-nonsense retired Blackpool fishmonger and Second World War veteran who was a decent snooker player in his youth and got into coaching later in life, developing a reputation for being one of the best. He's already coached Steve Davis, along with John Parrott and Terry Griffiths, among others, so bringing him on board to look at my game is a natural choice. And, from the off, we get on famously.

He's cantankerous, rude, funny, honest, and he doesn't give a stuff what anyone thinks about him – particularly Ian. That tickles me no end.

And he's good. Straight away, Frank notices my pumping cue action and suggests that instead I should pause, then deliver the cue. That extra second or two helps me focus on the ball and the pocket beyond and very quickly I notice my long potting improving considerably.

Frank is also keen to improve my safety play. This is a real bone of contention with me. My attitude towards safety shots, and defensive play in general, is that they get in the way of what I want to do, which is pot balls. I know Steve Davis uses the safety approach as an integral part of his game; he puts as much effort into a safety shot as he does a pot, and I don't. He almost always looks at the baulk end, or another difficult position, to place the cue ball for the opponent, whereas I would put it up there but not as carefully or tactically as he might. While I'm keen to learn from Frank, tying opponents in knots is not my thing. I just want to go for everything and win frames as easily and quickly as I can.

I make this clear to Frank. 'A safety shot is a negative shot,' I say, with all the confidence of an eighteen-year-old.

'Right,' Frank replies. 'I see. So if you play a safety shot, you force a mistake and you get in, what's negative about that? If there's no pot on, you just have to put the cue ball back up the table. Your opponent messes up, you're in again. Simple.'

I haven't thought of it like that, and while I'm still not fond of safety play I take what Frank says on board. He'll be with me for a few years and, off the table, he is good company and a welcome antidote to Ian's regular digs, rants and bollockings. Frank is an old-school player's player and has no time for Ian's flamboyant freewheeling style. 'Ignore him,' Frank will say to me after a tirade, 'he knows nowt.' Between matches, he and I play cards – kalooki, mainly – much to Ian's annoyance.

'He should be in his room relaxing,' Ian mutters, 'not messing about with cards.'

'He's exercising his brain,' Frank says, without even looking up. 'So let him be.'

After matches, Ian, my driver Tommy and I usually go out for dinner and, when he can bear to sit with Ian for more than ten minutes, so does Frank. Usually, though, he's on the hunt for a good fish-and-chip shop. Having been in the trade, he's a connoisseur when it comes to a battered cod. I introduce him to a chippy I've stumbled upon close to London's Wembley Conference Centre, where the Benson & Hedges Masters tournament is held every year. Surprisingly for a northern man, it becomes his all-time favourite.

Frank frets about the amount I eat. Or rather, the lack of it. Once a match is finished I've a great appetite but, in the build-up to it, I will eat nothing at all. Any morsel seems to knock me sick. I guess it's nerves, but Frank isn't happy. 'Ey, lad,' he says, 'you should eat summat. You need t'feed yer brain!'

He might be right, especially when the newspapers come calling over a supposed 'sex scandal' that never was. If I'd used my brain at the time, I could've have avoided it. By this stage I'm in my own flat in South Queensferry, having made the move away from home. It's not what you'd call a bachelor pad, as I have a steady girlfriend and rarely go out, preferring to relax between tournaments by watching TV or listening to music. But one night I come home quite late to find an American girl loitering in the hallway close to my door. She's a few years older than me and looks concerned by something. Politely, I ask her if there's anything the matter.

'I'm supposed to be staying with my uncle in this block,'

she replies, 'but he's not around and I have no key. I'm locked out.'

We stare at each other for a moment. I'm shy, but I know my manners. 'Well, maybe you could come in for a bit,' I say, 'and wait until he gets home.'

'Great!' she says, making towards the doorway. Slightly embarrassed, I put the key in the lock and usher her in. We chat for a while, but there is no sign of the uncle. Minutes, then hours, pass by. I'm tired and want to go to bed. Wherever the uncle is, he's obviously not coming home so I suggest she stays on the sofa, and that's how it remains for the rest of the night. In the morning she thanks me for putting her up and leaves. And I think no more of it until the following Sunday, when one of the tabloid papers does a 'Snooker ace's night of passion' job on me, with quotes from the lady herself.

We make our account clear to the paper in no uncertain terms. Ian is furious – he doesn't want anything to tarnish the squeaky-clean reputation of his star. And Mandy is none-too-pleased, of course, though she knows me well enough to believe me that nothing went on.

'But why did you let her stay?' she asks. 'That's just bloody stupid, isn't it?'

'I dunno,' I reply. 'She was locked out and I just felt sorry for her . . .'

The lesson continues over the course of the following week, as the newspapers look for further evidence of my fling. We're aware that I'm being followed, so when we go down to London for a match I swap rooms with John Carroll, a taxi-driver friend of Ian's who has by now become my driver and road manager since Tommy has been let go. True to form, John gets a 1am knock on his door and, dressed only in his boxer shorts, answers it to find a photographer and the American woman standing outside. John tells them where to go, and they're unable to locate me. The following Sunday the paper prints a retraction, making it clear that the story is untrue. Naturally, this is tucked away on page twenty-something, occupying a rather smaller slot than the original story.

The sex-scandal-that-never-was is a nuisance but nothing compared to what will follow. Since I've turned pro, Ian has been adamant that Mandy will not accompany me to tournaments, nor even stay over with me when I'm playing. Ian's argument is that I'm there to do my job – i.e. to win – and there should be no distractions, particularly of the female kind. I understand this; focus is everything, particularly in an individual sport like snooker. The minute you stop focusing, you lose. And neither Ian nor I want to give an inch. We are a team, he and I; the two of us against the world of established snooker, a pair of outsider Scots taking on an English-dominated sporting clique and literally beating them at their own game. Ian is draconian, for sure, but he has my best interests at heart and I obey the rules he lays down for me.

Well, most of the time I do. I'm also young – nineteen, twenty – and my girlfriend lives in England. We miss each other and when we do meet up there's always Ian to contend with. I resent having to ask his permission to see her, and to receive the inevitable lecture about missed practices and lost games after we've spent a weekend together. So when Tommy was my driver I got him to help me with a few clandestine liaisons with Mandy during tournaments. She took the train to wherever I was playing and while Tommy looked the other way she sneaked into my room. About half a dozen times we manage to get away with a night together without Ian being alerted.

Ian inevitably finds out about the illicit nights with Mandy and is furious, of course, and I get both barrels. But that isn't all . . .

I'd also tried 'poppers', amyl nitrate in a little bottle – it gives you a rush of blood to the head (and elsewhere . . .) and, in the late 80s, was used extensively on the gay scene. Mandy had obtained a bottle of this from some friends in Blackpool and we'd tried it a couple of times but it did nothing for me.

I'm down in London to play an exhibition match and, when I arrive back at my hotel, the Heathrow Penta, following the match, I see my Uncle Colin (my mum's sister's husband) standing in the lobby flanked by Ian and his business partner, a guy called Jim Marley. Immediately I sense that something odd is going on – Uncle Colin has had nothing to do with my snooker career so far but here he is, and the three of them are looking very serious indeed.

'We need to talk, Stephen,' says Ian. 'Let's go upstairs.'

Grimly, and in silence, we take the lift to my room. Once inside, Ian indicates that I should sit down. Like a dog, I obey.

'OK,' he says, 'I want to know all about your drug problem.'

I can't be any less surprised than I would if he'd told me I'd grown another head. I have absolutely no idea what he's talking about.

'What drug problem?' I say, open-mouthed.

Ian replies. 'The stuff you're sniffing. The stuff in bottles. Poppers – is that it? We all know now, so there's no point denying it. You'd better own up.'

'Oh, that! God, that's nothing. It's not drugs, it's just stupid stuff. All it does is give you a headache.'

I probably shouldn't have smiled when I said it, because what follows is a tirade from Ian that appears to rank me alongside Edinburgh's worst heroin users of the kind that will one day be seen in *Trainspotting*. Worse still, Mandy has the blame piled upon her for obtaining the poppers, and of course she's not around to defend herself due to Ian's blanket ban.

No matter how hard I try to underplay it, there is no calming Ian down. Uncle Colin isn't happy either. I've brought shame on the family, how could I ever have got involved in something like this, what about my career, etc., etc?

'You've really fucked up here, young man,' says Ian, 'so this is the deal. I want you to finish with Mandy. If this is the sort of thing you're going to be doing with her, then I want nothing more to do with you. Either you finish with her, or I'm done with you. And that's your career gone. Understood?'

Shit. Now this is serious. I've come this far, this fast. I want to be the best player in the world, nothing less. And I believe that only Ian can help me achieve this. If I have no career in snooker, I have no career in anything. I don't know anything else. Mandy's not to blame – we're just silly kids – but Ian is adamant that she's behind all this, and that basically she's career suicide. Do I have a choice? No.

Meekly, I nod my head in agreement. 'OK,' I say, 'I'll finish with her. But it's gonna be horrible. How would you like to have to do it?'

'You got yourself into this mess, Stephen,' Ian replies, 'and now you'll have to get yourself out of it. Make that phone call, go see her, whatever. Just do it, and let's move on from this.'

I should have gone to see her. It would've been the manly thing to do. But I'm no good with confrontation and so I phone her. The result is predictable and horrible; tears, anger, incomprehension.

'He's given me this ultimatum,' I say. 'Ian's making me decide on my career. I'm in a bad position.'

'And so you're just gonna sit by and let him do that?' she screams down the phone.

'I have to,' I say. 'I've got no choice. I'm really sorry.'

'OK,' she says, 'well if that's your choice you can fuck off!'

And down goes the phone, leaving me in a terrible state. I didn't want this to happen, and I feel that Ian has found the excuse he's been looking for to get Mandy out of my life. As ever, when there is trouble, I go back to the practice table. Snooker takes me out of my problems and places me in a focused frame of mind. If I wasn't aware of it before, I know now that snooker is my everything. Without it, I don't know what I'd be.

Unfortunately, my troubles aren't over yet. I'm at the club, practising for the upcoming 1988 Canadian Masters in Toronto. As I leave for the day I'm suddenly surrounded by a couple of reporters. One of them produces a little brown bottle from his pocket and, with a grin, says, 'Can I ask you about this, Stephen?'

My stomach turns over. Tight-lipped, I push past the journalists, get into my car and drive off quickly. All that week I'm aware I'm being followed, or that they're hanging around outside the club, and it's not a good feeling. One day, a couple of the guys from the club block in the journalists with their cars while I make my escape. But nothing appears until we get to Toronto, when there is a phone call to say that the *Daily Star* has run with the story: 'Snooker Star in Love Drug Shock', or something equally salacious. A few of the other players find out and I get the mickey taken mercilessly. I'm just thankful I'm out of the country, though when I arrive home (having been beaten by Steve Davis 9–5 in the semi-final), I receive a dressing-down from my mum. Evidently, I'm never too old to take a talking-to from my parents! Ian is also happy now he has his star player just where he wants him – practising, practising, practising for all the various tournaments, with little or no distractions.

I miss Mandy, but the renewed effort on the practice table starts to pay off. I get to the final of the 1988 UK Championship (losing to Doug Mountjoy 16–12 in a high-scoring game which sees Doug make four century breaks; I don't do too badly either, coming back from 16–6 and making a couple of centuries) and reaching the semis of the 1988 World Matchplay, going out to John Parrott.

But it's the Benson & Hedges Masters, to be played over seven days in January 1989 at the Wembley Conference Centre, that I'm most looking forward to. I'm now one of the top sixteen players in the world, so this is the first time I've qualified to play in the Masters. That itself is an honour but the opportunity to perform in this venue, which can hold 2,500 spectators, is a complete thrill. I've wanted to play here ever since the Masters semi-final of 1984, between Jimmy White and Kirk Stevens, which I video-taped and watched repeatedly as I tried to improve my own game by copying the greats. Kirk Stevens, one of the game's most flamboyant characters, wore a white suit and made a 147, which Jimmy answered in the final frame with a break of 124 to win the match. Afterwards, the pair were interviewed by none other than David Icke and all three were drinking champagne in celebration of Kirk's maximum. Those were the days!

The big crowd ought to be intimidating, but I find that I rise to the occasion when a large audience is involved – in contrast to my complete shyness off the table. Even at this stage I find it almost impossible to see that I have anything in common with the established players and although I'll say 'hello', that's about as far as conversation usually goes. When I've done my practice or played my match it's off to dinner with Ian and John and then back to the hotel for some time alone. No players' lounges or late-night card schools for me.

There's a real buzz about playing at the Conference Centre, even though I soon notice that most of the cheering and applause is reserved for Jimmy White – London boy and local hero. They're not quite booing me yet (though in time, that will happen) but there's a distinct feeling that as far as the crowd is concerned, there's only one contender for the title.

Unfortunately, I'm about to disappoint them. I beat Willie Thorne in the last sixteen then face Terry Griffiths in the quarter-final. Terry is a great player and an all-round nice guy. I enjoy his company and appreciate his dry sense of humour. I notice that he tinkers with his game on a regular basis – something I have little concept of at this stage in my career. Sometimes he's slow, sometimes he's speedy, and that can be unsettling. But I've played (and beaten) him a few times now and I have the feeling he knows he can't beat me. This makes me very comfortable indeed (though never complacent) and, true to form, he goes out 5–3 despite winning the first two frames.

This leaves me facing Steve Davis in the semi-final. We still haven't met in a final in the UK – a daunting prospect, yet one that I'm looking forward to – but I've already beaten him 9–3 in the semis of the 1988 UK Championship and, unlike a couple of seasons previously, I now feel that I'm in with a very good chance every time we meet on the table. This year he's defending Masters champion, but I'm buoyed with confidence and lead from the off. We both score a century break, but I'm just too good for him on the day and I beat him 6–3.

I can't believe I'm in the final at my first go in this competition. John Parrott is my opponent and he's a tough one – for me, he's up there with Steve and Jimmy as one of my most-feared opponents. In this match he fights particularly hard. He also has an annoying habit of smashing the pack open then turning away as if there was nothing on – before returning to the table to pot an easy shot. It's a bit of gamesmanship and I try not to let it wind me up as I sit in my chair, poised to get on the table.

After a long slog against John over fifteen frames, it's me who takes the trophy 9–6 – my biggest win since the 1987 Rothmans

Grand Prix. This, along with the World Championship and the UK Championship, is the icing on the cake in terms of targets each season and now I've achieved one – at the first attempt – I'm more than confident I can win the World in April.

Whether or not this confidence has led to me feeling a little less fearful of Ian I don't know, but a couple of months after the Masters comes a phone call out of the blue from Mandy. I'm delighted to hear from her. I've missed her and have never felt comfortable about the way I ended our relationship. After a few more phone calls we arrange to meet, in secret, at a hotel close to the M6 and halfway between our respective homes. We know we are in love, and that we don't want to be apart. Without Ian's knowledge several more meetings are arranged until, finally, I pick my moment and tell him that Mandy's been in touch. Then I ask if it's OK to start seeing her again. I feel ridiculous having to ask his permission – by now I'm twenty – but that is the nature of our relationship.

Ian sucks his teeth and doesn't look pleased. 'And are you sure you will put your career first, and always?' he asks.

'Yes, I'm sure.'

'Because so many good players have fallen by the wayside because they've been distracted by women.'

'Yes, I know that. It won't happen to me. I promise.'

'As long as you know what you're doing, Stephen,' he says. 'I don't want any repeat of the drugs stuff.'

I resist the temptation to repeat the fact that they were only poppers. 'Yes,' I reply, 'no problem. I understand.'

'OK, then you can see her again. But no more funny business. And remember your career.'

Lecture over, I phone Mandy to tell her the good news. She makes me happy, simple as that, and if I'm happy off the table surely that will make me a better, not a worse, player? So we get back together and within two or three years she will come up to live with me in the flat. We enjoy being together (when I'm at home, which isn't that often during the snooker season) and for now Ian is placated.

Mandy, however, will never quite forgive him . . .

Top 5 SNOOKER PLAYERS I'VE ENJOYED PLAYING AGAINST

1. Steve Davis
2. Ronnie O'Sullivan
3. Jimmy White
4. Alex Higgins
5. Mark Williams

CHAPTER 9

My confidence boost following the 1989 Masters win is perhaps a little misplaced, which becomes evident as the rest of the season progresses. I put in a couple of mediocre performances at the British and European Open events and Alex Higgins beats me 9–8 in the final of the Irish Masters, played at Goffs in County Kildare. This is a horse sales ring with seating all around the arena; when you're playing in the middle of this you feel surrounded on every level. It could be intimidating but as time goes on it becomes my favourite venue after the Crucible.

Backed by hundreds of Irish supporters, Alex proves that when he's on form he's still a deadly opponent. Unfortunately, he's not on form much these days, and is still in the tabloids for all the wrong reasons. Now it's for breaking a foot after jumping out of a window following a row with his girlfriend. During the first four frames, all of which I win, he's limping around the table and looks to be in real pain. Interestingly, when he settles into the game and starts to catch me up the limp miraculously disappears and by the end he's practically running to pot the balls. The crowd love it, and him. They're one of the most partisan

I've ever played in front of: Alex has the uncanny knack of being able to spread his confrontational personality and playing style far and wide.

The World Championship is, of course, in a different league as far as I'm concerned. I can't wait to arrive in Sheffield, settle in to the Hotel St George in Nether Edge (a couple of miles outside the city centre), visit my favourite restaurant, get on the practice table and enjoy the build-up to this event. However, the opening day, Saturday 15 April, is overshadowed by events going on in another part of the city. Liverpool are playing Nottingham Forest in the FA Cup semi-final at Hillsborough, and conversation among journalists in the Crucible's press room is that something major, involving multiple injury or even deaths, is going on down there. As ever, we players concentrate on our opening performances but when we catch the TV news later in the day we can hardly believe what we're seeing.

In the first round of the tournament (in which I'm seeded for the first time, at No. 4) I achieve a narrow 10–9 win over Gary Wilkinson. I dominate the game until 7–3, at which point Gary makes an impressive fightback and harasses me to a deciding frame. In the opening rounds of any tournament you want a quick win, particularly in the World Championship because you don't really feel you're involved in it until the later stages, so to be part of a decider in the first round is very pressured. The last thing you want is for your tournament to be over before it's even begun.

In the decider I make what is becoming one of my trademark shots – knocking in a raking long red with position attached and following up with a high break that wins the frame and the match. I'm finding myself doing this regularly now and getting something of a reputation for it. That's no bad thing – anything that gives me a psychological advantage over my opponent is to be welcomed. Also, I'm learning to cope with pressure at the biggest events, knowing that if I keep my cool I can deliver.

Such belief carries me through the next rounds, and I breeze past Willie Thorne and Terry Griffiths (13–4 and 13–5 respectively). In the match against Terry I win nine frames in a row and make a break of 141 – my highest so far at the Crucible.

The results put me into the semi-final against Steve Davis. He hasn't had the best season and I've beaten him three times already. But while Steve's form may not be quite what it was (and the bookies' odds narrow as the tournament opens, with me running a close second to him), he's still my hardest challenge. If I can beat him in this semi-final, I can win the tournament for sure.

Steve, however, has other ideas. If he beats me and goes on to win the title, it will take him to his sixth, equalling Ray Reardon's record. If this doesn't make him focused, nothing will. Despite all my protestations and promises, I haven't even been in a World Championship final yet, let alone won one. When I look at Steve's record I see a very large mountain ahead.

Steve outplays me with superior match-play and by the first session of the second day he's 10–4 ahead. I'm furious. I jab my cue into its case and slam the stage door behind me as I get into the car which will take me back to the hotel. Ian and John sense my mood, and during the journey to the hotel there is nothing but silence.

'I can't believe how fucking lucky Steve is,' I suddenly blurt out, 'getting such a good run of the balls.'

'Is it luck,' replies Ian, 'or is he just outplaying you?'

I don't reply. I really believe that I can win this, and I'm not prepared to accept that Steve might still be too good for me. But it is true. At this point I'm still not a complete enough player to beat him over the distance of a four-session match. Time and experience will eventually solve this. For now, though, I'm livid and full of frustration.

Increasingly, though, I'm finding that I'm at my strongest when the chips are down and I'm angry, and I fight back, recovering to 12–9. But it's not quite enough – Steve has the edge and earns his place in the final with a score of 16–9. His opponent is John Parrott and in cracking form Steve wins 18–3. John claims that fatigue has got the better of him, a result of seventeen days of long matches, but I don't really buy it. To me, the World Championship is the greatest test of stamina, concentration and technique and you just cannot allow yourself to think that you're tired. You must snap out of the mindset and get right back on it. If you feel tired, or you convince yourself you're feeling that way, there is no chance of winning a tournament like this.

So the final is simply no contest and what lies ahead for all of us is the realisation that Steve will play his hardest next season to earn his seventh world title, becoming the record holder. I've previously boasted to the *Sun* that I'll retire when I'm twenty-four, but only if I've won the world title at least twice. The idea of buying a restaurant and a snooker club, which I share with the newspaper, may have to remain on ice for a little longer.

Still, there is much to be optimistic about as the 89/90 season begins. I know I've hit great form and there's no reason for this not to continue and improve. Every time I open a newspaper I am being talked about as 'Steve Davis's successor'. There is still the occasional reference to 'Golden Bairn' or 'Wonder Bairn', a couple of nicknames that are planted on me at the start of my career (the latter by the racing commentator John McCririck, who occasionally pops up on ITV to give his opinion about betting on snooker) but haven't really stuck. There are no Hurricanes or Whirlwinds, or even Nuggets, sitting between my first name and surname. The best I get comes from Ted Lowe, who invariably calls me 'young Stephen' or 'this young man'. Sometimes he goes further and announces me as 'the Scottish Sensation' and, as I've mentioned, 'the young prince of potting'. In the future, he will often refer to me as 'the world's number-one star'. Forget Michael Jackson or Tom Cruise – I'm the man! Usually, though, to all and sundry it's just 'Hendry', and often I hear players in interviews saying things like, 'Yes, I've beaten Terry and Jimmy, and next I face Hendry.' No matter. It's the game, not the nickname, that counts.

There is a pre-season jaunt to the Far East, and for the first time we visit Thailand. Thai player James Wattana has broken through into the big time and the whole country has gone snooker mad. To capitalise, the first ever 'Asian Open' has been scheduled for a ten-day stint in a Bangkok TV station. I'm deeply impressed by the flavour and the buzz of this most extraordinary of cities. One of my fellow players takes me on a tour of the city and doesn't hold back when it comes to ushering me into live sex shows and the like. This isn't my scene at all, but for an innocent kid from Scotland it's a complete eye-opener, and away from the seedy side (and the ping-pong balls!) I love the vibrancy of the place. And after a few tentative tastes of Thai curry and spicy salad, I'm even getting to like the food.

However, I seem to be one of very few players who appear to enjoy travelling such distances to tournaments. Almost as soon as the plane takes off from Heathrow, the moans and groans about the impending couple of weeks begin in earnest. I find it hard to understand what they're grumbling about; I love packing for the airport, chilling in the lounge, sitting in first class, staying in a nice hotel and looking round an amazing city, the like of which you've never experienced before. There are worse things in life! Even so, the mumblings and mutterings continue, with players almost looking forward to losing in the first round so they can fly straight home to the UK. Terry Griffiths is well known for having his case packed before a match so he can get to the airport immediately, should he lose. I don't get it – but then I'm not a family man yet.

The Asian Open ends in a 9–6 victory for me in the final against James Wattana, though I almost lose my cool in one of the frames when, inexplicably, a fly somehow gets inside my shirt. I can feel panic rising – I have a phobia of flying insects – so while James builds a break, I'm frantically slapping my chest. I manage to get the beast and continue to dominate the game, though there seems to be an attitude among the Thais that because James is one of theirs, I ought to have let him win. Later, I have to explain that it doesn't really work like that, and particularly not with me. Even if I were up against my granny, I wouldn't even give her a chance to win.

Before we leave Thailand I pick up a souvenir of my visit in the form of two large oriental-style brass lion ornaments which I've spotted in a shop opposite the hotel. I pay a couple of hundred quid for them, but because of their weight they cost around £600 to send home. Ian won't be pleased, that's for sure . . .

Back in the UK, my season gets off to a great start with a 10–1 win over Terry Griffiths in the Scottish Masters final and a 9–2 victory against Doug Mountjoy in the first ever Dubai Classic. Steve beats me 9–4 in the final of the International Open but I take my revenge in the UK Championship final, beating him 16–12 in what is my first defeat of him in a long-frame, two-day final. In February 1990 I take my second Masters title, beating John Parrott again. If I win the World Championship this season, I will have done snooker's 'Triple Crown' – UK Championship, Masters and World Championship in the same season. But it's a big 'if'.

Before that, there is a significant event in January – my twenty-first birthday. A surprise party is held at Ian's club in Stirling and it's a great gathering of friends and relatives, despite the fact I'm not much of a party animal. Coming of age is an important event in anyone's life, of course, but for me, being twenty-one means fulfilling the public promise I made six years previously to be World Champion. I'm wealthy (on paper, at least), I own my own house, I drive a nice car, I have an amazing girlfriend, and I have great trips abroad both for work and leisure.

I also buy whatever I want, even if Ian thinks that spending £4,000 on a leather Versace jacket is 'ridiculous'. He claims that for every pound I spend, I pay more than double in tax. Maybe he's right, but I'm not interested. Personally, I think nothing of blowing a few thousand on clothes for Mandy and me, and there will be years when our clothing bill will come to something around £50,000. No wonder the Versace shop in Glasgow welcomes me with open arms and champagne. When I look back now, I shudder at the thought.

At this point, though, snooker has brought me countless rewards – and yet the biggest one, the prize I truly crave and work relentlessly towards, has so far eluded me. This year, of all years, I need to take home that World Championship trophy. Otherwise I'm going to look a bloody fool.

Somewhere in the general build-up to the Crucible, I play an exhibition match in Essex. Even though I'm making very good money, I still play exhibitions here and there as a way of earning extra money between tournaments and to keep myself sharp. There is nothing exceptional about this event, except for the presence of a fourteen-year-old boy who is put up against me. He has quite an entourage of supporters with him, including his dad, and they're very vocal in their opinion that he's 'the next big thing'. I hear this a lot about unknown players, and mostly take no notice, particularly when it comes from biased friends and relatives. But I've heard good things about this intense kid and when he gets on the table, grudgingly I have to admit that, for once, his supporters might be right. Straight away I can tell he's got 'it' – the magic ingredient that marks out the best from the rest. Maybe I'm impressed because I see he plays like me: attacking, going for everything, forgetting about safety play. We play a frame, I beat him, and I wonder whether he might do the same to me one day in the not-so-distant future. His name? Ronnie O'Sullivan.

For now, though, it's my name which appears to be on everyone's lips as we approach the April date with the Crucible. The newspapers are full of it. 'Has Hendry's time now come?' 'Will he do it this year?' 'Can anyone stop him?' Helpful as ever, Ian tells the *Daily Star* that I've got five years left before I burn out. 'If anyone's game starts to slide,' he warns, 'they will be following it a bit sharpish.' As ever, the paper follows up this dire prediction with the reassuring news that I'll be a millionaire by then and won't need to worry.

I try not to take too much notice (and, in fact, I will add to it by promising a tournament full of 'blood, sweat and tears' to the *Daily Record*) but in a way, maybe Ian is right. It's now or never. My gut tells me that yes, my time has come, and that I can finally beat Steve Davis on his territory, so to speak. My game is fine-tuned enough for a World Championship win and I'm well prepared mentally. I want to be the best player in the world, nothing less.

In the early rounds I beat Canada's Alain Robidoux, Tony Meo and Darren Morgan comfortably enough. Steve is also doing well, of course, but as we enter the semi-finals the trajectory we're on is blown off course by Steve's shock 16–14 defeat by Jimmy White. Jimmy is a superb player, but so far the title of

World Champion has eluded him. This is hugely frustrating for him and his army of fans. They find it hard to see why he hasn't won it so far because he has all the talent in the world – but often, talent alone is not enough, and the top professionals know this.

Am I more confident now that Steve's not in the final? Yes, in a way, because him not being there makes my task that bit easier. I don't fear him, or anyone, but I'd rather have an easy run to the top than a huge battle. And if I need a boost of confidence, it comes in my semi-final against John Parrott. I win 16–11, and after the game John Carroll rubs it in with John's manager Phil Miller by shouting 'Unlucky, Phil!' as he goes by. I look away in embarrassment – I like winning but I'm not the sort to gloat in front of my opponents after a match. Unlike Ian, of course, who makes himself ever more unpopular among the clique of managers that regularly gather in the players' lounges. He is very vocal about who's good and who isn't, and when I see the other managers standing together and whispering, I know for sure that it's Ian they're talking about.

That said, Ian, John and I all have reason to be cock-a-hoop following the John Parrott match because now, according to the rankings system, I am officially world number one for the first time. To say this is massive for me is an understatement. In less than ten years I've gone from being a kid who got a small snooker table for Christmas to becoming the best player in the world. And the youngest player ever to have achieved this, to be followed by a place in the World Championship final against Jimmy White, my hero, my idol; the player I most admired as I potted balls obsessively on my little table and tried not to think about schoolwork. I can hardly get my head around it. It feels amazing. In the post-semi-final interview, I say that I'm nervous about meeting Jimmy. I'm not. If I'm nervous about anything, it's about not winning the title, or completing the Triple Crown.

And really, I'm not very nervous about that at all. The way Jimmy plays suits my game down to the ground. It will be open and attacking, not tight and defensive (as it would have been had Steve been the opponent). Jimmy can be inspirational, but he's also the kind of player you know you will get chances against. He has easy misses in him. I'm the world number one and, while I don't have much time to really dwell on this, the final coming the day after the Parrott match, I can't see any way of losing. Even so, there is a secondary battle going on between me and Jimmy – that of our hairstyles. In this first year of a new decade we both sport classic 1980s mullets, though Jimmy's is thicker and more luxuriant than mine, which seems to be a variation on a Jason Donovan theme. Within the year mine will be replaced by something much slicker; Jimmy, however, will stubbornly resist the shedding of the '80s rock star' look for a while to come.

The moment I come through the curtain and down the steps leading to the floor of the Crucible for the final is one I will remember forever. The thrill is indescribable – even if I am announced as 'the Wonder Bairn' and the applause for me is nothing compared to that for Jimmy, who has walked out first. Jimmy is their darling; he's played his heart out during the Davis years, entertaining and charming audiences who don't always want Terminator-style snooker. Jimmy has lost in three world semi-finals and two world finals. 'If it's anyone's time now,' his fans are thinking, 'it's Jimmy's . . .'

The hush descends as the game begins. I know my family and friends are here, though – unlike Jimmy White, who spends half his time before the final running around trying to sort out tickets for his nearest and dearest, I leave visiting and hotel arrangements to Ian and John. I'm kept out of all that; although we meet beforehand and chat, even Mandy isn't allowed to stay in my room until the final is over.

Jimmy and I are evenly matched for the first few frames, the pair of us dodging and weaving, watching, waiting, anticipating. We're both looking to find the rhythm that will nudge us ahead, force each of us into defensive safety play or, worse, into making mistakes. I inch into something of a lead, but I can't afford to take anything for granted, especially when Jimmy soon pulls it back to make us even at 5–5. When this initial sparring session subsides, however, I edge in front again and this time start to feel that old tingling sensation, the one that whispers, 'This is where the tide begins to turn.' At the end of the first day I'm leading 9–7, and when we reconvene on day two a high-octane mixture of excitement, anticipation and nerves is making me sick. Quite often I feel this way before a match. As I read the paper in my dressing room, I can feel my breathing becoming shorter and shorter, the feeling of wanting to vomit only subsiding when I'm at the curtain, ready to be announced, and I go into 'match mode'. I just want the waiting part to be over as quickly as possible.

I can detect a change in Jimmy – the one which signals that he's desperate to win, yet secretly knows he will struggle. It's almost imperceptible – a tiny inwards movement around the eyes, a fleeting nip of teeth on lip – but it's there. I move slowly around the table when I'm on, shutting out everything else other than this moment of pure focus. When I'm not at the table I sit in my chair and let my head hang down. As the camera zooms in I could be taken for a player in deep dejection, facing a crushing defeat. But I'm not defeated, far from it. I'm just trying to exclude everything else and concentrate on the moment. 10–7, 11–7, 12–7, 13–7, 13–8, 13–9, 14–9, 14–10, 15–10, 15–11, 16–11 – the waves wash back and forth but the tide has long since turned. Jimmy is as pale as his surname as he breaks off for what will turn out to be the final frame, at 17–12. He needs a miracle now. As I pace the table I'm momentarily distracted by a rustling noise a few feet from the floor. There are low murmurs, the sounds of something being prepared. I realise that in the backstage area, the officials and sponsors are gathering for the end. They know something, and so do I. In a matter of minutes, I will be World Champion. I shouldn't allow myself to think about that, for the dangers of taking anything for granted are obvious, even at this stage. Especially at this stage. But I do think about it, and when I do I begin to play as though I'm back in Dunfermline, knocking balls across the battered baize of Maloco's or the slicker surfaces of the Classic, as older guys sip their pints, pull on their fags and comment on how I'm 'no' bad for a wee boy'.

Jimmy's head has gone. He sits in his chair and pokes his fingers into the top of his eyelids. He gets back on the table and misses an easy red. He sits down again and chews his finger. I tighten my jaw for a second before breathing out into a more relaxed posture. Referee Len Ganley dutifully replaces the colours as I take a determined, clear-eyed aim at my next target. This is how I've dreamed it would end and, with a break of seventy-one, it does. There is a roar.

I've done it.

I've done what I said I'd do.

I am World Champion.

I just don't know how to react. I'm not the sort to have prepared a celebration ahead of victory – I'd just feel stupid – and I'm certainly not going to break down in tears. So I lift my cue above my head and puff out my cheeks. Ian walks on, beaming, and grabs my head in his hands before pulling me to him. In the audience, Mandy looks amazing and my mum is crying.

My mouth hangs open in shock and I run my fingers through my hair. At the side of the table Jimmy is standing with his hands in his pockets, trying hard not to show his disappointment.

Nevertheless, he nods and gives a tight-lipped smile – which is more than I do, at least until I have my hands on that trophy. When I lift it over my head, out comes a lop-sided grin. 'Stephen Hendry – Snooker World Champion'. My new title. At twenty-one, the youngest ever to achieve this. I feel elated and weird and surprised, yet not surprised, all at the same time. What next?

Top 5 VENUES I'VE PLAYED

1. The Crucible
2. Goffs (Kildare, Ireland)
3. Wembley Conference Centre
4. The Guildhall, Preston
5. Queen Elizabeth Centre, Hong Kong

CHAPTER 10

In the immediate aftermath of the win there is a flurry of family hugs, kisses and handshakes, then straight into press interviews. 'How do you feel?' I'm asked. Now it's beginning to sink in. 'When I turned pro at sixteen I said I'd be World Champion at twenty-one,' I reply, 'and now I've done it, it feels amazing.'

'What's next, Stephen?' ask the reporters.

To keep winning, of course. What else?

There is an after-final party hosted by Embassy at the Grosvenor House Hotel in Sheffield. I'm not keen on this place – it's a bit of a dump, to be honest, but it's close to the Crucible and everyone descends on it for the final fling before the season closes. The press are allowed in, too, and after a few drinks the questions are less about the professional and more towards the personal. How much money have I earned? How will I spend it? What's it like to be a millionaire at twenty-one? I'm always on my guard at these events, being careful not to have any more than a couple of glasses in case I say the wrong thing. Out of the corner of my eye I see Ian giving interview after interview. He loves the attention and the sound of his own voice. Whether I like it or not, tomorrow's papers will be as much about my earnings as they will about the win, because Ian will tell them.

After Sheffield it's back to Scotland, and my 'hero's welcome'. An open-top bus tour of South Queensferry, where I live, has been arranged and I do my best to look like I feel comfortable about it. I'm honoured that I'm thought of in this way but in truth, I'd rather just go home after the win and make very little fuss about it. The victory itself has been labelled in the Scottish press as 'one for Scotland' and while I believe it's more a win for me than for anyone or anything else, I'm happy to go along with the theory. For many years Scottish snooker was very much in the shadows compared to what was going on down south. Ian and I have challenged the English status quo in the most visible way possible. Scots players have previously been seen as not having the bottle to play on TV. It's very satisfying to overturn this idea spectacularly.

And yet, this is still small-minded Scotland – the country that moans when its heroes remain local ones, and moans even louder when they have major success. My family is gathered for the bus tour through South Queensferry, and amid the cheers and clapping I can hear the odd voice shouting from the pavement about 'hangers-on' and the like. No doubt they've read all the pish in the papers about earnings and youth and success. It's stupid and annoying but I'm going to have to get used to it. Like it or not, I'm now 'famous' in that people want to know as much about me as they do about my game. There are requests for 'lifestyle' articles – I do a couple but try to keep the answers to the questions as close to snooker as possible. There are requests for public appearances, too. I'm more than happy to take the World Championship trophy to Tynecastle Park for one of Hearts' first matches of the season and walk on to the pitch with it at half-time, to a massive cheer. I'm less happy about the sartorial rules imposed on me that day; I turn up in a smart suit and shirt, but with no tie. Ties are obligatory in the directors' box, where a reception is being held, so I'm forced to borrow one that doesn't match my suit or shirt, which irritates me somewhat.

So life has become more than just playing snooker, but in fairness I'm shielded from much of the extracurricular attention by a combination of Ian's deflection and living in Scotland. The scrutiny I get is nothing to what it would be if I lived in London, and I've no intention at all of going there. I'm happy just to do the occasional bit of publicity and otherwise keep my feet on the ground.

The summer break consists of a holiday in the sun, time spent with Mandy and her family in Blackpool, and playing golf. I am more visible now – it's hard not to be when you've been in close-up on TV for the past few weeks – and people do greet me in the street. They're generally polite, friendly and older. As ever, there's quite a bit of 'My granny loves you,' or 'Can I get an autograph for my mum?' If there are hordes of young screaming groupies following snooker players around, they haven't yet discovered South Queensferry . . .

Following the summer break, the plan is to smash all the records Steve Davis has set. Tournaments won, maximum breaks, ranking points and – the daddy of them all – the six world titles he has amassed. I'm already alongside him in winning the Triple Crown and momentum is right behind me as I go into the 1990/91 season, though Jimmy White has already reminded me that it will not be a walkover by beating me 5–2 in the semi-final of the Hong Kong Challenge late that summer.

Still, I win the first four ranking tournaments of the season – the Rothmans Grand Prix, the Asian Open, the Dubai Classic and the UK Championship. The Rothmans is marked by a heart-stopping moment when I discover my cue has been stolen. There is a dedicated practice room in the Ramada Hotel, right next to the venue. I'm there practising and after an hour I nip out to get a Coke. When I return, the cue is gone, prompting complete panic all round.

Now, incredibly, this is still the £40 Rex Williams cue that I picked from the rack in the Classic Snooker Centre in Dunfermline simply because I liked the design on the handle. It's a cheap bit of wood, to be honest, and it has been the butt of other players' jokes for ages. Frank Callan has always insisted that I need another cue, claiming that it isn't strong enough to play a long shot to pot a red, screwing the cue ball back to the safety of the baulk end of the table. It's a bone of contention with Frank but I insist on sticking with the Rex Williams for the reasons that it's my first proper cue and because it suits my small hands. And with it, I've won a lot of silverware, including the World Championship trophy. Its loss is a massive blow.

Ian swings into action, contacting the press immediately. He tells them there is £15,000 on the table for anyone who can get it back. Pretty soon it is discovered in a bin (even the thieves appeared to have had a laugh over it) and returned. It's a tad damaged, but otherwise no worse for its ordeal and there are sighs of relief all round. Well, in some quarters at least. In the first round I'm drawn against a player called Jon Wright and as we stand in the wings, waiting for the announcement to go out, he says, 'I see you got your cue back.' I confirm this to be the case, to which he replies, 'Fuck!' As well he might – I beat him 5–2 and go on to win the championship, beating Nigel Bond 10–5 in the final.

There's no doubt I'm on a roll and I know it, and sometimes that leads me to shoot my mouth off uncharacteristically. One of these moments occurs at the Dubai Classic in November 1990.

Top left: As a schoolboy with great hair

Top right: Keith and I with the 'Grinder', Cliff Thorburn

Centre: Me (*front row, right*) looking aged about eight with other players at the World Amateur in Dublin, actually aged fourteen

Right: Representing my country with George Carnegie

Left: Starting my trophy collection, 1983

Right: With Mum and Dad, my biggest supporters

Below left: Wearing the leather waistcoat that caused problems with my cue action

Below right: At sixteen, I was too young to drive this 120mph Volkswagen Scirocco GT

Right: Me and the 'Hurricane', 1987

Left: Promoting tour of Scotland with Steve Davis, 1986

Centre left: First time on the table at the Crucible

Centre right: Still too young to drink this

Right: *Daily Record*, October 27, 1987

Above left: First of
four finals against my
boyhood hero, Jimmy
White

Above right: 'I've done
it!' First world title won
at age twenty-one

Right: My teammate
and doubles partner,
Mike Hallett

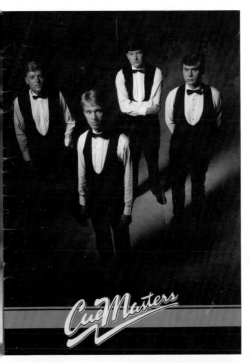

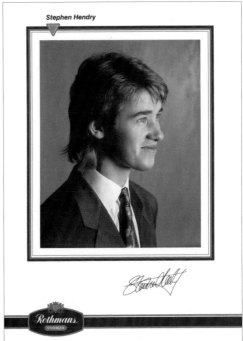

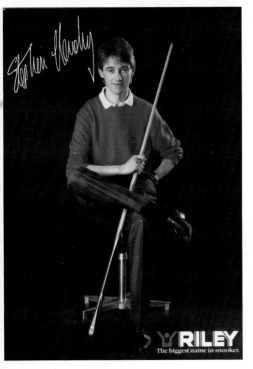

A selection of programme covers for 1980s tournaments

Below right: Signing my first contract, for Riley – Ian as ever looking over my shoulder

Top left: A frame in the desert with Steve Davis, 1990

Top right: Looking more like Shakin' Stevens

Below: Photo shoot in the snow with Lord Lichfield for the Sweater Shop

Hendry king of snooker

STEPHEN Hendry's third world title in four years earned him £175,000, took his official career prize money to £3,048,011 and confirmed the No.1 world ranking he has held since he became the youngest-ever champion in May 1990.

He has made 36 centuries in the Embassy World Championship since 1977, four more than former three-times champion, Steve Davis.

His total of eight in this year's championship equals the record set by Davis and equals that two years ago by John Parrott.

Hendry is in any case the most prolific breakmaker snooker has known. Davis has taken 15 years on the professional circuit to make 202 tournament centuries. In eight, Hendry has made 206. Davis has won 67 professional titles, Hendry 43 — so far.

Statistics say something but do not convey the strength of mind, the quality of concentration, the nerve, the killer instinct that make an exceptional champion.

Tactically, Hendry's cue action is as straight as a human being can get it. This, and the ability to keep still on his shot even when he is quivering with tension, produces the hand-eye co-ordination

Scots snooker star Stephen Hendry has the world at his feet after his fabulous display to clinch the world championship. Snooker expert and TV commentator CLIVE EVERTON reports.

••••••••••••••••••

which makes him a deadly potter.

At close quarters he has the deftness of touch, the control, the intelligence of shot selection to reel off fine winning breaks one after another. In his capacity to raise his game under pressure — notably his 9-8 victory over Mike Hallett in the Benson & Hedges Masters final three years ago from 8-2 down — he has no peer.

His best is clearly better than anyone else's. His less-than-best grows more formidable as his tactical game and knowledge grow stronger by the year.

Even so, off-peak, he can be beaten by a first rate percentage player like Davis.

Hendry will inevitably lose a few best-of-nines, the staple fare of most tournaments, and any of the top half dozen players on a given day could turn him over in

a best-of-17, but, at the Crucible, where matches start at best-of-19 and work up to 25, 31 and for the final, 35, he has lost only once in four years.

His strength of character has been shown by his recovery from a poor start to the 1991/93 season. Having won nine titles in 1991/92 he felt capable of ten in the new campaign, but in the first two finals he lost to Parrott 6-5 in Peking and 9-8 in Dubai.

A freak 6-5 defeat from 5-1 up by Gary Wilkinson in the quarter-finals of the Scottish Masters in Motherwell in September was an irritant; the series of death threats from a woman now on probation for these offences fractured his concentration for the Rothmans Grand Prix at Reading in October, where he lost to a Welsh journeyman, Tony Chappel.

Inconsistency

He played to form only in spasms until he won his fifth consecutive Benson & Hedges masters at Wembley in February, then lapsed into inconsistency until he won the Sky Sports International at Plymouth in early April, making ten centuries, a record for a world-ranking event.

At 24, Hendry has few more worlds to conquer, only similar ones to conquer again and again.

Money, though never irrelevant, is more an index of his worth than a spur to endeavour. Shrewdly managed by Ian Doyle, who is negotiating contracts such as the lucrative ones he now

ON TOP OF THE WORLD: Scotland's snooker ace Stephen Hendry with the trophy he won for the third time yesterday and his manager Ian Doyle.

Left: 'King of Snooker' with my manager Ian Doyle, *Daily Record*

Right: A Scot made King of Wembley, 1993

Left: Proud day in 1993, collecting my MBE at Buckingham Palace with Mum, Dad and Mandy

EXCLUSIVE! *TITLE TREBLE PUTS SCOT OUT ON HIS OWN . . .*

SIMPLY THE BEST!

Hendry's No.1 of all time

By *JOHN DOCHERTY*

DEADLY RIVAL . . . Steve Davis

STEPHEN HENDRY is the best snooker player – of ALL TIME.

And here's the exclusive picture that proves it – the Scot with the three big championship trophies.

Hendry is the only player to have held the World, European and UK titles at the same time.

A few people in the Steve Davis camp may disagree.

But when you examine the record books, I've got to put my neck on the table and say that Hendry is in a league of his own.

The rivalry between Hendry and Davis is well known and the burning question among millions of TV fans is – Who is the Greatest?

Golden boy Hendry, who celebrates his 26th birthday on January 13, won't get drawn into the Great Debate.

"I believe I'm the best in the world," he said. "But as for being the greatest ever then that's not really for me to say."

Hendry's manager Ian Doyle, however, insists: "In my book, Stephen is the finest player to grace a snooker table.

"He's a legend. Steve Davis is a legend – but even at his peak he was never as good as Stephen."

Confidence

After the festive break, Scotland's sporting king will be back at the table, sharpening his cue for the Benson and Hedges Masters at Wembley in February.

Hendry won that tournament FIVE years in succession before being toppled by fellow Scot Alan McManus in last year's final.

But after his 9-3 triumph over John Parrott in the recent final of European Championship in Antwerp, Hendry heads for London full of confidence.

And no doubt he'll be hoping to put another one over arch rival Davis.

GLITTERING PRIZES . . . Stephen Hendry shows off the silverware that makes him the No.1 – the World, European and UK Championship trophies   **Picture: CHARLES DONNELLY**

How they measure up

	HENDRY	DAVIS
Age next birthday	26	38
Turned pro	1985	1978
World No.1	5 years	7 years
Prize cash	£3,991,442	£4,198,327
Best season	£694,056	£661,490
	(90-91)	(88-89)
Major finals	65	92
Major titles	50	69
Average tournament wins per season	5	4.05
Ranking titles	22	27
Age at first major title	18	23
	(Grand Prix)	(UK)
World titles	4	6
World and UK same year	3	3
Highest break	147	147
	(Matchroom League, 1992)	(Lada Classic, 1982)
Centuries	269	234
Most centuries in a tournament	12	8
Most centuries in World Championship	8	8
Head-to-head wins	23	14

Hendry was youngest ever World champ at 21.

Who do you think is best?

SO who is the greatest? Team Sweater Shop would like to know what Record readers think.

Send your verdict to: Daily Record Sports Desk, Simply the Best Snooker Competition, Anderston Quay, Glasgow.

First name drawn will get two tickets for Scotland's premier tournament, the Regal Masters, at Motherwell Civic Centre, from September 19 - 24.

We are also giving away 10 special Team Sweater Shop sweatshirts.

Alex off hook

SNOOKER bad-boy Alex Higgins won't be carpeted for calling a referee "incompetent".

The Hurricane blew his top after being beaten by Dave Harold in last month's UK Championship.

He added that respected ref John Street should "take an eye test".

However, the WPBSA's disciplinary committee decided yesterday that Higgins hadn't broken the rules.

Earlier this week, the WPBSA handed Higgins a £5000 fine and one-year ban, suspended for two years.

King for a day

SCOTLAND'S Billy Snaddon won the King's Cup in Bangkok yesterday – then dashed off to get married!

The 25-year-old from Alloa defeated Noppadon Noppachorn 8-4 to capture the £3,000 first prize.

Within minutes, he was heading back to the Bangkok Palace Hotel, where he married Tracey Johnston.

"What a wonderful wedding present," said the world No.35, who donned a kilt.

"I've never won a major title either as an amateur or professional before."

The country is an emerging market for snooker and we players haven't been going there too long, so it takes a bit of getting used to. In 1990, Dubai is nowhere near what it will become as the decade progresses. The city is expanding, but just beyond its limits is a whole lot of desert and we are having to drive many miles across barren wastes just to get to the Emirates Golf Club, where we play expats during downtime. Our snooker practice takes place at the Dubai Police Club, and it's not at all uncommon to be up against players in full flowing Arab dress. I like the place and find it interesting, though any chance of experiencing some night-life is stymied by the fact that there is little to no night-life to be had. In 1990 Dubai is still a very conservative, traditional Arab country.

I win the final very comfortably, beating Steve Davis 9–1. Afterwards, I do a TV interview during which I'm asked if I have any regrets about the tournament. Without thinking, I reply, 'Yeah, I wish I'd beaten Steve nine–nil instead.' Immediately I realise how arrogant that sounds, and how it didn't really need to be said. I was trying to express how much I enjoyed winning, and winning well, but it comes out churlishly. Off the table, I'm not an arrogant person at all, though it has been said that when I am playing, I move around the table with an air of arrogance. At dinner that evening I apologise to Steve and explain that it came out the wrong way. Credit to him, he just laughs it off.

If I am arrogant, it's only because I'm enjoying being world number one, and World Champion. There is a respect towards me from the other players that I used to notice when Steve Davis was top dog. He cultivated a certain aloofness and now I feel this too. The guys aren't in awe of me, as such, but I sense that I'm being treated differently. The days of being 'the kid' in the corner are over. I love having the attention from within the game that being number one brings. It was hard getting here, and it will be even harder to stay, but for the moment I'm really basking in the sun – and not just around the pool of our Dubai hotel.

As a gift of thanks for attending the Dubai tournament, all the players receive a watch. Mine is a Cartier and I'm delighted because I have a thing about nice watches. Steve doesn't even look at his, and when he turns up to the airport the following day, looking tired and almost missing the flight, his first action once safely on the plane is to open the box. Whatever is in there is obviously not up to his standard.

'Well,' he says, snapping the lid shut, 'that's the final boot in the bollocks from this trip.'

We all laugh, but when we arrive at Heathrow Customs the smirks are replaced by downturned mouths. Duty is payable on the watches, and some of us must cough up tidy sums. I'm stopped by a customs officer, who asks if I'm in possession of one too.

'Yes,' I say, 'they gave it me for winning the final.'

'Ah,' the officer replies, 'that's different rules. Off you go, sir.' And I walk out of the airport to mutterings all round!

This particular trip to Dubai is one that some wives and girlfriends attend, and they spend their days sunning themselves while we battle it out indoors at the Al Nasr Stadium. Mandy isn't among the party, but this isn't because she doesn't want to come. In truth, it's me who would rather be alone, and this goes for most of the travelling abroad that comes with the job. I don't want to worry about her being bored while I'm working. Neither do I want to feel under pressure to do things when I'm not at the table. When wives aren't invited I see them in tears at airports and players phoning home several times a day. I just don't feel that way, and I don't particularly miss being at home. It sounds callous and selfish, and maybe it is. But I just enjoy my own space, and the experience of visiting new places.

Understandably, Mandy finds this difficult to accept but as soon as I walk out of the door of our flat and towards whatever venue I'm playing, I'm off to work. My desire to be alone while I'm playing abroad will be a fixture of our years together – sadly, problems will arise because of it.

On arriving home, Ian is very keen to get me to take part in a sports-related TV show being made at Thames Television in London. Forceful at the best of times, he's unusually insistent that I do this and so we turn up at the appointed hour to the studios in London's Euston Road. There seems to be something going on that I can't quite put my finger on, especially the way the blonde receptionist is trying to hide her face – then all is revealed when Michael Aspel steps out of nowhere and tells me that, 'Stephen Hendry, tonight, This Is Your Life!' Mandy reveals herself as the 'receptionist' and from behind some screens emerges a gang of snooker players, Joe Johnson and Terry Griffiths among them.

I'm stunned. 'But I'm only twenty-one,' I reply, genuinely surprised that anyone might be interested in such a short life as mine.

After I get over my blushes I'm led into a studio full of familiar faces. I take a seat next to Mandy, who has known about this for months, as have my parents and Ian. A parade of players is brought on, the first being Alex Higgins, who describes the time he and I practised for money ('just to make it interesting, you understand') and I had to borrow £100 from Ian. A couple of hours later, I took the stake back to Ian intact, plus an extra £20. After he tells this story, Alex kisses me on the cheek and waltzes off. Cliff Thorburn, Willie Thorne, Ted Lowe and Jimmy White all make appearances, as does my gran and Conrad Whitelaw, my teenage snooker pal. Conrad has made the effort to come to London and has never in his life stayed in a hotel. Later he tells me he even got lost walking up to his room from the lobby. It's great to see him, but the times we pretended we were Jimmy White and Alex Higgins seem like a lifetime ago. It's not just family and snooker-related guests: I'm delighted to see star striker John Robertson and chairman Wallace Mercer sending a few words from the pitch at Hearts.

After all this there's barely time to breathe before I rejoin the tour for the 1990 UK Championship held, as ever, at Preston Guild Hall. This year I'm the defending champion, having beaten Steve 16–12 the year before, and he'll be out to take back the title. I know I'd feel the same if I were in his shiny shoes. I have little trouble getting to the final and, predictably, so does Steve. My confidence is such that five frames in, I've skipped comfortably into the lead and Steve is nowhere. Good job, then, that I never underestimate him because he holds his nerve and battles me back to 10–7. From there on it's a real tussle. Steve's game is superb and at the start of the final two frames he's in the lead at 14–15. So much for an early advantage, and by now I'm pretty sure I'm beat. I've played Steve enough times now to know when he's in sight of the winning post. When the pressure builds he keeps his cool whatever the circumstances.

Or will he? Catching sight of the end of a match, when it's going your way, is fraught with danger. The situation can really faze players, and cause mistakes they would not otherwise make. As I sit in my chair at the start of the penultimate frame, watching Steve make a steady break, I'm hoping for one of those mistakes. And on forty-four it comes, letting me in – until I fail to pot a tricky red and I'm off the table again. Then Steve misses an easy red to the top-right pocket, there is a groan from the audience and I'm back in the frame. But now it's my turn to make a simple miss and on we go, with Steve closing in all the time. However, his default safety play won't allow him to split the reds and, as the tension mounts, he gives me yet another chance, one of several in this frame. I start the break with a great red, but I also know that the positioning of the blue, hard up against the cushion, is going to cause me problems later on. Even so, the break builds and even though any miss can cost me the match, and the title, I plough on with confidence. I really want to move the blue from the cushion but it's now impossible because of the angle I've left myself on the brown. An option – the only option, most players would argue – is to play a safety shot off the blue. But that doesn't cross my mind at all. I'm going to have a crack at this. I've made a great break and I simply don't see that I can't pot the blue. It's a crazy shot that few players would attempt, especially under these circumstances and made even more difficult by the fact I have to use the rest. If I twitch it Steve will clear up and win the match. Backstage, Ian is speechless with horror that I'm going to attempt it. But to hell with all that. I'm in the zone and I know I can do it.

I breathe, pull the cue back and hit the white perfectly. The seconds seem to slow down as it hits the blue, knocking it in cleanly. There is a short gasp followed by applause from the audience. It was an outrageous shot to take on but I've been rewarded for my bottle. Frank Callan, who is watching the game, tells me later that he can now 'die happy', having seen me build what will be one of my greatest career breaks culminating in that potted blue.

I know Steve will have been willing me on to take it, assuming I'd miss. When I don't, he's clearly rattled. The shot is the jolt of electricity I need to keep in the game; if anyone had said to Steve just two minutes previously that he'd be in danger of losing, he'd have written you off as mad. But this is snooker. The ebb and flow can go on right down to the wire. Steve has had a handful of chances to win this, and he hasn't taken them. As I'll say in an interview later, going into the final frame felt like a whole new match, especially when Steve inadvertently splits the reds on his opening shot and I get in. The winning post is ahead, and now it has my name on it. I try not to think about that and stay calm, focusing, keeping my breathing steady, yet still going for everything on the table.

In the players' lounge, Ian has already told anyone in earshot that I'm finished in this match. He seems to make a habit of this when things appear to be going badly; in fact, there are times he will have already shaken the hand of my opponent's manager to congratulate him, only for me to come back and win. Unfortunately for Ian (and Steve) this is heading to one of those moments. Steve sits and suffers as the reds and colours go down, and at 16–15 it's finished. I hang on to the UK Championship, Steve is vanquished and there is talk that his era is over – and that mine has well and truly begun.

The restless relentlessness of the season marches on and I'm out for every trophy I can get my hands on. I'm desperately keen to win a hat-trick at the Benson & Hedges Masters event and the tournament goes well. So well, in fact, that up to the final I lose a total of just two frames. The path appears clear for the treble, but standing in my way in the final is Mike Hallett; stablemate and doubles partner. He's a great player but I'm not aware of too many difficulties involved in beating him.

That's where I'm wrong. To everyone's surprise, not least my own, Mike storms to a 7–0 lead. He's been practising like hell for this one following a terrible 9–0 defeat by Steve Davis at this competition in 1988, and time spent at the practice table is really showing. I hadn't expected this at all, and I'm thrown by his sheer determination to win. After this first session I go back to my room, feeling terrible. I pick at some food and stare at the ceiling, still in shock and wondering how I'm going to pull this back, if at all.

At the start of the evening session there is hope as I pick up two frames. Mike gains another and now, at 8–2, he's almost at the point of sending me home on the long drive up to Scotland. Having potted an easy blue he's nearly cleared the table and needs to use the rest on the pink. I close my eyes for a second as he takes aim . . . and misses. I jump towards the table, potting the pink before Mike's barely sat down. Now it's 8–3 and I'm off the hook, temporarily at least. An interval follows immediately after the frame and Mike's frustration is there for all to see as he stomps back to his dressing room ahead of me, thumping his cue on the floor with every step. In my dressing room I sense what he's feeling and realise that I'm now in a good position to take advantage of his annoyance. He's the second player Ian has brought into the Cue Masters stable – the team that Ian has built to rival Barry Hearn's Matchroom line-up – and I know he considers himself a touch 'second best'. So there is a bit of needle here, and he's very keen indeed to beat me at a major event. Yet he's the underdog, and as any snooker player in that position knows, the final frame is always by far the hardest. If I can keep the pressure on him, just concentrating on every shot and winning each frame, I can really rattle him.

As predicted, when we come out after the break Mike is thrown. In his confusion, agitation and disappointment he becomes nervous and makes mistakes, leaving me to build the fightback: 4–8, 5–8, 6–8, 7–8, 8–8. 'Has anyone got a rope?' Mike asks plaintively at one point. He puts up a fight in the last frame but it's too late. It's a scrappy frame and he leaves me a tricky brown which, again, a lot of players wouldn't take on. Again, it doesn't enter my head to think or care what other players might do. I have to play it with a lot of right-hand side to pot the ball, which I do, taking the cue ball off three cushions to get on to the blue. And with the pressure, the blue isn't easy, either. I must hit it really well to get the desired action that will land me nicely on the pink. Subsequently I pot the pink into the bottom-left pocket and almost punch the table in triumph. Now I've won three Masters titles in a row and years later, in an interview about this match, Dennis Taylor will say he's never seen emotion like that from me. It's from a place of celebration, but relief too. The mental effort of this fightback, the biggest of my career so far, is draining and although I never give my opponents an inch, I do feel for Mike – especially when he's having a few drinks in his hotel later that night and is informed that while he's been playing me, his house has been burgled. Robbed twice in one day, poor guy.

Top 5 FAVOURITE HEARTS PLAYERS

1. Bobby Prentice
2. Eamonn Bannon
3. Drew Busby
4. John Robertson
5. Craig Levine

CHAPTER 11

The glamorous life of a star snooker player continues with a visit to the Alwyn North oil platform in the North Sea, during the early part of 1991. The platform is owned by the Total company, who also own glue manufacturers Bostik, one of our sponsors. Mike Hallett and I have been asked to play an exhibition there and following an extensive safety briefing in Aberdeen we're taken on a two-hour trip over the North Sea by helicopter and on to the platform, which is geographically closer to Norway than it is to Scotland. As the helicopter hovers over its landing point I can see the swell of dark water below us and I look away in terror. I'm not a nervous flyer, but this is something else.

Safely touched down, we are given a tour of the place before we get on with the match, to the delight of the guys working in this remote place. The only downer is that we have to stay the night – the accommodation is basic, to say the least. Ominously there are no locks on the doors in case we have to suddenly evacuate the platform. The food, though, is amazing and all in all it's been an interesting experience, though I've never been so glad to get back on dry land.

The tour of unlikely venues continues with a visit to Polmont Young Offenders' Institution near Falkirk. This is also a scary experience, but for very different reasons. I've agreed to play a few frames of pool against some of the young guys currently incarcerated, and a prison officer has already warned me that in such places, everyone wants to prove how tough they are. There are four sets of seats surrounding the table, and the occupants of the various wings are brought in one wing at a time. When the sex offenders' wing arrives there are boos and hisses right around the hall.

The heavy atmosphere doesn't dissipate once the pool starts. Every time I miss I get abuse, real hard-edged stuff, and my opponents aren't guys I'd like to meet on a dark night on any street corner. I try to clear the table as quickly as possible because I just want out of here. Yet when we finish I take time to sign autographs and chat to some of the inmates, and I find that on a personal level they're friendlier than I expected. As I leave I'm presented with a gift made by some of the lads working in the carpentry shop. It's a kind, thoughtful gesture.

These surroundings are in sharp contrast to the splendid Hampstead home of the son of the Sultan of Brunei, one of the world's richest men. The man who will later become Crown Prince Billah is a snooker fan and has employed a succession of top players to coach him, including Steve Davis, Jimmy White, Willie Thorne and Dennis Taylor. When I become World Champion I also get the call, and although I'm cancelled at the last minute ahead of our first meeting, we eventually get together a second time at his home. It's like a scene from the Eddie Murphy film *Coming to America*; suddenly a convoy of three luxury cars appears and the Crown Prince appears from the middle one, surrounded by security. Politely he escorts me into his house, in which a competition-standard snooker table

ME AND THE TABLE

is set up ready for action. The Crown Prince chats while his security staff remove his jacket. He's a nice guy, and obviously very into his snooker. My problem is that I know little about coaching, so I suggest we follow my usual practice routine. He turns out to be a decent player, and we agree to play alternate shots until we've cleared the table. This lasts for an hour or so. Then our session is over, and security reappear to replace his jacket and whisk him off in convoy. For my pains I'm paid £5,000 and given a penknife embossed with a diamond and a triangle of red rubies. Not bad for an afternoon's work.

By the time the 1991 World Championship rolls around I've won no fewer than eight tournaments (including five ranking events) and I'm still World number one. In April, I arrive at the Crucible like the conquering hero, the result of the tournament a foregone conclusion (in my mind, at least).

What do they say about the best-laid plans? And pride coming before a fall? It is a fall, too; a big one. I hear stories about something called the 'Crucible Curse', which apparently affects players who are defending the World Championship the year after their first win and, by some strange means, manage to lose it. I think it's all bollocks, of course, and given my track record this season there seems no way that such a thing can apply to me. And then I go out in the quarter-final to Steve James.

Now, many reasons are put forward for this shock defeat, the main one being that I'm completely exhausted from a season which has seen me play out of my skin and win almost everything in sight. In short, I'm burned out and I don't have enough left in me to get over this final line. It seems a very plausible reason and one I'd be happy to accept if, like the Crucible Curse, I didn't think it was even more bollocks. I'm the World Champion, I'm number one in the rankings and I'm still very young. I have bundles of energy, and all the confidence needed (and more) to pull myself to a second world title. That I don't manage to is purely down to the fact that Steve James is a very talented player and, on his day, can beat anybody – including me. In my blind expectation of winning, I simply haven't entertained that. He beats me 13–11, winning each of the last four frames, and I'm completely devastated – I haven't even made it to the semis, never mind the final.

That night, straight after the defeat, I pack my case, get into the car and we head for home. John Carroll is driving, and the only word I say during the whole of the journey from Sheffield to South Queensferry is 'thanks', when he drops me off. The loss has cut deep, and for the next few days I don't answer any phone calls or even leave the flat. I'm speechless with fury at myself. Ian doesn't ring. And I don't want to speak to him. I'm not yet ready for the inevitable inquest.

While I sulk, the tournament continues. John Parrott emerges as the deserving winner, and the latest player to stamp all over Jimmy White's hopes in the final. I don't watch a second of it, of course. Why would I? I should still be there, intimidating opponents with my reputation. Eventually, I'm summoned to Stirling for what I expect will be a large bollocking that I feel I fully deserve. Ian, though, is strangely OK about it.

'You're knackered, son,' he says. 'You've had a hell of a season. Let's forget this one, if we can.'

'I should've won,' I say, still down in the mouth. 'That guy should no way have beaten me.'

'So you keep saying. Don't be too hard on yourself. There's always next year.'

It's true, and within a few days I'm putting it behind me. I didn't feel tired or burned out, but I know for sure I was overconfident. Steve James was up against the defending champion and he played to win. So did I – my problem was that I thought I'd won before I'd even got to the table, and it didn't quite turn out like that. Simply, I was outplayed by a guy who raised his game specially. Lesson learned, it is back to the practice table. Fifteen reds, six colours. Red-colour, red-colour, red-colour, red-colour, red-colour, red-colour, red-colour, red-colour, red-colour, red-colour, red-colour, red-colour, red-colour, red-colour, red-colour. Yellow-green-brown-blue-pink-black. And repeat . . .

It's September 1991, and our Boeing 747 touches down on to the hot surface of Indira Gandhi International Airport, Delhi. Mentally I tick off yet another country that, being a professional snooker player, I'm lucky to visit. Billiards is huge in India but although snooker has its roots here, thanks to the British Empire, the Indian snooker scene is only just developing as a popular pastime.

Nevertheless, here we are at the inaugural Indian Challenge event, to be played over three days at the Taj Palace Hotel, Delhi, where we're also staying. We've come straight from fixtures in Hong Kong (where I beat James Wattana 9–1 to win the Challenge final) and Bangkok (the Thailand Masters, in which Steve Davis has beaten me 6–3 to take the trophy) and we've had a great time in both places. The hotels we've stayed in have been fabulous, too. So I'm very much looking forward to seeing what Delhi, and India, has to offer.

Something of an answer comes as our minibus nears its destination. I'm gazing out of the window, just people-watching, when I spot a guy squatting at the side of the road. Is he doing what I think he's doing? No . . . he can't be . . . not in the street. Oh Christ, yes he is!

Feeling my stomach turn over I look away and suck in a lungful of air-conditioning. I've just witnessed a guy taking a crap on the pavement, and in broad daylight. What kind of a country have I come to? While I feel bad for anyone having to do this in the street, this sight isn't the greatest of welcomes.

We arrive at the hotel and disembark from the minibus. By now, I've a pretty good idea of the kind of hotels I like staying in, particularly abroad. I'm an unapologetic hotel snob, and from the second I enter the lobby of this place I know it's not going to be for me. It doesn't look or feel right, a suspicion confirmed when I open my room door and see that the bathroom looks decidedly below par. If I could check out now I would, but not knowing an inch of this vast city, I wouldn't know where to go. I'll just have to put up with it, and I resolve not to touch any food other than items I'm completely sure about.

It sounds like paranoia, but when my fellow players quickly succumb to 'Delhi Belly' after less than twenty-four hours in India I'm very glad that I've stuck to a diet of tomato soup, bread, and little else. I'm told that curry is the safest thing to eat as it stays boiling in the pot all day. This sounds like a recipe for disaster and so it is – I'm the only one who doesn't become ill. Poor Gary Wilkinson gets it so bad that he's forced to take three or four impromptu breaks during one of his frames to run to the toilet. There is some relief for us all when we visit the British Embassy in Delhi, where we're served traditional sausage and mash, complete with HP sauce.

Maybe it's no surprise, then, that I win the tournament (which includes a win against the incredibly named Indian player Sonic 'Boom' Multani, who plays out of his skin and narrowly loses 5–4), though I'd like to think it's due to my playing being superior to everyone else's, and not because they're in varying stages of collapse. In the final I beat John 'sick-as-a-parrot' Parrott and the minute I'm off that table my case is packed and I'm in the lobby, waiting for the minibus to take us back to the airport. Never have I longed so much for aeroplane food . . .

Back in the UK, I'm delighted to beat Steve Davis 10–6 in the final of the 1991 Rothmans Grand Prix. A few weeks later

ME AND THE TABLE

Steve is witness to a nasty little incident involving me and Alex Higgins. We are facing each other in the first round of the UK Championship in Preston; only a year ago, making an appearance on my *This Is Your Life*, Alex had nothing but kind words of praise for me. Despite his reputation, I've always got on well with him. Now, though, something has changed – and it is that he recognises my stock is rising rapidly, while his is in free fall. To say he doesn't like this is an understatement.

Alex likes to have enemies. As I've mentioned, the target for his mutterings, utterances and digs in the press used to be Steve Davis when Steve was winning everything. Now I'm winning (not everything, but a very good percentage) his laser-eyes have locked on me. Everything he says appears to have a barb attached to it. Resentment pours out of him like a spilled pint; he is The One – the talent, the genius. Woe betide anyone threatening this. He's also going through bankruptcy and early next year he will face a World Snooker Association disciplinary hearing for 'bringing the game into disrepute'. It isn't the first time and it won't be the last.

This early round comprises eight tables, four on each side of the auditorium, and a corridor in the middle. The players, including myself, are waiting in the corridor just before the games commence. Alex comes in, walks towards me and I offer my hand for the customary shake. He takes it, looks me right in the eye and says, 'Shake hands with the devil . . .'

Steve Davis is standing nearby, and he catches the remark. Alex notices he's heard it and, with a nasty grin, says, 'I'm going to fuck him tonight, Steve.'

Steve doesn't reply, but raises an eyebrow, Roger Moore-style, in my direction. He's had plenty of this kind of behaviour before and he hasn't allowed it to faze him. So I won't either. The best way to deal with aggression is to ignore it and try to get the match over as soon as possible. I beat him convincingly 9–4 and throughout the game he's snapping and snarling. At the end, I offer my hand again; again, he takes it, gives me the death-stare and mutters, 'Up your ass, you cunt.' There's no answer to that and I don't even bother trying. In the after-match press conference the journalists who've noticed Alex muttering things in my direction ask him what he's been saying.

'Oh, I was just saying, "Well done, you were a bit lucky",' he replies, looking like butter wouldn't melt. Perhaps Alex gets some satisfaction when I eventually lose 9–2 to Jimmy in the semi-final, though by this stage he has enough problems of his own to worry about.

In London I win the B&H Masters for the fourth time, beating John Parrott 9–4. There's something about this venue that inspires me to play well at it and I always rise to the occasion there. And the prize money is amazing too (as the press are always keen to note), but if 'Hendry is going home with a cheque for £105,000 in his back pocket' he isn't finding much time to spend it. Below is the breakdown of my schedule for March 1992, a typical month in the life of a top snooker player, circa early 1990s:

MARCH 1992
Sun 1. Matchroom League -v- Foulds
Mon 2. Travel home
Tues 3. Practice or possible event in Monte Carlo
Wed 4. As above
Thurs 5. As above
Fri 6. As above
Sat 7. Travel to Warwick. Fly to Birmingham – 2.45pm
Sun 8. Matchroom League -v- Wattana, Warwick University
Mon 9. Travel home. Evening dinner at Partick Thistle

Tues 10. Practice

Wed 11. As above

Thurs 12. As above

Fri 13. Dinner Dicksons, Perth / Travel to St Helens,
    9.30pm

Sat 14. Matchroom League -v- Wilkinson, Town Hall,
    St Helens

Sun 15. *Question of Sport*, Manchester

Mon 16. Travel home.

Tues 17. Practice

Wed 18. As above

Thurs 19. As above

Fri 20. Travel (destination to be advised)

Sat 21. Matchroom League -v- Meo, venue to be advised

Sun 22. Matchroom League -v- Davis, Concert Hall,
    Glasgow

Mon 23. Practice.

Tues 24. As above.

Weds 25. As above.

Thurs 26. As above.

Fri 27. Help the Aged exhibition, Grosvenor Hotel,
    Glasgow, 6.00pm

Sat 28. Travel to Gatwick, Matchroom League -v- Fisher,
    8pm, Gatwick Stirling Hotel

Sun 29. Matchroom League -v- White, The Hawth, Crawley

Mon 30. Travel home

Tues 31. (left blank)

Finally! A free day at the end of the month! The schedule is typical of every month of every year, barring about six weeks off over the summer. Being a pro snooker player is well paid and prestigious and all that, but let no one say it isn't demanding.

The day after my much-needed rest day I fly to Ireland for the Irish Masters in County Kildare. The local favourite is Ken Doherty, a talented player similar in age to me, and who beat me in the quarter-final of the British Open back in February 1992. Ken isn't the heaviest scorer but he's a clever player, particularly when the balls aren't in easy positions. He has lots of bottle and is good under pressure. They don't call him 'Crafty Ken' for nothing. This time I'm determined not to let him in and in the final I'm 3–1 up against him at the mid-session interval. Ken, though, is dogged, never letting up even when he begins to trail, and eventually squares me at 4–4. I make three good breaks in a row but even then Ken doesn't give up, winning a couple of frames before I finally finish him 9–6. It's a been a good scrap, and one in which Ken has shown his mettle.

The win sets me up – if I need setting up – for the World Championship. I have a lot to prove this year, not least that the 1990 win wasn't just a fluke. I want to be World Champion again – and again, and again. Doing it once will never be enough for me. And there are external pressures too; an interview I give to the *Scotland on Sunday* newspaper the day before the World Championship begins includes the line 'The word on the street is that Hendry is heading for a burnout'. Again, it doesn't feel that way to me, though judging by the schedule above my life is very, very busy indeed. In addition, I've won no fewer than six titles so far this season. By anyone's standards this would be brilliant. But I'm not just 'anyone'. The implication is that I need to be winning everything, and the fact that I haven't quite cleared the table this season seems to be a sign that I'm heading for the rocks.

It's not true, of course, but had the press widened their focus somewhat, they might have spotted that a talented trio of players were all about to turn pro and would eventually become the new young guns of snooker. School-leavers like me, the three have come up through the junior ranks to take their places among the rest of us. Before long, they will be serious contenders for tournament titles and the arrival of this 'Class of 92' will be proclaimed as a new 'golden age' for snooker. Their names? John Higgins, Mark Williams and that kid called Ronnie who I encountered at the exhibition in Essex.

More of them later. For now, my focus is to cut my way easily through the early rounds at the Crucible, taking nothing for granted, until I'm safely into the final. The semi-final draw is a comfortable one; I'm up against Terry Griffiths, a player I haven't lost to so far, and true to form the game goes my way resoundingly. I'm ten frames up before he even starts to get a look-in. And the handful of frames he snatches barely puts me off my stride. At 16–4, I'm into the final with my confidence set at maximum.

My opponent is feeling pretty good too. Like me, Jimmy White lost out last year and, having been my scalp in the 1990 final, he's more than keen to put that right. He's already made a 147 in this tournament – only the second player ever to do so at the Crucible. He and I always seem to be the first players into the practice room in the mornings. I can see that Jimmy has remained focused and played well to get this far; like me, he saves his best snooker for the Crucible, making him one of my toughest opponents here.

With the final under way, it doesn't take him long to prove this. I win the first frame comfortably, but Jimmy picks up his form and we scrap it out hard. Jimmy begins to take the advantage. He's playing like his life depends on it and I'm just about hanging on to him as we go 4–6, 5–6, 5–7, 5–8, 5–9, 6–9. Now he's broken away, taking the score to 14–8, with two frames left of the third session. I'm trailing, and although I haven't lost hope or focus it would seem that if Jimmy continues with this form he will be lifting that trophy by the end of the day.

Ian has already given me a bollocking in the dressing room following the end of the second session. In my mind's eye I see him talking to Jimmy's entourage, telling them that this year it really is their boy's turn for the trophy. A flush of anger ripples through me. Despite my predicament there's no way I'm going to let Jimmy get the better of me. I need to win the next two frames. If I don't, I'm sunk. Jimmy's fans sense their hero is on the brink of something amazing and, as we enter frame twenty-three, his demeanour is calm, while I face trouble, needing ten frames to win. I've been outplayed by Jimmy but I still hang on to the belief that I can turn this around. I make a stupid mistake and let him in. But after he splits the pack he misses a red and lets me back on the table. Even under this pressure – maybe because of it – I'm still going for whatever I can sink. The pressure is immense, and we feel it acutely. Mistakes are made on both sides. Jimmy misses a long pot and I clear up to take the frame. There is a faint breath of relief, although there is still the matter of the next frame. As I force the pace I make a foul and I'm back in my chair, head down, eyes closed. Jimmy has me for the taking. It can only be a matter of time now before he pulls ahead once again. Then, with a break of forty-two under his belt, he uses the rest for a pot to the corner pocket and misses. I'm surprised, as he's usually excellent with the rest, but I now have a chance to get in and hopefully make a clearance. I slot away a few easy reds and try to move the pink away from its place hard up against the cushion but it's not for shifting. The blue is somewhat easier, and I screw back for it, only to come straight on it, leaving myself unable to get good position on the yellow. The obvious move now would be to play the cue ball on to the black and snooker Jimmy on the yellow, behind the blue and pink. As ever, I don't go for the obvious; instead I decide to take on the brown – a tough shot because the cue ball is in the middle jaws of the pocket. It's awkward cueing and if I miss I will be six frames behind at the start of the final session – a mountain to climb. Later, John Virgo will say it's the bravest shot he's ever seen. Others might describe it as suicidal. It will be one of the biggest and boldest shots of my career.

To my relief it goes in, and the boost it gives me helps me clear the table. It's one of the best breaks I've made and now I'm just four frames behind and feeling more confident about the rest of the match.

Back at the hotel, the wait before the start of the evening session seems to last forever. I didn't want to stop; having to go back to the hotel when I've found momentum is agony. I sit quietly on my bed, read the paper and listen to some music. Ian and John know better than to bother me now. I don't want any pep talks or to deal with anything other than what is ahead, the outcome of which lies completely in my hands. What Jimmy is doing I don't know, but it's a safe bet that he's chatting away to his family and friends as they tell him he can do this. I don't need to hear any of that – I know I can win if I just focus and concentrate.

The evening session begins and quickly I notice Jimmy is really feeling the pressure. He's hitting the ball too hard and he's sweating as he runs his fingers constantly through his hair. His edginess boosts my confidence. If I can hang on, take advantage of his nerviness and put him under even more stress, there might be a chance.

The frames begin to tumble. From perching like vultures around the arena just a few hours ago, Jimmy's fans seem to have collectively slumped into their seats. 11–14, 12–14, 13–14, 14–14 – I make a break of 128 in that 28th frame and we're even.

Jimmy's positional play starts to unravel and I'm now firmly in the zone. I think he knows I'm about to take control of the match and even though I'm still making mistakes he can't quite capitalise on them and snatch away the game. 15–14, 16–14. The finishing line is close ahead. I'm on a roll, feeling totally relaxed and, as Ted Lowe observes from the commentary box, 'It's like having a game in a pub.' Glancing at Jimmy, I see his face as a picture of despair and misery. Snooker is a game that challenges all your mental faculties. You can be so many frames down, on your knees, and your opponent riding high. Then there is a sea change – a careless shot or one easy miss, and now it's you who's in the ascendancy.

Jimmy's gone. He's offering nothing now. All he can do now is sit and bite his lip. In the final two frames I make breaks of 134 and 112 to finish him off. I've won ten frames in a row and at 18–14 it's all over. I've held on to my bottle and fought back to produce one of the best wins of my career. The relief is etched into my face as Ian comes on to shake my hand and I raise the trophy in the air, managing a brief smile. Then David Vine arrives to host what he always refers to as 'wages time' – the presentation of the cheques. This phrase always irks me slightly. The money is good – fantastic, I should say – but it's not what this or any final is about. For me, it's the winning, first and always.

Jimmy takes the defeat in good spirit, in a way I could never do. He arrives at the after-final party and he seems fine, chatting with everyone and having a laugh. If I'd suffered such a defeat I'd be wanting to crawl under a stone. Next day, he tells the papers that someone would have to 'play like God' to beat him, and I did that. 'He won playing fantastic snooker. It's the first time I've ever not felt sick at losing,' he says.

Never one to shy away from a reporter's notebook, Ian says that he 'wouldn't like to say' that I'm the game's greatest player but I'm 'certainly the greatest winner'. He adds that I might get out of competition snooker soon because of the 'pressures', though not before I equal Steve Davis's record.

My own judgement of the event is a little more economic. 'It was a night I'll never forget,' I say.

Top

5 FILMS
1. Godfather II
2. Godfather 1
3. Sideways
4. The Wolf of Wall Street
5. The Insider

CHAPTER 12

Mandy and I are scanning the brochures we've been sent from the estate agencies. I turn them over and over, not quite getting my head around the idea that someone like me could be living in places as glamorous-looking as these. I'm not much of a homebody. Living out of a suitcase is second nature and I'm quite happy to sleep in hotels and eat in restaurants, if they're good ones. But circumstances are different now and settling down seems to be the thing to do.

Mandy has, by now, moved up to Scotland. At first, we lived in the flat before buying a detached house in South Queensferry. The place is nice, but we're looking for something with more land. Mandy is a keen showjumper – always has been, even before she met me – and she wants to stable her horses closer to home. At present they're in a livery yard. Horses aren't my thing at all. I will help muck out if necessary, but it's almost always a case of 'Oh God, do I have to?' However, I can see the equestrian life is something Mandy has always loved and having her horses on land we own will make life a lot easier for her, especially when I'm away.

'How about this one?' she says, passing me a brochure. 'I can really see us in there. It looks amazing.'

She's not wrong. Westfield House, in West Lothian, seems huge. Four bedrooms, the same number of reception rooms, beautiful gardens, twelve acres of land and outbuildings that can be converted into stables. And it's between Edinburgh and Glasgow too. The place is up for auction with a guide price well into six figures. The brochure stresses that the property requires some 'modernisation', which is usually shorthand for a lot of money needing to be spent. Can I afford it? The answer is 'yes', even if I abide by Ian's rule for the purchase of property, which is to buy it outright. He doesn't see the need for a mortgage if you can afford not to have one. The thing is – what will Ian say about our plans?

'What will Ian say?' is my default reaction to almost everything involving money, and it irritates the hell out of Mandy. 'I don't know what you're worrying about,' she says, when I bring up my concerns over Ian's reaction. 'You've earned it, haven't you? Who's winning all these trophies – you or him?'

She's right, of course, but I can't envisage having much success without Ian's influence. Sure, his motivational methods leave a lot to be desired. The summer after winning the second world title, Mandy and I decided to take a luxury holiday for a few weeks. Just after we arrived home I attended an engagement with one of the sponsors of Cue Masters. One of the sponsors' representatives asked me had I had a good summer. Before I could reply, Ian chipped in, 'Yes, he has, he's been acting like Elton John for six weeks.' He wasn't quite knocking me off my World Championship pedestal, but he was certainly rattling it.

When I ask him about Westfield House there is the usual umming and ahhing and sucking of teeth until he gives me permission to bid for it. So we go for it – and we win. There is a lot to do, including the complete renovation of a flooded cellar, and these repairs plus other improvements will cost around

£75,000. Nevertheless, Mandy and I are delighted to be owning such an amazing place.

'So what did you pay for it, then?' Ian asks when we next meet. I knew he would ask and I've been dreading telling him.

'Around £300,000. It's expensive, I know, but—'

'You paid too much for it,' he snaps. 'You'll need to be practising hard this year to pay that off.'

Duly admonished, we move in once the renovations are complete. Like the pair of excited kids that we are, we wander around the place, barely believing it belongs to us. It's an old house and although we've modernised it, it still comes with age-old problems. Specifically, it has mice. We spot the tell-tale signs of shredded paper in the cupboard and one evening, when Mandy's sister is visiting, we're watching TV by the fire when one of our dogs (we have two, a Rottweiler and an Old English Mastiff) leaps up from by the fireside and starts chasing something he's just spotted creeping under the door. There is a kind of *Tom and Jerry* moment as we all run after the unfortunate creature and eventually I trap it beneath the dog's water bowl before letting it go in the garden. No doubt it will be back in ten minutes . . .

At this point in time, however, a mouse isn't the worst invader of my privacy. A series of letters, photographs, phone calls and even the text of a play (in which I'm the leading character) has been received by Ian's office. The communication is from a woman in Manchester, and her letters are becoming more obscene, more threatening and weirder with every new one that arrives. It appears I have a stalker.

At first, we try to laugh it off but as time goes on we've little choice but to take this seriously. In one letter, she points out that security at snooker tournaments is very lax. Anyone could carry a gun into one of them, and shoot a snooker player, she says. The play she sends is called 'The Death of the Snooker Player' and in it I'm subjected to all sorts of unspeakable acts (some carried out by other snooker players) culminating in my murder.

At this point we've had enough. The police are called, she is quickly identified as the sender and is arrested. At Stirling Sheriff Court she admits sending the letters and making obscene phone calls and is placed on probation with the condition that she seeks psychiatric help. Whether she does or not I will never discover, but she will later appear on a daytime TV show, in a programme about stalking, and say that all she wanted to do was 'wish Stephen good luck'. All I can say is that she has an unusual way of doing this; when she's re-arrested the following year, after turning up at Stirling Police Station posing as a lawyer in a bid to get more details about her own case, I can't say I'm surprised. A restraining order is served on her and luckily we never hear from her directly again.

Ian, John Carroll and I talk about security in the light of what's been happening but none of us feel the need to go overboard. John has always looked after me very well and I see no reason to surround myself with bodyguards or anything like that. I don't truly believe someone will run on to the floor of the Crucible and shoot me. Still, it's a weird and somewhat unsettling time, especially when a few months after this woman's court appearance, the tennis player Monica Seles is stabbed by a stalker while playing in a match in Germany. It will be two years before she plays again, such is the trauma she suffers, and it proves that no matter how safe you might feel, where there's a will there's a way.

Meanwhile, I have a snooker career to get on with. Just before the start of the 1992/93 season I visit the Chinese mainland again, playing in the Kent Classic tournament in Beijing. John Parrott gets the better of me in the final, winning 6–5. It's not the snooker but the city I'm most struck by. I didn't like it much when I first visited in 1987 and it still feels vast and teeming, dark and smoggy.

There is little choice in terms of international food and the hotels are poor. Yet it has an old-world charm, typified by the sheer number of people who travel everywhere by bicycle. Even so, you get the sense that the place will change, and is doing so already. In a few short years China will be almost unrecognisable from the one we're visiting during this tournament. And it will also play a very important part in my life and career.

For the moment, though, John Parrott seems to be on something of a roll, particularly when he's playing me. He squeaks to a final-frame win in the 1992 Dubai Classic and beats me again (6–3 this time) at the Humo Masters event in Antwerp, Belgium. In many ways it's a scrappy season for me; I win the Masters for the fifth time in a row, beating James Wattana 9–5 in his first major UK final, and to mark my achievement the organisers of the tournament give me the trophy to keep forever. I'm delighted – this event, the UK Championship and the World Championship are the main targets of my season and I love playing at the Wembley Conference Centre. The Masters is always very well run by tournament director Jim Elkins, and the atmosphere is never less than electric. I've come to believe that I'll never be beaten here, despite it being filled with a partisan crowd who will support anyone with a familiar accent – step forward, Jimmy White.

For the next few tournaments I kind of limp along, getting through the quarters and semis but not doing much else until I beat Steve Davis 10–6 in the 1993 International Open in Plymouth. The win has broken something of a drought and has set me up nicely for the 1993 World Championship. If I take it this time, it'll be twice in a row of course, and I will be halfway to equalling Steve Davis's record. Excellent motivation, should I need an extra dose.

Overall, it's a great tournament for me. I have very little trouble from anyone I play as I head towards the final and although I play some good players, Darren Morgan and Nigel Bond among them, I'm always confident I can beat them. This is the Crucible – it's where I'm at my best, and where I fear nobody. Every match feels like a breeze. I'm here to win, simple as that. There is one moment, however, where uncharacteristically I throw my toys out of the pram, and it's before the semi-final against fellow Scot Alan McManus. Somebody thinks it's a great idea that we're both led out by a bagpiper, to the amusement of the crowd. But I'm not laughing – this isn't an exhibition match and if there's one thing I can't stand it's the sound of those bloody pipes. I'm furious, but there's little I can do other than grit my teeth and get on with focusing on the game.

Running parallel to me as I move closer to the final day is our old friend Jimmy White. He's also had a great tournament and as he and I enter the practice room on the morning of the final he smiles and gives me a wink.

'Me an' you again, my son,' he says. 'I'm surprised anyone else bothers turning up for this thing . . .'

As ever, Jimmy's entourage are all over the place, backslapping him and shouting their encouragement. Jimmy's dad Tommy is a gem of a guy; he always brings a dinner suit to the tournament, which he says he'll only wear when his boy is finally presented with the trophy.

The final starts at 2pm. I haven't eaten. Frank Callan thinks I'm mad ('you need to feed your brain' is still his mantra) but the only appetite I have is for getting out there and winning. After a final warm-up practice I sit in my dressing room alone and read the paper before curtain call. At this stage I'm beyond speaking to anyone or listening to advice or encouragement. Ian and John Carroll know this and keep away. Their 'good lucks' have already been communicated. Now I'm alone, and I prefer it that way.

Today is Jimmy's birthday and he steps out to rapturous applause and whistles. As I arrive and head to my chair to pour out a glass of water, the cries of 'G'wan, Jimmy!' are still ringing around the auditorium. Jimmy is the 'People's Champion' and while I'd like to be as popular as he is, I also know that I'm there to win for myself, and not for everyone else. Having the support Jimmy has must be great, but it also comes with its pressures. Referee Len Ganley quietens them down with a warning about shouting, and we're off.

Jimmy's break-off is a bit loose, allowing me to get my hand on the table for the chance to pot a long red to get on to the black. It goes in without trouble and almost immediately I relax into my stride. Calmly I clean up, putting the first frame on the board without Jimmy getting another shot. It's a total clearance of 136 and if anything will do psychological damage to my opponent at this stage, that will. However, Jimmy displays the form that has got him to the final and takes the next frame, to his visible relief. But not for long. I circle the table, looking for an opening and an opportunity to win the frame in one visit.

At the interval I've won three frames out of four. We retire to our separate dressing rooms for twenty minutes. I pick up the paper and continue the article I was reading before the start of the match. Then the silence is interrupted by the arrival of Alan Stockton, Jimmy's manager, in his client's dressing room.

'You're a bloody disgrace!' he shouts at Jimmy. 'What do you think you're playing at? Three frames down already . . . that's 'cos you were out last night. Till bloody five in the morning!'

The walls are paper-thin. I can hear everything, and I sit quietly as Alan continues the bollocking.

'I wasn't out last night,' Jimmy protests feebly, 'I was just in the hotel, playing cards. I wasn't hammered. I only had a couple of joints.'

I'm open-mouthed. We all know Jimmy. His public love him

for it, though. I just smile to myself. Jimmy and I are chalk and cheese. I wouldn't even have half a lager the night before a final, never mind anything else. And yet, he's seemingly living life to the full, having fun with his mates while I'm here, on my own with only the newspaper for company and totally committed to doing what I do best. Four times he's been here, four times he's been disappointed. People say that if Jimmy was more dedicated he would win the World Championship – to which I reply, if he didn't live his life the way he lived it, maybe he'd never even get to the final. People are just the way they are.

Alan Stockton tells him how I'm already dominating the match, how I'm going to keep my focus, how I never lose it under pressure. It must be hard for his player to hear.

'Don't worry about Stephen,' Jimmy says, ''cos I ain't.'

Jimmy's dressing-room confession, advantageous though it should be, doesn't make much difference to my game. I only need to keep cool and rack up the pressure on him. If he isn't worried now, he should be, and although we share the next four frames to take the score to 5–3, after this point he never gets back in the game. I strut around the table like a peacock, confident in my cue action and positional play, ready to take chances wherever possible. It's as if I'm saying, 'Look what I'm doing to you.' 6–3, 7–3, 8–3, 8–4, 9–4, 10–4, 11–4, 12–4, 13–4, 14–4, 15–4. Jimmy's posture as he sits in his chair is all too familiar; tense, stressed, disappointed. It's the afternoon of the second day and by now, the Crucible crowd are pretty sure they're not going to see any more from us this evening. I've made three century breaks in this match, taking my total to eight across the championship and equalling the record set by Steve Davis.

And with a final break of seventy-three to make the score 18–5, it's finished. 'I don't even feel I've played,' Jimmy admits later. 'I've just been dragged along the sessions.' I started as I meant to go on, and I've done it again. Ian takes my cue and grabs my fingers in a sort-of shake. Then I'm presented with a cheque for £175,000 and the trophy. If Jimmy were in my position he'd be racing round the auditorium with the thing on his head. I crack a smile, but only just. I don't take winning for granted, yet I knew I was going to win this, and maybe I don't feel it's that big a deal. In fact, so confident was I that before the tournament I suggest to Mandy that she brings down a black-and-white check Versace jacket that I like wearing, because it will look great at the party afterwards!

Because the match has finished a session early, something must happen for the crowd who expected some snooker in the evening. So Jimmy and I return to the table and, with the help of John Virgo, we put on an improvised version of BBC TV's *Big Break*, the snooker-themed game show. Neither of us are particularly keen to do this; I'd rather just celebrate my win. But we do our best and by now the alcohol has been broken out. Although I'm still no drinker I get on the beer early. Big mistake . . .

The after-final party at the Grosvenor in Sheffield is the usual boozy affair and I don't hold back. I'm pictured in the papers spraying photographers with champagne and slow-dancing with Mandy. Me, dancing? I must be drunk.

The following morning, I wake up with a pounding head and a reminder from John Carroll that I'm due to make an appearance at Sheffield's Meadowhall shopping centre. One of my big sponsors, Sweater Shop, wants me to visit their store with the trophy and sign autographs. The sponsorship deal with them is very lucrative and at this point in time the brand is everywhere. They're very generous; after the first round at the Crucible there is always a six-day break between matches and very often the company will fly me back to Scotland in their own helicopter, landing me on my front lawn. They'd pick me up from the same location and deliver me to Sheffield when it was time for my next match. I'm often photographed wearing their garish jumpers and generally being an all-round clean-cut walking advert for them, so I'm in no position to excuse myself with a terrible hangover. Besides, what would Ian say?

Feeling horrendous, Mandy and I get ourselves together and John drives us to Meadowhall. I make a half-hearted attempt to hide the fact that I'm dog-rough but at least three times I need to stop signing autographs and posing for pictures so that I can nip to the loo and throw up. It's an undignified end to what, for me, has been my best performance in a final, and a championship in which I've dominated everyone I've played. Queasy stomach aside, I'm still on an absolute high and I'm playing as well as I ever will. Even Tommy White, whose dinner suit must go away for another year, has a good word for me. 'To beat my son 18–5 is something amazing,' he tells the *Edinburgh Evening News*, 'it is beautiful. It might make Stephen Hendry a better player and it might make my son a better player too.' And Jimmy is nothing if not persistent, as we will see in the next season.

Top 5 PLAYERS NEVER TO WIN THE WORLD CHAMPIONSHIP

1. Ding Junhui
2. Jimmy White
3. Judd Trump
4. Matthew Stevens
5. Paul Hunter

CHAPTER 13

Sheffield, April 1994: It's the early hours of the morning and I'm lying on the bathroom floor of my hotel room, wondering what the hell has just happened and why I am in so much pain.

I've got up to use the loo and haven't bothered to switch on the light. No need to – I always use the same room in this hotel and I know its layout like the back of my hand. Except this time, in a semi-conscious state, I've somehow lost my footing on the carpet and shoved out my left arm to break my fall. My elbow has taken the brunt and now I'm in a world of pain. Later today I have the second session of a second-round World Championship match against Dave Harold to finish. I'm leading comfortably – but I made that lead with two hands. Suddenly it appears that one of those hands – or the arm, to be more specific – isn't working too well.

I crawl back to bed, hoping that by the time the alarm goes in a few hours the pain will have subsided. No chance. The reality is that it throbs for the rest of the night, and when I wake up again I realise I can't straighten my arm. Not a great situation for a snooker player to be in, to say the least.

I lie in bed and think about the panic that will ensue when I tell Ian and John what's happened. Then I get up and try to dress myself, in an attempt to minimise the pain.

Shit.

I can just about get my clothes on, but it is horrendously difficult. The consequences of this unfortunate accident are beginning to sink in, and I'm thinking three things:

a) 'I can't go on with the match.'
b) 'I'm out of the tournament.'
c) 'Someone else will become World Champion.'

I slump back on the bed. It's almost too much to bear. I lean over and look at my watch. It's only just gone 8am. There is still time to see a doctor if I make the call now. With a heavy heart I ring reception and ask to be transferred to Ian's room.

If I must relinquish my title over a stupid accident, this season will have been something of a disaster for me. I'm still world number one, and I've won the European Open and Dubai Classic events, but I haven't excelled myself at the tournaments I'm always keen to win. A rising new talent, Peter Ebdon, has knocked me out in the second round of the Rothmans Grand Prix, and in the final of the UK Championship I lost 10–6 to Ronnie O'Sullivan. He's only been professional a year and this is his first ranking win – at seventeen, he's the youngest ever to achieve this. After the match there is the inevitable 'young pretender' style headlines, and speculation that Ronnie could be my biggest threat in the future. For once, they're not wrong. Ronnie is the real deal and, like me, he really steps up to the mark at the biggest events, going for everything on the table. I admire his cue-ball control and break building, plus his attacking flamboyancy and the speed with which he clears up – these are my strengths and I identify those in him. But he has personal challenges to contend with too; a couple of days after his win, he is photographed in the press taking his trophy to HM Prison Gartree, where his father is serving a life sentence for murder. Dealing with that can't be easy, yet determination and sheer talent seem to be seeing him through darker moments.

I turn the tables on Ronnie in the final of the European Open but disappointingly, I lose in the final of the Benson & Hedges Masters event to Alan McManus. At 9–8, it's a hell of a scrap and I fight all the way in the hope of gaining a sixth consecutive title. I feel I own this event; having won it so often it truly belongs to me. But this time it's not to be and I'm nothing less than devastated. I concede in the deciding frame and I'm completely gutted to see Alan holding up the trophy this year. The looks on our faces say it all; neither of us can believe it's happened. A week or so later Alan nails me again in the quarter-final of the 1994 International Open, slaughtering me 5–0, followed by Ronnie's victory against me in the semis of the British Open.

All in all it's not been a great season, at least on my terms, and as a frantic Ian rings up one hospital after another, trying to track down a specialist who might be able to patch me up so that I can continue the World Championship, I can only dwell on the fact that in snooker, like all individual sports, sometimes things just don't go your way, no matter how much you want them to.

Finally, Ian hits lucky with a private hospital near Sheffield that can see me immediately. We tear over to it, and straight into the X-ray department. Ian bites his lip as the doctor holds up the image against the lightbox. I feel despondent with pain, hoping against hope that my arm isn't broken.

'I'm afraid it is broken,' says the doctor. 'If you look along the elbow you can see a fracture about an inch long.'

That's it. Over with. Finished. Jimmy's dad will finally be able to wear his best suit with pride. And if it's not him, it might be Ronnie, or Steve, or any of them. Anyone but me, in fact. It is down to Ian to ask the million-dollar question: can I continue the tournament?

The doctor catches the look on my face. 'Normally I'd say no,' he says, 'and really, your arm should be in a cast. But it might be that if we drain some fluid from around the fracture, and if you promise to keep your arm in a sling at all times when you're not playing, then maybe there's a chance.'

There is no hesitation. The fluid is drained, and I find I can straighten it enough to get it into a position where I can just about support my cue. From the hospital we rush to the Crucible. Waiting at the stage door, a look of sheer panic on his face, is a well-known professional gambler called Harry Findlay, better known as 'Harry the Dog'. Harry is famous for betting long odds-on matches; for example, if I'm 15–1 on to win against Dave Harold, Harry will put £15,000 down and pocket a grand. It's just a way of making quick money on near dead certs to win. But having a broken arm means I'm no longer the safe bet and a very worried Harry is here to check if I'm still able to play. Having reassured him that I should be OK, I rush inside and find a quiet practice table. As I lower my hand down, the pain is terrible, but less so once it's on there. I make a bridge and hit a couple of balls.

'What do you think, son?' Ian asks anxiously. 'How does it feel?'

I'm playing today, I've decided, no question. If I can get down on that table I can do this, pain or no pain. Ian is delighted, and to my astonishment immediately gets on the phone to the Sweater Shop, explaining that a photo of me with my arm in a sling (over the top of a Sweater Shop jumper, of course) will make great publicity. I can't be bothered to argue – I just want the thing over with so I can get on with the tournament. And although it's agony at times, I resume the match against Dave Harold. I'm

6–2 up so I'm comfortable, but who's to say this pain won't get worse as the match proceeds, and I have to concede?

Taking advantage of my initial timidity, Dave pulls a frame back, but if he thinks it's all over he has another think coming. In the next frame I let loose a break of 124, despite my discomfort, and after this all the momentum is in my direction and I take the next five frames for a 13–3 victory with a session to spare. Obviously, winning this so convincingly with a broken arm gives me a huge boost. There are now five days before my next match, so at least there's time to rest the arm, follow the doctor's orders and secure it in its sling.

In this downtime I still attend practice and discover that making awkward bridges really hurts. But there is no giving up. The idea of handing myself the perfect excuse not to carry on doesn't even occur to me. I've a fair idea of what the other players might be thinking and all I want to do is go back to the Crucible and disappoint them. But Jesus, when that pain kicks in . . .

Trying to put it to the back of my mind, I return to the venue, and a quarter-final match against Nigel Bond. I open proceedings with a break of ninety-one, but Nigel is a top player and, understandably, he doesn't want to be beaten by a guy with a busted arm. We tussle until the score reaches 7–6, at which point I get into the zone and I'm off to a 13–8 win. As much as I can I try to blank out the pain, though I still need to ask the referee if he can pick up the rest and place it on the table for me when I want to use it.

After Nigel, I face none other than Steve Davis in the semi-final, and if anyone will show me no mercy, it's him. The way the rankings are this season, a win in this match will send him to the top of the table, displacing me as world number one. And if he is victorious, there is a strong possibility he may do the double and become World Champion. The prospect of this fills me with equal amounts of dread and determination. Being number one means more to me than being World Champion; I love being the best in the world, simple as that. It's a title worth fighting for and although Steve wins the first two frames we really lock horns for the first two sessions until it's 9–8 to him and I need to do something decisive to gain control of the situation and put some space between us.

What happens next is almost a textbook example of momentum in a long-frame match and how a break delivered under pressure can change the course of play significantly. I'm aware that the rivalry between us requires me to go in with determination and I do, making a break of seventy-five to win the frame. Suddenly, I've found an extra gear and pull away spectacularly, winning the next seven frames with several fifty-plus breaks. As the momentum builds I can feel Steve weakening, yet when I pot the pink to win the match comfortably at 16–9 I drop my head down to the table, relieved that not only have I retained my number one slot but stand a very good chance of becoming World Champion again. There is another mountain to climb in tomorrow's final but I'm still there at the top of the tree, albeit hanging on by one arm.

If I need it, there is one extra reason for wanting to be 1994 snooker World Champion and it is that if I win, the Sweater Shop have promised to give me a Bentley Continental. Almost £200,000 worth of car, for winning the tournament. The mind boggles but, as ever, such a carrot isn't necessary to motivate me as I go into the final. Still, as I enter the practice room on the morning of 1 May I can't help picturing myself at the wheel of that very impressive motor. Already at the table, and looking a lot fresher than he did last year, is the man who is out to shatter those dreams. Hello, Jimmy . . .

Here he is again, for his sixth visit to the final and his fourth against me. From the beginning I notice he's more alert, more focused. He must be heart-sick of being the 'bridesmaid' so often in this event. This, surely, is his big day, and if he wins it won't be because I'm somewhat incapacitated. It'll be because he has the form and the determination and the talent. His time will have come.

As ever, my aim is to get in, clear the first few frames and stamp my authority on the match as soon as possible, putting Jimmy under pressure. At 5–1 up I think I'm doing just that, but maybe this year I underestimate him. Far from wobbling, Jimmy wins the next six frames and now it's me wondering if this is going to be a trickier game than I'd anticipated. He's well back in the flow and, no matter what I try, he's hanging on to me for dear life, and vice versa. 9–9, 9–10, 9–11, 10–11, 11–11, 11–12, 12–12, 12–13, 13–13. We're like two fighting dogs who've locked jaws, neither willing to let go. At 16–14 I'm two frames up, but we're both seeing the winning post and Jimmy's desire to get there first seems to be propelling him on, faster and faster. I've missed chances to win this final and now I'm wondering whether I will get another one.

With the score on 17–17 you can almost taste the tension in the auditorium. They so want Jimmy to win. Every ball he pots is greeted with a thunderous round of applause and 'C'mon, Jimmy!' ringing out all around. In a deciding frame all you can hope for is the one chance to get in and clean up. As I sit in my chair, watching Jimmy break, my other hope is that I'm the one who doesn't allow that chance to happen. In this situation all technique goes out of the window. It's all about who wants it most, and who has the biggest balls to make it happen.

With an assuredness that comes with the anticipation of a longed-for win, Jimmy steadies himself to do the honours. Now he's aware of every single movement he's making. Although you're playing shots you've played a million times, a decider seems to increase their difficulty tenfold. But Jimmy's confidence is winning through and the position of the reds and colours are giving him gift after gift. I'm beat, I know, and momentarily I look up into the audience and spot my Irish friend Paul Mulligan sitting on the edge of his seat. I give him a fleeting look which says, 'It's over . . .' Backstage, Ian has already shaken Jimmy's dad's hand and congratulated him, telling him Jimmy deserves the title this year.

But then, on thirty-seven points, Jimmy goes for what should be an easy pot on the black from its spot. He twitches it and I'm out of my chair so fast that I seem to have a rocket up my backside. The groans of disappointment from around the Crucible have barely subsided before I'm lining up on a straightforward red. Jimmy can only sit there, a picture of misery, as I take full advantage of his horrendous mistake.

Now under any other circumstances (while practising, for example) the situation on the table would be straightforward and, in all honesty, you could clear up with your eyes shut. But this is the deciding frame of the World Snooker Championship, and as such you can add a huge amount of pressure into the mix. Plus, there are 980 people on the edge of their seats, the cameras surround me like a pack, focusing right into my face, and there is the issue of a Bentley at stake, as well as the World Championship title itself.

Yet when I lean down to start the assault, all that external focus falls away and, as ever, it's just me and the table. My whole world becomes a 12ft by 6ft rectangle of green baize. I blank everything out and just concentrate, shot by shot. Call it a trance or 'going into the zone'; whatever it is, it's an essential state of mind in a situation where acknowledging pressure can be fatal.

And although I'm in control I find myself making several risky shots to the middle pockets which usually I'd try to avoid and, with the rest, I pot a pink which rattles in the knuckle of the corner pocket before going in. You'd prefer not to have little wobbles at such moments, but the thing is to keep cool and just focus on the next shot. The first two or three pots are when you're mostly likely to miss, until you settle and find your rhythm. When I get perfect position on the yellow, I know I've won this. At this moment the image of the Bentley floats across my mind. Never mind the World Championship – I want to be driving that car! I push the image aside, pot the yellow, get perfect position on the green, then focus on brown and blue, willing them to go my way. And finally, with the pink safely in the pocket, the triumphant moment has arrived. Once more, I've taken the World Championship. And won a Bentley too. Amazing . . .

The guy I've just beaten steps up and wraps both of his hands around mine. 'Unlucky, Jim!' is the cry and for once I agree, because I know I haven't played my best and have almost been outclassed. A stunned Ian comes over, kisses me, then smacks me hard on the cheeks. I laugh and smile, and I'm pleased I've won but I can't say the same for my performance. It should've been Jimmy's, by rights. Still, it's been an exciting final and an amazing Monday night at the Crucible. As ever, Jimmy is gracious in defeat. 'He's beginning to annoy me!' he quips, as David Vine asks the crowd for their appreciation of him. I stand stock-still, knowing that he'll always be their favourite. In fact, I appear glum enough to be the loser; however, that might be the nagging pain in my elbow that has been exacerbated by a long tournament. It's been OK while I've been playing but, as soon as the match is over, it comes back straight away. The photographers ask me to hold the trophy in one hand and a bottle of champagne in the other, but I'm unable to manage this. Even worse, there will be no golf for me during the summer break as the arm must now rest properly.

* * *

A couple of months after the World Championship it is announced that I've been awarded the MBE. Someone (Ian, I assume) has approached our local MP and in turn they've mentioned it to 10 Downing Street. The awarding of the honour is a big surprise for me; as ever, I find it a bit hard to understand what I've done to deserve something like this.

This feeling of embarrassment continues the day I go to Buckingham Palace to receive the honour. I'm accompanied by Mandy and my parents, and we're all dressed to the nines as we walk across that huge frontage and line up by the entrance to the palace itself. It isn't the first time I've been here; a few months previously there was a reception for sports people that I was invited to attend. I was unable to bring a guest and, not wanting to seem rude by turning the invitation down, I went alone. I can always manage small talk when I'm invited to snooker-related events or corporate occasions when I'm the focus, but I'm shy and awkward when I'm plonked in a room full of people I've never met. That first time I was standing alone, too shy to introduce myself to the famous faces I saw all around me. Then, in the opposite corner of the room, I noticed Ryan Giggs, of Manchester United, looking equally uncomfortable and alone. He caught my eye and somehow we edged towards each other. We started chatting.

'Are you feeling as daft as I am standing here?' I asked. Ryan nodded in the affirmative.

'Painful, isn't it?' he commented.

'In that case,' I said, 'if you're ready to go, so am I. We could always walk out together.'

I've never seen anyone look so relieved, and together we left the swishy reception and went our separate ways, pleased to be away from the social discomfort.

There is no such early escape from an MBE presentation,

though, especially when it involves the Queen herself. So I look on it as a day out, and my parents and Mandy are thrilled to be here. The recipients of the award are separated off and kept in a room until our names are called. When it's my turn I step forward, flushed with embarrassment. There are hundreds of people here being honoured for services to charity or the emergency services. Mine is for winning snooker tournaments. It all seems a bit weird, really, but I make my bow as I've been taught, and she pins the award on me. Then she asks me when my next tournament is. I answer, she smiles, and I move on. I can't imagine she knows who I am, but you never know – I find out later that there is a full-sized snooker table somewhere in Buckingham Palace.

I'm invited down to the factory in Crewe to choose the spec of the promised Bentley. I have to choose the colour of the car, the interior, the wood trim, the carpet, the colour of the seats; there are so many options that the whole process feels like decorating a house, not picking a car. I choose classic Racing Green for the body, along with a black leather interior. Eventually, the Bentley arrives and when I see it gleaming on my drive at first I think my birthdays have all come at once. It's a beautiful car, but also huge and I realise I don't have storage space for it in my garage. Neither is it the kind of car you want to leave parked outside your house. It's a lovely thing to have but impractical. I drive it twice, at the most, and on one of those occasions I take it for a spin through the village close to where we live. As I pass through the main street a couple of guys clock the car and its driver and immediately give me the shaky-hand gesture that means only one thing: 'wanker'. As I pass them I think, 'This isn't for me.' I've always liked quality clothes, good food and a nice car, but I'm not one to flaunt all that. So I arrange for the car to be housed in the Doune Motor Museum in Perthshire and after a year or so I sell it.

Not so long after, Westfield House itself is also up for sale. We love the place, and having enough land to accommodate Mandy's horses, but the area around it isn't much to our liking. We want as normal a life as possible, which includes being able to go to the local shop for a pint of milk without enduring growled responses or menacing glances. I'm just a guy who plays snooker, not an aristocrat or lord of the manor, and when a bottle of 'Buckie' – Buckfast tonic wine – is thrown through the window of our house one night, we start to think that perhaps we'd be better off elsewhere.

By this stage I'm a member at Gleneagles golf club and I like to head over to the famous course as often as I can, especially when the weather is good. In the summer months I'll often finish practice an hour early so I can take advantage of the evening sun. I grow to really like the area – it has great natural beauty and I'm never treated in any other way than with unassuming friendliness – so when Mandy begins the house-hunting process all roads seem to lead in the direction of Perthshire. Also, there is the small matter of a wedding to think about . . .

Top 5 GOLF COURSES I'VE PLAYED AT

1. Loch Lomond
2. Sunningdale
3. Gleneagles (Queen's Course)
4. Bel Air Country Club, Los Angeles
5. Emirates Golf Club, Dubai

CHAPTER 14

By 1995, Mandy and I will have been together for ten years.
Now and again we're asked by family and friends when
we're likely to get married. I don't mind admitting that I'm
somewhat awkward about these things. Being the centre of
attention in a capacity not related to snooker is out of my
comfort zone. But I know Mandy would like to get married and
to start making a fuss about it would be churlish.

I never look at it in any other way than 'This is what we
should be doing by now'. We're very different personalities;
she shows her emotions easily, whereas I don't. I'm not keen on
confrontation or arguments and tend to keep quiet when faced
with such moments. But it's the normal stuff of relationships
and we're very happy together, albeit I'm not at home much.
She understands this; she met me when I was an unknown and
had nothing, and now my career is more successful and busy
I'm away from her a lot. Working with her horses or spending
time with her family in Blackpool makes the times I'm away
easier for her.

I'm not a great romantic, but when our shared future
surfaces as a topic for discussion we agree that we would like

to be married before we have children. So I buy an engagement ring and, one afternoon, when she's up at the stables working with her horses, I pay her a visit and ask her to marry me. I reckon she'll be pleased to get a proposal of marriage in the place she's happiest, close to her horses, and she is. For me, it's the nearest I will get to a grand gesture. We will marry in the summer of 1995, when the World Championship is over.

Meanwhile, Mandy continues the house-hunting and, before long, she sees a property we immediately fall in love with. The house, called Norwood, is in the small town of Auchterarder, less than two miles from Gleneagles. Although it doesn't have stables, there are five acres of land on which to create equestrian buildings. In the meantime, Mandy will be able to keep her horses at Gleneagles. The house itself has four bedrooms, three bathrooms, a games room – complete with full-sized snooker table, which is what catches her eye when she's browsing – and a garage with space for three cars. There is more than enough room in which to raise a family. It's not far from Stirling and getting to Edinburgh or Glasgow airports is easy.

Ian's rules about buying property still apply, so I purchase the place outright at around £350,000. The problem is that Westfield House hasn't yet sold and there seems to be a lack of interest in it. So now I'm the owner of two substantial properties, one of which I would like to move to and the other I'm nervous about leaving empty in case it's broken into.

The problem is solved by a somewhat snide article in the tabloid press. The *Sun* picks up on the fact that I've bought one house and can't sell the other, so the tone of the article is the usual 'look at how much this boy is earning'. I take no notice of it, but I'm delighted when, as a direct result of the article, someone comes forward with an offer and we sell Westfield

House. A big thanks to the *Sun* for an excellent piece of free marketing!

These are good days. Mandy and I have a lot to be grateful for, and much to look forward to. We have property, money, cars, horses and nice clothes. We're a happy couple. We do whatever we want to do, go wherever we want to go, buy whatever we want to buy. I'm the best snooker player in the world and still proving this year after year. I see no reason why all this shouldn't continue, even when Ian calls me into the office one day following a practice session.

'We need to talk about money, son,' he says. 'About how much you're spending . . .'

Here we go again. This has been a familiar conversation for some years now. He thinks I'm spending too much. As ever, he warns me that I'm not thinking about the tax man, about how every thousand spent actually costs me two thousand, and so on. All this goes in one ear and out the other.

'I'm earning it, though, aren't I?' I say defensively.

'At the moment, yes,' he replies, 'but you need to know about the tax situation.'

'Oh, the office always takes care of that,' I say. 'I'm not in any trouble, am I?'

'Do you know how much tax you owe this year? No? Then let me show you this.'

From his pocket he produces a cheque and hands it to me. It is made out to the Inland Revenue, from Stephen Hendry Snooker Ltd. My eyes widen in astonishment when I read the amount on it.

'Two hundred and seventy grand? That can't be right, can it?'

'I thought that'd make you sit up,' Ian says. 'Here . . . go ahead and sign it.' He passes me a gold pen. I take it and scrawl my signature in the box. It's a painful experience, but even as I do it I'm thinking that it will all be OK, as I have another season coming up in which to be even more successful.

As it turns out, the season gets off to a shaky start for me. I lose 9–7 to Ken Doherty in the final of the 1994 Scottish Masters, and only get as far as the semi in the Dubai Classic. I'm hoping for better things at the 1994 Grand Prix (no longer 'the Rothmans' – tobacco sponsorship is being squeezed out of sport and the event is now sponsored by Skoda) but I go out in the quarter-final to Dave Harold.

In the semi-final of the UK Championship – a tournament always on my yearly target list – I'm pegged against Peter Ebdon. By now we've played each other three times, with the tally at 2–1 to me, and this semi-final will be an interesting encounter. Peter hasn't been long on the scene – a couple of years, perhaps – but has already made an impact, not least for his very confident approach around the table, his ponytail hair, garish waistcoats and his fist-pumping. He's about as far from my approach as it's possible to get, yet not really like other flamboyant personalities such as Jimmy White or Alex Higgins because he's also very into the modern methods of motivational psychology.

While all that sounds like criticism of Peter, it's not meant to be. His approach to snooker is like that of a tennis player, which in hindsight makes perfect sense. Both are individual sports requiring huge amounts of focus, concentration and psychological strength. It's just that this highly tailored attitude is quite new to us players and, to be honest, all the fist-pumping and supreme belief in his own ability gets up some noses, as it's never been seen before in this game. If I win a World Championship I might allow myself a quick 'cue in the air' moment, but that's it. It certainly doesn't happen after every shot, as that seems to run contrary to snooker as a game in which unspoken tension and restraint is everything. It isn't a flash, brash sport but with Peter's arrival it appears to have taken a step in that direction.

All that said, Peter is a unique player because he seems to play shots that no one else would play and take risks where others wouldn't. He plays with supreme belief in himself and confidence in his ability. He will come back at you, again and again and again, and he's no quitter, even when you've established a good lead. In short, he must be beaten properly and that means not relaxing for a second. He could be six frames behind and still be relishing the challenge of getting back into a match that others would now see as hopeless. I admire him for that, even if I don't wholly understand his game in the technical sense. He gives pints of blood away with every shot and as a competitor I have the utmost respect for him.

Off the table, I don't mix with him at all. He spends a great deal of time with his coach, Chris Henry, a former player who has really bought into the whole American-style self-belief/ motivation thing and is now sharing this with Peter. The rest of us are suspicious of this new approach but, in time, there will be many among us who will also adopt it in a bid to rescue their careers. Indeed, in a few years' time Chris Henry will be coaching me.

As ever, I make a quick getaway in the match against Peter, going four frames up. He fights hard, bringing the match back to 6–5 and punishing me for a few careless mistakes. I pull back a couple of frames but let him in again and he forces a decider, which I win after he misses a green. In the post-match press conference, Peter observes that he's 'got what it takes' to be World Champion, and that I know what he's made of.

And so to the final against Crafty Ken. He's proving himself a great player now and, like Peter Ebdon, he doesn't roll over easily. He's a scrapper too, and my frustration when playing scrappy games often shows in a loss of patience and points. If I can't get in, pot balls and make big breaks I'm not at my best. 'Winning ugly' is not a strength of mine because I'm my own worst critic and become frustrated if I'm not playing as I should. And in this final, of all the finals I've played (and will ever play) I'm more than happy with what will unfold. Far from being ugly, the snooker I play in this final is some of the best I will ever play. And, I might add, a lot more pleasant to look at than Preston Guild Hall. To get there from the hotel we must walk via the town's infamous concrete bus station. It's not a pretty place but at this time, in the mid-1990s, many of Britain's towns and cities are no different. Snooker is, by and large, a working-class sport and is played in tough working-class areas, the kind of places you wouldn't linger in late at night. In years to come such towns and cities will develop and modernise, but for now it's a case of do your job and focus on the tournament rather than the surroundings.

Ken goes a frame up and I equalise with a break of 112, followed by frame-winning breaks of 114 and 130. It's enough to rattle any player worth his salt but Ken takes the next to make it 3–2. Again I make a century break (109); again Ken pulls one back. And he still looks like he's enjoying himself; Ken is a typically gregarious Irishman, cheery and positive whatever the circumstances. And even though I'm making century break after century break, I'm thinking that it's still not easy to shake Ken off. He could still win this.

The thing is, I love making century breaks. Even when the frame is won mathematically I just want to continue potting and potting, almost as if I'm at the practice table. It's a psychological thing – keep potting and keep your opponent at bay. I'm well into the zone now, looking at the table and mentally working out how to open it up and build the break. When I'm in this mood there is no stopping me – I'm out to destroy whoever is sitting in his chair.

From the commentary box, Dennis Taylor observes that 'we're watching unbelievable snooker here'. My concentration is at its peak and the audience seems to know this; my cue-ball control is perfect but there is no applause, just a stunned silence as the points pile up because I'm making this look easy. This is as good as I will ever play, and when I make it 8–5 with yet another century break, I know I don't want to give Ken a single second's chance to get in again. If he wins one frame he might win another, and it would be unthinkable to make seven centuries in a final, only to lose it if it goes to the wire.

I will not allow that to happen, and at 10–5 we're done. Seven century breaks in one match is a new record in snooker and I'm also the first player to record six centuries in eight frames. Additionally, I've beaten my own record by making twelve century breaks in a single tournament. I'm pleased but, as usual, not visibly so. In fact, I look like a plumber who's just fixed someone's boiler. My attitude is that I am there to play well and win the match, and I have done my job. Yet this final has been cited as one of my best performances ever, and I would hardly disagree.

After the match, Ken and I are interviewed together by David Vine. Despite BBC advertising regulations, we are resplendent in matching 'Team Sweater Shop' T-shirts that fit badly and, in hindsight, look horrendous. Ken is generous in his assessment of the match, in that there was nothing he could do to stop me. 'I've never played against anyone who's played so well,' he says. 'Without pumping him up, of course . . .'

My own view on the match, as transmitted to David Vine, is that I played well, but wish I 'could play like that more often'. It's a curious comment in some ways. Although I've had an amazing win, the critic in me still finds space to find something negative. Now, with the benefit of hindsight, I see it as the tiniest, hair's-breadth crack in my own sense of invincibility. As I explain to the presenter, I regularly make multiple century breaks in practice; to do this in a match is a very different thing altogether. 'I do it maybe once a year,' I say, 'and perhaps I could do it more often.' Is there an element of doubt creeping into that statement? Time will tell . . .

As far as the rest of the season goes, it is a mixed bag. There are a few more tournament wins but the bigger events seem to elude me, including, most disappointingly, the Masters, at which Peter Ebdon beats me 5–4 in the quarter-final. Ebdon does it again in the final of the Irish Masters, a close shave at 9–8 but a win nonetheless.

The 1995 World Championship hits the headlines almost immediately, but for all the wrong reasons. Jimmy White's first-round fixture against Peter Francisco comes under scrutiny because of a large number of bets that it will end in a 10–2 win for Jimmy – which is exactly what happens. An inquiry is launched and, after both players are interviewed, Jimmy is cleared of any wrongdoing. Francisco is later banned from playing for five years for 'not conducting himself in a manner consistent with his status as a professional sportsman'. However, he is cleared of match-rigging.

My quarter-final appearance is against Ronnie O'Sullivan. He's one of the best players in the world by now and I can see he will be one of my toughest opponents. I enjoy playing him because we have the same type of game; we can both go into one and reel off five or six frames in a row – very little tactical play and more like a boxing match, going at each other punch for punch. Despite him fighting hard I build a reasonably comfortable lead at 9–6, but then he takes two frames in succession, in the second of which I don't even pot a ball. Suddenly there is a fear that he may gain momentum, and during a short break in proceedings Ian pops his head around the door of my dressing room.

'They're saying you're finished, you know,' he says. 'They reckon Ronnie's gonna do this.'

'Who's "they"?' I ask.

'Reporters. Everyone. It's the end of the road, son. Ronnie's the man now.'

'Fuck off, Ian,' I say, and he does. But his work is done. He's got to me. If everyone's saying I'm finished, the only way I can answer that is to get back on the table and prove they're talking rubbish.

I stride out of the dressing room in anger, yet filled with determination. And, without hesitation, I put my foot to the pedal and reel off four frames including breaks of 88, 84 and 133 to finish Ronnie off and win the match. 'There,' I think, 'that'll show you all.' Backstage, Ian shakes my hand. 'Sorry about that, Stephen,' he says with a smug little laugh, 'but you needed a good kick up the arse there. I knew what I said would do the trick.'

He's got to me again, wound me up into a fury. And again, it's worked. It's a tactic that doesn't sit comfortably with Frank Callan, who has never been at ease with Ian's treatment of me, and it's around this point that Frank and I part company. There is nothing acrimonious about it; I'm on a winning streak and I don't think my game needs any tweaking. As Frank says about our practice sessions, 'I dunno why I'm here – all I seem to do is pick out the balls from the pockets.'

As ever, Jimmy White is hopeful of the elusive world title but to get there he'll have to beat me in the semi-final. This might strike a note of disappointment for Jimmy's fans, but the match is no less memorable than the battles we've had over the past few years. And not just because we've both had a change of hairstyle: Jimmy has opted for a greased-back look this season, while I'm sporting a closely-cropped affair with a nod to the Britpop 'Blur vs Oasis' era that I've had done at a barber's in Sheffield after the first round. No, this match is significant because it includes my first ever 147 break at the Crucible. At this point I've only ever done this once in a tournament, during the 1992 Matchroom League event, and only two players had achieved it at the Crucible before the 1995 championship – Cliff Thorburn in 1983 and Jimmy himself in 1992.

The maximum comes in the twelfth frame, with the score 7–4 to me. I've already made two century breaks so I'm getting into that zone, down on the table and potting as much as I can to create distance and psychological advantage. When I take six reds and six blacks, however, the pressure of winning the match steps aside temporarily in pursuit of this much shorter-term goal – and a bonus prize of £147,000, plus a £20,000 'high break' prize, if I achieve the maximum. A total of £167,000. Just breathtaking.

It's a huge amount of money – enough to make you twitch if you think too hard about it. Which, at the beginning, you don't. You're just concentrating on winning the frame and keeping a nice pace around the table while thinking two or three shots in advance. Here, it's all about cue-ball control, giving you a choice of two or three reds. Reaching seventy-three points, so that your opponent can no longer win the frame without snookers, is the moment there is a change in atmosphere. You can feel it, but you can't allow yourself to take notice of it. Your job is just to stay in the zone.

From his corner, Jimmy watches me intently. As Len Ganley collects the balls from the pockets and replaces them on the table, I have just a moment's chance to size up the opportunities for perfect positioning.

In a maximum, the hard work comes during the red-black combinations. When it's the turn for the colours all you're thinking is, 'Don't miss now.' I pot the yellow with the rest, and even at this stage my thoughts are already on the pink and blue because they're in awkward positions. I just concentrate as hard as I can on the brown, knowing I can only play for the blue into the opposite corner pocket. The most important shot of this break is getting on to that blue. If I pot it into the yellow pocket I will be able to cannon the pink close to the left-middle pocket. I pot the blue, then send the pink towards the middle pocket. The angle on the pink means I have to send the cue ball up and down the table, so it must travel around twenty feet to get on the black. I pot the pink, the cue ball comes off the baulk cushion and I'm thinking, 'Stop, stop, stop!' I know I've hit it too hard, but all I'm hoping is that it doesn't arrive at a point where, after potting the black in a corner, the cue ball will automatically go in the centre pocket. Fortunately it doesn't.

There is £167,000 resting on this final, awkward shot. If you think about that for a second, you'll bottle it. Yet, making a 147 in these circumstances is just about the biggest buzz you can have playing snooker. And if I pot the black it will be my first 147 at the Crucible. I just have to stay in the zone.

Keep momentum. Strike. The black ball goes in and the white doesn't go in after it. The audience rise to their feet and the noise that comes from all around the auditorium is greater than for any final I've ever won here so far. Jimmy grabs my hand and shakes it warmly. 'That was fantastic!' he says. He knows exactly how this feels. 'Well done, son,' says Len Ganley. The adrenalin rush is massive. I can't believe I've done it. I'm as thrilled as I could ever be.

But not for long. After an interval in which I get my breath back we head to the table again and Jimmy promptly takes the next three frames. Perhaps I've lost concentration after what's just happened and making the maximum has thrown me off what I should be doing – winning the match. Whatever – I do know that I'm furious by the end of this session, and when the press ask me to pose against the table with the balls in a '147' pattern I refuse. The drive with John Carroll to the hotel is a silent, tension-filled one.

Back in my room, I calm down a bit and realise that, yes, I've done something I should be very proud of. And not forgetting the bonus, either. A couple of days later, the *Daily Record* will gleefully report that I'm planning to give the £147,000 cheque to Mandy as a wedding present. Where that piece of fiction comes from I've no idea, but I imagine the tax authorities will find the story particularly interesting.

Once again, I'm the barrier to Jimmy's chances of a world title. I find my momentum again and although Jimmy rallies towards the end, a final score of 16–12 sees me into the final for the fifth time. My opponent is Nigel Bond, an attacking player but one I have little fear of. I expect him to come out and play well from the beginning, rising to the occasion of a World Championship final, but if I keep focused I know I can go through the gears and keep on top of him over a four-session match.

Nigel is a stablemate, also managed by Ian. He's a talented snooker player but at the time I don't think he has the killer instinct needed to dominate the sport and be a repeat winner. He is capable of winning tournaments but is maybe too nice to be world number one, season after season. It takes selfishness and a bit of unpleasantness to be able to bully, harass and psyche out opponents. I have all that in spades – on the table, at least. And I see it in the sportsmen I admire: Nick Faldo, Michael Schumacher, Tiger Woods in years to come. We want to be the best, not the most popular.

Although I still have a couple of mountains to climb, Steve Davis's record of six World Championship titles is now under serious threat. Me being me, I want to hurtle past that and make it seven, eight, even ten titles. Why not? It seems that every year the Crucible is mine to own. Successes at other tournaments might not be coming quite as easily as they did, but when I'm here the sheer magic of the event lights up my game spectacularly.

As predicted, Nigel comes out all guns blazing and we're tussling to 4–5. Then I put my foot to the floor and pull away from him, winning ten frames in a row. I like getting opponents to the stage where they just can't see themselves winning another frame and begin to tire of my relentlessness. Nigel is a good player, as I've mentioned, but he's not a Ken Doherty or a Peter Ebdon; he's not going to hang on to me kicking and screaming to the bitter end. In fairness, at 14–5 Nigel wins three frames in a row and suddenly looks hungry but he'll not keep me out for ever. Although Nigel makes a decent 111 break to win the penultimate frame, I finish him off in style with a 103 break to take the title. Before I played Jimmy in the semi I knew I'd have him, and when I was drawn against Nigel I had to stop myself thinking, 'I've won the World Championship already.'

Instead, I told myself before it began that the final was mine to lose. Yet from the beginning I sensed the match would happen for me and that no matter what my opponent did, I would enjoy myself. In a four-session match I almost always have one session in which I completely dominate and that becomes the bedrock for winning. My aim is always to build up a lead that is so strong that you can afford one or two mistakes later on, should these arise. So this is a very satisfying win in terms of my technique, but perhaps not surprising. On his day, Nigel is a match for anyone. However, this is the Crucible – my natural home, just as it was for Steve Davis in the 1980s. And like Steve, I dominate by reputation. I can intimidate players into resigning themselves to defeat in Sheffield before they even get to the table. I also find I have the ability to will them into making mistakes. It's an odd thing, but I do notice this happening regularly. I sit in my chair and think, 'You'll butcher this,' and they do. At this moment, the general attitude is that 'Hendry is in the final again, and there's bugger all we can do about it.'

With the world title safely in the bag, my next date with the cameras is one that I'm very nervous about: 30 June 1995 – the day of my wedding to Mandy at a church in the village of Muthill, to be followed by a reception at Gleneagles. I stay overnight at the hotel and play a round of golf there on the morning of the big day to steady my nerves, while Mandy stays at home to get ready. The preparations for the wedding have been huge and, at times, fraught; the invite list is massive and hard to manage.

It is a very big occasion. More than 200 guests arrive for the service, with around another sixty attending the evening event. It's one huge party, and an expensive one, too; the total bill, including our honeymoon, comes to more than £250,000. That maximum break prize will certainly come in handy!

It isn't a celebrity occasion, though many of the snooker guys are here, and there are one or two other famous faces. Kenny Dalglish has become a friend, so he's here. Actor Sean Connery is staying at Gleneagles that night and he mistakenly thinks that a red carpet installed for us has been rolled out for him!

Mandy's father makes an incredible speech, bringing the house down with laughter. My best man, Scott Howie, who I met at Miller's club in Broxburn when I was fifteen and with whom I became good friends, is great too. Unfortunately, I don't rise to the occasion in quite the same way. Focusing on the snooker season has left me very little time for preparation and I forget to thank some very important people – my mum chief among them. That's what happens when you only write your groom's speech the night before and I should've put far more thought into it than I did. I should've treated it with the respect that the biggest speech of your life deserves, and to this day I regret not making more effort.

On the recommendation of a friend we book our honeymoon for Honolulu, and after a night in Glasgow we leave for the Hawaiian resort. When we arrive, we wish we'd never bothered. The place is a total disappointment – an American version of Magaluf. We wander around dispiritedly for a day or two until we can stand no more. I phone the travel agent I always use for personal trips abroad – I could use the guy who books my journeys for snooker but if I do, Ian will find out how much I've spent! – and he books us one week in San Francisco and another in Los Angeles. We enjoy the experiences we're having but, oddly, the time away doesn't feel like a honeymoon. While we're still in love, we've been together for a decade and we're more like an old married couple than a pair of newlyweds. The honeymoon is more of a holiday than anything else.

Shortly after we arrive home we finally move into the house in Auchterarder and our conversations turn to the idea of having children. We would like to start a family, albeit that because I'm away so often the hard work of bringing up babies will largely be down to Mandy. It'll be tough for her, we know, but life on the road and regularly being apart from loved ones is just part and parcel of the life of a professional sportsman.

Top
5 SPORTING HEROES

1. Tiger Woods
2. Michael Schumacher
3. John McEnroe
4. Nick Faldo
5. Tony McCoy

CHAPTER 15

My dad is on the phone and is annoyed. 'Did you really say that, Stephen?' he asks. 'I'm surprised you're thinking that way. Kind of disappointed too. How do you think it's going to look?'

I understand Dad's fit of temper. I've been reading today's copy of the *Daily Record* through my fingers. The headline is bad enough: 'Hendry in tax exile shock', or words to that effect. The story is that if Labour win the next general election, as seems likely now Tony Blair is leader of the Party, I will have to 'consider leaving the country'. The reason is that Labour might raise taxes for top earners in Scotland.

The story has been planted by Ian. He and I do talk about tax but, as we've seen, I only sit up and take notice when he makes me sign a large cheque to the Inland Revenue and tells me to curb my spending. I have very little interest in my financial affairs and no idea how much I have 'in the bank'. The papers are always much more curious about this stuff than I am.

However, Ian and I have never talked about me leaving the country. I've no intention of leaving Scotland, not even to live in London, where connections to flights that take me to tournaments abroad are much less complicated. It's just not on the agenda. Yet Ian's comments to the paper cheer up Scottish Conservatives, who reckon there will be a flood of Scots out of the country once new tax increases are announced. Meanwhile, Labour insist they will not put up taxes in Scotland.

I'm in the middle of a political argument that I haven't started and am not at all interested in. How Ian thinks this will be good publicity for me is baffling. I'm left looking a complete arsehole and a few days later my dad's prediction comes true when I get a pile of abuse via various letters pages in the papers. Dad even does an interview in the *Sun* to stress that it isn't me who's said this, but the damage is done and for years to come people will ask me if I really plan to be a tax exile.

It's very annoying, and I try not to let it distract from the snooker season. After a relatively poor performance in 94/95 (excepting the UK and World Championships, of course) I need to assert myself away from Sheffield and the Crucible. I need more consistency in my game, and to hold to the idea that I can dominate in any arena.

I make a good start with victories over Peter Ebdon in the 1995 Scottish Masters and John Higgins in the Grand Prix. I meet Peter again in the final of the 1995 UK Championship and the rivalry that has developed between us is demonstrated in a contest which concludes with me making a 146 break to close the final frame. The result is a commanding 10–3. Earlier in this tournament I make a 147 against Gary Wilkinson – the first ever to be televised at this event – and in total I've made no fewer than eleven centuries during these matches.

There is a great result for me at the 1996 Masters, which I take for the sixth time after a 10–5 win over Ronnie, the defending champion. It's particularly satisfying to win at Wembley again, and against Ronnie, who has now taken over from Jimmy as the fans' favourite and is clearly demonstrating that he has what it takes to dominate the game. There is no doubt in my mind that one day he will be World Champion – and I'm aware that day could come sooner rather than later.

This season, though, the thorn in my side is Ken Doherty. He beats me on no fewer than four occasions and increasingly I'm not enjoying playing him. I'm not in fear of his game but I've made my mind up, wrongly, that he always gets the run of the balls when he's playing me. This puts me on the back foot straight away and I know I must just concentrate on my game when he and I meet. Some players I know I can bully into submission; Ken (and Peter Ebdon) will stand up to any demonstration of that and aren't fazed by my reputation. In fact, they even seem to relish playing me, and that makes me irritable in a way I've not noticed before.

In the past, sitting in my chair while my opponent is making a break, I've kept focused on the game as it's unfolding. I've watched for chances to open up, planned for ways to make clearances from whatever position the balls are currently in. In short, I've concentrated 100 per cent on my game and not really cared who's on the other side of the table.

Now, something different is starting to happen and it catches me unawares. For example, Ken sometimes wears a black velvet suit and something about it really annoys me. I don't know why (only it's not the kind of thing I would wear) and yet I can't help but home in on it. The same goes for Ebdon's jazzy waistcoat, though I don't expect I'm alone in disliking its garish flashiness. But I really shouldn't be bothered about such stupid details as players' clothing. It's what I'm doing that counts, not what they're wearing. I tell myself I need to pay more attention to what I do; if I do, I will be more successful.

Also annoying is the posturing and bantering which seems to

have crept into the game. A newer generation of players and managers are no longer reticent about criticising fellow players, especially in the press. There's a lot of 'I'm gonna do this to him . . .' or 'He hasn't a chance against me . . .' etc. While I've never been a good loser, or even particularly complimentary about other players, the occasions are rare that I've criticised anyone unfairly. Now, though, managers talk as if they know chapter and verse about snooker and will sit in players' lounges making snide remarks. Ian has always done this and hasn't held back when it comes to criticising me in front of others. I've become used to that and have found that the best way to shut him and others up is simply to win. Now, though, such banter has come from behind closed doors and into the press and it's increasingly hard not to become riled by it.

Having reclaimed the Masters and won the UK Championship, I'm understandably keen to do the Triple Crown again and win the World. Whatever else is going on, I'm always well prepared and focused for this event, and 1996 is no different. For me, every tournament is a build-up to the World Championship. The bigger the occasion, the more inspired I am. And there is no bigger occasion in the game of snooker than the Crucible.

I have a familiar routine for when April comes around and Sheffield beckons. John Carroll and I will travel down on the Thursday before the tournament starts to be ready to play the opening match on Saturday, traditionally reserved for the defending champion. I begin to feel the buzz as soon as we've turned off the M1. Ian usually turns up the following day in his own car. We always stay at the same hotel (and I have the same room every year, despite the occasional bout of bathroom-floor slippage) and we eat at the same Chinese and Italian restaurants.

After practice on Thursday night it's early to bed. The following day is the press call, at which the top players will give their views and predictions on the tournament ahead. I'm always asked if I will win it; I always reply that if I'm focused and on form, then I stand a very good chance. There's nothing worse than bragging about something that you can't live up to.

I enjoy the pre-match interviews. I'm world number one and I admit, I like the press attention it brings. At this stage, their scrutiny – on the subject of snooker, at least – is all positive and I don't find their questioning a chore in any way. That said, it's different when I lose. Then, the bad loser comes into play and my answers are just 'yes' and 'no' – if I bother answering at all. This year it's all friendly questioning about whether I will equal Steve's record of six World Championships.

My approach to the pressure of long-frame matches in the premier event of the snooker season is to relax, practise, eat well and get to bed early. As in other aspects of my professional life, almost every match day I'm at the event is timetabled, and for a 10am start it goes something like this:

7.30am: Alarm goes. I switch it off and have a couple of snoozes.

8.00am: I get up, shower, don't bother with breakfast. I watch thirty minutes or so of TV then put on my suit.

8.55am: John Carroll is waiting in the car outside the hotel. Ian is in the back seat. I sit in the front – I always do, as John doesn't take kindly to my jokes about him being a chauffeur!

9.10am: If the traffic is with us we arrive at the stage door of the Crucible. John and Ian will chat among themselves, but I don't say a word on the journey there: I'm too busy thinking about the match to come and anyway, I'm not a 'morning person'.

9.15am: There can be up to a hundred autograph-hunters
waiting at the stage door but on match days I will
only sign a handful. 'Keep walking' is the advice.
If it's just a practice session I will spend longer
outside.

9.20am: I enter my dressing room, take off my coat
and remove my cue from its case. I walk to the
practice room.

9.25am: There are two tables in the practice room and
four players waiting their turn to get on. I will
play for twenty minutes, just to loosen up, and
will pick out the balls from the pockets when
I've potted them. Oddly, I'm one of the very few
players to do this themselves – most of them
bring a coach or a helper along to assist. In all
my time playing I've never seen Jimmy or Willie
Thorne retrieve a ball.

9.45am: I return to my dressing room and flick through
the paper. I'm feeling tense, and the words I'm
reading are barely registering. John Carroll asks
me if I want tea or coffee. I always shake my
head. He always asks anyway.

9.50am: The tournament director knocks on my door
and says, 'Stephen, five minutes.' This gives me
enough time to use the loo. I feel sick with nerves
but know they will pass once I'm at the table.

9.55am: The final call. It always reminds me of a boxing
bell – ding-ding, round one. Now I'm like a
coiled spring. I pick up my cue and walk through
the backstage corridor towards the entrance to
the auditorium. Other players will be waiting
silently there.

9.57am: The MC introduces us in turn, the defending World Champion always coming out last, and to a wall of noise. I walk carefully down the stairs, always reminding myself not to trip up.

10.00am: I shake hands with the referee and my opponent. A coin is tossed to decide who breaks first, and off we go.

There's seventeen days of this stuff so occasionally it's nice to break out and do something different. At this point, in the mid-1990s, distraction comes in the small-but-formidable shape of 'Prince' Naseem Hamed, World Champion featherweight boxer, Sheffield resident and all-round flamboyant character. Naseem likes snooker and loves winners; he becomes my biggest fan and we strike up an unlikely friendship. He invites me over to his house, where we play some snooker and enjoy fish and chips, then he takes me for a drive around Sheffield in his Lamborghini. Naz is so small he can barely see over the steering wheel, but what he lacks in height he makes up for with foot-to-the-floor acceleration. His driving is so terrifying I can feel my stomach turning over with each corner he cuts, scaring the shit out of me.

This year's tournament holds few surprises. I progress to the final against Peter Ebdon with relative ease, but I know he will not be an easy opponent. And so it proves. Peter starts quickly, winning the first frame, and although I begin to break away at 5–4 he hangs on to me and I can't shake him off. I find it difficult to stamp my authority on the match but, that said, I have enough in the tank to keep me ahead and don't feel in much danger. The last session is a comfortable one and at 18–12 Peter concedes the match after needing snookers and missing a shot – the first and only time at the Crucible that the winner of the final doesn't take the last shot. 'You're a hard bastard to beat,' I say, when I shake his hand. I've made it five in a row for me at the Crucible and I've also achieved the Triple Crown again. This final is also significant for the fact that 'Whispering' Ted Lowe, the legendary commentator, announces his retirement as our match draws to a close. I'm honoured to have played in Ted's last appearance as commentator; ever since I first met him on the set of *Junior Pot Black* he has shown nothing but kindness to me and my family. He's also been very generous with his broadcast comments about me and I have nothing but respect for the man who helped to bring snooker to a huge TV audience.

The World Championship result is massive for me. Finally, I have equalled Steve's record and the path is now clear to breaking it. That is the theory, at any rate – and it's not just my game which will put me ahead of the field. For winning the world title, my sponsors, Sweater Shop, kindly give me a red Ferrari 348 convertible, which Mandy and I are duly photographed with, looking very pleased. In addition, Sweater Shop's owner, Graham de Zille, flies the both of us in the company's private jet to the Mugello racetrack in Italy so that I can have a spin around the circuit in a few Ferraris. The 348 is a great-looking car but the gearstick is stiff, and it doesn't have power steering, making it hard to drive. After a couple of months I decide to trade it in and, having added £20,000 to the deal, I come away with a 355, which does have power steering and is a much more comfortable drive. I pick it up from a dealership in Surrey and drive it all the way home to Scotland. Unfortunately, I've forgotten to order a stereo with it, and so I spend the entire journey listening to the sound of its distinctive engine. For the first thirty minutes this is thrilling but six hours of it is enough for anyone, so my first port of call is to the auto-electricians to have a sound system fitted.

In the autumn of 1996 the Ferrari comes in handy for quick

trips to the hospital in Perth, about fifteen minutes from where we live, to visit Mandy and our newly born son, whom we've called Blaine. At the end of the 1996 final, David Vine 'outs' me as a new father-to-be during our live TV interview, to my embarrassment, and although I'd rather have told the world in my own time, I'm delighted and proud to be the father of a healthy baby boy, who is so beautiful he is often mistaken for a girl. We look for a name that can't be shortened so we choose 'Blaine' because it's unusual and only one syllable long. The baby is in breech position, resulting in Mandy having a Caesarean section and needing to stay on the ward for a few days afterwards to recuperate. John eventually drives us home from hospital and from then on we face what every new parent does – the surreal experience of having a baby in your midst and no book of instructions accompanying it. We fret and we worry and we feel exhausted, but soon Blaine settles down and sleeps through the night. He's no trouble, which is just as well because I need to get back on the snooker circuit and will be away from home for days at a time.

During the pregnancy and birth, I hear the same mantra from fellow players and people I know, and it's that my game 'won't be the same again'. My outlook and priorities will shift, and I will no longer be the player I was. I don't wholly buy that – my practice routine continues with regularity and I'm still winning matches and tournaments – but I do recognise that something has shifted. In the months following Blaine's birth I find that I no longer sulk as much when I come home following a defeat. In the past, I might have been moody for a day or two; now, there is no time for that and, should I be heading for a sulk, Mandy quickly reminds me that there are other things in life than snooker matches.

She's right, of course. Having a child is a huge responsibility and when I'm at home I do my bit to help Mandy in establishing Blaine's routine. But setting aside time to brood after a defeat hasn't, in my experience, always been a bad thing for my game. I need to 'hurt' a bit following a loss in order to spur me on next time. Pushing that 'grieving time' aside to prioritise family matters is necessary – and yet it does influence my playing. I still want to win and be number one, of course, but now Blaine's here things feel different. That said, if I lose and I hear people say, 'It's because he's a family man now,' it irritates me, but it's obvious they're looking for the easiest reason to have a dig.

My being away for much of the time necessitates that we bring in some help for Mandy and the baby. A local woman, Ann, is employed as a mother's help and she works part-time so that Mandy can have a break and look after her horses. My mum also moves to the village with her second husband, Steve. Unfortunately, the relationship between Mum and Mandy is fractious and will worsen as the years go by. There is no need to go into the whys and wherefores in these pages – suffice to say I'm often caught in the middle of their disputes and, for someone who consciously avoids conflict, that's not an easy position to be in.

Otherwise, life is great. I have a great marriage and a nice lifestyle, and I'm a proud dad and a sportsman at the very top of his game, even if that game takes me away from my family. A few weeks after Blaine is born I'm off to Thailand for the Snooker World Cup, representing Scotland with team mates John Higgins, Alan McManus and reserve Billy Snaddon. Billy is a local boy from Stirling who's turned pro and has been my regular practice partner at the club. He's a great guy who always brings a lot of jokes and laughs to our sessions. When John Higgins is with Cue Masters he and Billy will always argue about football – Billy is Rangers while John is Celtic. John and I both develop an interest in the Australian TV show *Neighbours*, and we always time our lunch breaks for the time it's being shown. Other players around the club include Alain Robidoux (who is hilariously funny), Marco Fu and Fergal O'Brien. We have a lot of fun down there and it's always a buzz going into work.

The Scotland team are favourites to win, and there is a distinctly laddish atmosphere to the whole event, particularly because we're playing in teams rather than as individuals. And we're there for two weeks, so the event feels more like a holiday. As expected, we do well as a team and reach the final against the Republic of Ireland with little difficulty. We start well, and the Irish guys give us plenty of chances, which we take mercilessly. Eventually we beat them 10–7 after a decent struggle and between us we pick up a cheque for £105,000. I phone Mandy every night and if I happen to mention that I'm tired, she'll remind me she's the one at home, looking after a tiny baby. Point taken . . .

After the win we celebrate hard and all become very drunk. I manage to crawl into bed at 3am but the other lads stay up all night. Somehow, they persuade a maid to let them into my room and I awake to find three people standing over me, giggling away. I'm so befuddled through drink and deep sleep that I think I'm being mugged and put the covers over my head. The hi-jinks continue the following day, and on the evening flight back to the UK the actress Su Pollard is aboard the plane. A steaming John Higgins can't resist shouting 'Hi-de-Hi!' in her direction every two minutes.

Back in the UK, the team spirit we four Scots fostered falls back into rivalry as I narrowly beat John Higgins to take the 1996 UK Championship. At one stage I'm 8–4 up but John stages an impressive comeback and the match is decided in the last frame.

I play what is becoming a trademark shot – knocking in a long red and going on to clear up. Players often say to me that as soon as I pot that red, they know the frame is over.

There is also one of the best wins of my career – it's against Ronnie O'Sullivan in the final of the Liverpool Victoria Charity Challenge, held in early January 1997. I make a century in the first frame and steam ahead to 4–0. At 8–2 it's looking like a decisive win. Then O'Sullivan really finds his form and by 8–8 there are six centuries on the scoreboard (three to me, three to Ronnie) and I must find something special if I'm going to take the deciding frame and win the tournament. At this stage many players would be feeling that it was all over for them. Not me. I know Ronnie has played superbly to get back in the game and I haven't had any solid chances to win the match so I've nothing to beat myself up about. We've both played excellent snooker up to this point – in that sense it's been a great match to be part of.

The deciding frame begins. Ronnie and I play three or four quality safety shots until I have an opportunity on a long red. The cue ball is close to the baulk cushion, so I need to keep perfectly still, but a trademark shot looms, and I play it with top spin to follow through off two cushions for the black. My technique is perfect, and I stroke it in, getting great position on the black. At this stage, of course, all my thoughts and efforts are focused on winning the frame, nothing more. And yet, as the reds go down I feel something of a tingle up my spine. The position of the balls is excellent. Could there be something amazing in store for this frame?

I can't think that way. Not yet. I need to make the frame safe first. After all, I'm trying to win the match and taking unnecessary risks to pull off a 147 in a deciding frame is madness. No wonder it's never been done before. But I've now potted eight reds and eight blacks and not had to make any hard decisions that might lead to catastrophe and a match thrown away. And the positioning is still very advantageous.

'It's not possible,' says commentator Rex Williams from the box. 'I thought miracles stopped happening 2,000 years ago . . .'

No they didn't, Rex, and this miracle is happening with a £40 cue that bears your name.

Thirteen reds and thirteen blacks. It's happening. The final red is just past the middle pocket, so I need to have exactly the right angle on it to come back for the black. There is a chance that if I get it slightly wrong I will snooker myself behind the green. Luckily for me, it falls perfectly.

Ronnie knows he will lose the frame and the match, that's for sure, but he never expected it to go this way. I play a shot with the rest on the yellow to come around off the angles. Now it's 122. The applause and the cheering grow louder with each shot. I use the rest again to pot the green: 125; 129; 134. The pink makes it 140 and with the final black, that's it.

'What can we say?' gasps Rex Williams. 'Absolutely incredible.'

A maximum break in the deciding frame of a final. It's never been done before, and I've just set a record. Amid a standing ovation I walk towards Ronnie with my arms outstretched, as if to say, 'You did amazing to get back in the game, but I'm the best in the world and look what I just did.' And I don't mean to be boastful; at this moment I'm just incredibly pleased with myself and it's showing. Even today, people say this was one of the greatest snooker matches ever played on TV, and not just because of the 147. We've both played outstandingly, and at the very height of our powers.

However, a month later, Ronnie brings me down to earth, knocking me out 6–4 in the quarter-final of the 1997 Masters. I'm bitterly disappointed, as I'd hoped to start reclaiming this one after last year's win. Still, I win the 1997 International Open, easily beating Tony Drago 9–1, and although I lose to Nigel Bond in the semi-final of the Thailand Open, I beat Wales's Darren Morgan to take the Irish Masters title. I suffer defeat at the hands of another Welshman, though, in the shape of Mark Williams, in the final of the 1997 British Open. Overall, it's not been a bad season and though the prize money earned isn't quite what it was in 95/96, I'm still top of the rankings and looking forward to what I hope will be a record-breaking World Championship win. That is, until the postman arrives one morning and drops an innocuous-looking letter through our box.

Top

5 CITIES I'VE
VISITED
1. Hong Kong
2. Bangkok
3. Las Vegas
4. Shanghai
5. London

CHAPTER 16

There is no postmark and it isn't even addressed properly. Nothing particularly unusual about that. People often write to me, addressing the envelope, 'Stephen Hendry, Snooker Player' or 'Stephen Hendry, Scotland' and it still reaches me.

Mandy opens this morning's mail. I'm just about to leave for practice at the club in Stirling but when I see the look on her face I stop in my tracks. She is as white as a sheet. 'Read this,' she says, holding out a piece of paper.

As I read, my stomach lurches over. In a scribbled hand, the writer sends a warning about the forthcoming World Championship. He (or she – it's anonymous) claims to know where I live, and where Mandy walks with Blaine in his pram. If I win the world title this year, the writer promises they will throw acid into my child's face. The final sentence reads: 'Black ball, black death.' Lovely.

I've had threats before, of course, and not only from the woman who wrote the play about my death. There are times when there's been some discontent, especially at exhibition matches, and muttered threats from audience members. I take no notice and, in any case, I always have John Carroll around to deflect any unpleasantness. There was an occasion when shit (dog or human – we never delved too deeply) was sent through the post, and again Mandy had the unfortunate experience of opening the envelope in which it was contained. None of this is nice, but I've come to realise that it's part and parcel of being in the public eye. A direct threat to my child, however, is something else altogether.

Mandy and I stare at each other in shock and horror. 'They're just trying to wind us up,' I say. 'It's a load of rubbish. Let's not worry about it.'

But I am worried about it. If I attend the tournament I'll be away for more than two weeks (assuming I reach the final), leaving Mandy on her own, and vulnerable. It might well be a crank letter. Should I take that chance, or should I pull out of the competition altogether?

Really, there is no choice. I won't be prevented from doing my job to the best of my ability. I will be going to Sheffield as planned. I share the news with Ian and the management team and the police. The latter investigate it, but with little or no evidence to go on they're unable to arrest anyone for sending it. Otherwise, we don't publicise the fact that it's happened. Even if they don't intend to carry out their threat, they would no doubt enjoy knowing that their actions have upset me and my family. I do wonder what kind of a mind would threaten an eight-month-old baby over a game of snooker.

We keep an eye out for anything suspicious in our neighbourhood and Mandy's sister arrives from Blackpool to spend some time with her while I'm away. Mum and Steve are also around to assist, so I know Mandy is in good hands. I arrive in Sheffield and slip into the old routine – same hotel, same room, same restaurants, same practice schedule – and try to put aside the anxiety generated by the letter. As ever, once it's just me and the table and I get down to potting balls and making clearances, whether in practice or in a match, I'm able to block everything else out and simply concentrate on the moment.

And yet, late at night and in the back of my mind, the contents of the letter flash in front of me. I keep wondering what will happen, if anything, if I win the final? The first round comes and goes without incident, although there is something of a kerfuffle in the quarter-final when Darren Morgan, my opponent, asks for Number One Stephen Hendry Fan Prince Naseem Hamed to be moved from his place in the front row. Naz's presence is putting him off, he claims, though it might have something to do with the gleaming silver jacket he's wearing. My boxer friend is duly offered another seat and the game resumes. I admire Darren for being single-minded enough to request that he's removed from the front row. It certainly can't have been an easy call to make. Naseem or no Naseem, I win 13–10 and I'm into the semi-final against James Wattana. It's a high-scoring game, with three century breaks from me, and a tussle until 8–8, when I find form and build the breaks I need to take me to the final. To a casual observer, my game hasn't altered much since last year's tournament. I'm doing what I always do – playing to win, and win well. However, only I know that I'm not playing at 100 per cent. I don't have the same intensity and focus as usual, and the thought that if I do lose in the final nothing will happen to Blaine or Mandy creeps into my mind. I try to avoid such thoughts because in normal circumstances I would never give myself any excuses; even a fractured elbow didn't put me off my game. This, though, has rattled me and I go into the final not with the will to lose, but certainly without the same level of intensity and expectation as usual.

My opponent is Ken Doherty: friend, stablemate and hard-fighting snooker player. I haven't told him or any of the other players about my difficulties, therefore no one is giving me any concessions whatsoever. I step out on to the floor of the Crucible determined to win, and despite making no fewer than five centuries and outgunning Ken in terms of points won, he proves a very worthy and tenacious opponent. He punishes me for the first ten frames and although I stage a comeback from 11–6 down to make the score 15–12, it isn't enough to derail Ken. Simply, it's his time, and he wins the championship fair and square at 18–12.

As he pots the final pink I offer him my hand and say, 'Well played.' It's as much as he's likely to get from me at this stage but at the party later I make a speech that congratulates him properly. He's won because he's played better than me and, while I'm gutted, I can't say I'm as devastated as I might be under any other circumstances. In truth, the loss feels like a weight off my shoulders. Something has been missing from my performance this whole tournament, and I'm glad it's over. I never thought I'd catch myself thinking this, but I console myself with the fact that there is 'always next year'. Ken, meanwhile, is receiving all the plaudits for the win, including the obligatory 'hero's welcome' open-top bus tour of Dublin.

Ian says very little to me after the final. He's just pleased that two members of his team are in the world's premier snooker tournament final. The inevitable post-mortem comes a week or so later, when he tells me I wasn't focused enough, and that Ken outplayed me. We don't discuss the ins and outs, which is fine by me because now it's over and no harm has come to my family, I just want to forget about it all.

The following season is patchy, to say the least. I'm still reaching quarters, semis and finals, but titles this year are elusive. Ronnie O'Sullivan beats me three times, including

Left: Trying to look happy in this pose requested by photographers after winning the World Championship in 1994

Right: With Naseem Hamed after my sixth world title in 1996

Left: Me and Mark Williams square up for the Masters, February 1998. I'm smiling now . . . I wouldn't be later that night thanks to THAT miss on the black

Top left: Deep in concentration at the semi-final of the 1999 World Championships at the Crucible

Top right: Celebrating seventh World Championship same year with Mandy and Blaine

Below: At the Hungarian Grand Prix in 2000 with Chris Evans as guests of Benson and Hedges

Right: The loneliest seat in snooker (Embassy World Championship final, 2002)

Left: With my best mate on the circuit, Mark Williams, at the Betfred World Championships in 2009

Right: Cheers to another Crucible 147

Left: Checking to see what I've left for Jimmy at the 12Bet.Com UK Championships in 2010

Left: Betfred World Championships April 2012 – the only time I played John Higgins at the Crucible Championships

Right: Stretching a bit to pot the red

Below left: The last walk from the Crucible arena after losing my final match there to Stephen Maguire, 1 May 2012

Bottom right: Taking the applause after announcing my retirement the next day

Top left: In the BBC studio with 'crafty' Ken Doherty

Top right: Post-match interview after beating Jimmy in Hong Kong in an exhibition match

Middle left: Not sure Steve is agreeing with me here

Below: Walking out to play Chinese 8-ball match in China, 2013

Top left: The Great Wall

Top right: One more question, please

Below left: Fresh out of the oven. One of my favourite things to eat – Beijing duck

Below right: A random street in my favourite city in the world – Hong Kong

Above: Exhibition match with Ronnie O'Sullivan in Sofia, Bulgaria, in 2017

Below left: Ready for my appearance in the *Celebrity Masterchef* kitchen

Below right: With the chef from restaurant 'Made In China' in Beijing

Right: I was never this happy after winning a snooker match!

Left: With the team at ITV Snooker enjoying a night at the poker table

Below left: Charity event in London in 2015 with Lauren

Below right: Winning the Poker Stars celebrity event in London, 2017 – my one and only poker trophy

a 10–6 defeat at the 1997 UK Championship. By now he's displaying his fantastic talent and you'd be forgiven for thinking he'd been pro for many more years than he has. He outplays me and I've no excuses for it. The guy is hungry for success and I know exactly how that feels.

I reach the final of the 1998 Masters event, pitched against Mark Williams, the second member of the Class of '92 ('the Golden Trio') and this proves to be a memorable match in that it comes down to a black-ball game. Mark opens strongly but I overtake him to establish a reasonably comfortable lead at 9–6. Then I make a couple of costly mistakes and Mark catches up to make the score 9–9. As the frame progresses we're on fifty-six points each and it becomes clear the final will hinge on the re-spotted black. I smile briefly as the crowd goes wild, acknowledging the fact that it's come down to this cliffhanger.

I know I've had chances to win this match and it should've been over by now. There will be no elegant play ahead; in a black-ball final all you want to do is slot that black away or keep it very safe if you can't. Everything you've learned goes out of the window and it's as much as you can do to keep your head when there is so much excitement and anticipation swirling around you.

Mark wins the toss and puts me in to break-off. Famously, the last major final that came down to a black-ball game (albeit not a re-spotted one) was in 1985, during the World Championship match between Steve Davis and Dennis Taylor. Dennis happens to be commentating on our match, and he knows exactly how tense we're both feeling. We both miss shots we wouldn't normally have too much trouble with and the crowd is at fever pitch. I make something of a mess of a safety shot, leaving Mark a chance to pot the black. It's too much for him and, again, he misses. Now it's my turn to make what should be a relatively simple pot to the centre pocket – maybe not quite as easy as it looks, but nothing that you wouldn't slot away ninety-nine times out of a hundred in practice – and because of the angle I have to play it slowly. And I miss. Finally, the tension is broken as Mark sticks the black away to take the trophy. In truth, I lost the match a few frames previously. I had chances I didn't follow up on and at 9–8 I needed to pot blue, pink and black, and was unable to put the pink away.

So I can't complain about losing it on the black ball but still I'm naturally gutted, and in years to come it will become almost more famous than my six Masters wins. Mark will regularly rib me about it. Off the table we're good mates; we share a similar sense of humour and enjoy going out to restaurants or having a hand or two of poker. For me, having 'mates', as opposed to acquaintances, is at this point in my career something quite new. As I've explained, previously I've tended to keep away from other players, partly because I'm shy and feel that I don't fit in, and partly because Ian isn't keen on me mixing with players – he wants me to possess the same mystique as Steve Davis, and for very good reasons.

That was all fine when I was a teenager. Now, though, I'm a married man with a young child and I'm closing in on thirty. It strikes me that I can't play the iceman forever – at some stage I might want to loosen up and enjoy life a little. Behind the scenes of any snooker tournament there is always banter and mickey-taking, and so far I haven't participated in any of that, feeling unable to compete with the likes of Jimmy or Willie for quickfire wit. But as surprising as it seems, I'm not without a sense of humour, even if it doesn't always look that way on screen. And increasingly, when I do enter the players' lounge, I sit with Mark or Ken or John Higgins and we have a laugh. We take the piss out of each other and in tune with the times our banter is knockabout and laddish. People who previously thought I was aloof and unapproachable are now beginning to say, 'I didn't know you were like this,' as if they've just discovered that I'm a human being after all!

What's happening – although I don't recognise it yet – is that I'm becoming one of the crowd. Another talented player in a sea of talented players. A winner, certainly, and an outstanding sportsman in his field, but one who seems to be happy that friendship and fitting in are finally finding their place in his life. We laugh and joke. We go out to dinner and have a few drinks. 'We' are something of a gang, and no matter what Ian Doyle or anyone else says, I'm enjoying discovering this previously unexplored side of my life.

Ian doesn't say much these days. He wonders why I'm associating with other players, but this is never relayed to me directly – it always comes via John Carroll and he never says, 'No, Stephen, you can't do that,' because he wants to stay friends rather than be the one who wags the finger. The hold Ian has had over me is loosening – these days he's involved in other players' careers and other aspects of his business. Ostensibly I'm still number one in his eyes, and the ambition to overtake Steve Davis is undimmed, but life has changed considerably for both of us since it was just me and him against the world.

So I begin to frequent the players' lounge more often and I chip into the banter. The ice is slowly melting and with it, perhaps, the aura that has surrounded me since I turned professional. I see players looking at me as I chat and laugh, and I seem to know what they're thinking: 'He's not that invincible after all – he's just one of the lads.' There is a chink in my armour which might give them a tactical advantage. Suddenly, I'm no longer above them; I'm one of them, and that's going to cause me problems as time goes on.

One of the more memorable and infamous nights out comes

after a fixture in Bangkok. Mark Williams and I decide to go out for something to eat and we hit Sukhumvit Road, the longest in the city. A few drinks later, we realise we need to find a taxi back to the hotel. As we start the process of hailing one, Mark says, 'I'll bet you wouldn't dare drive it back . . .'

Now, let's make it perfectly clear that I'd never advocate drink-driving. Somehow, though, I get caught up in the mischievousness of this moment and accept Mark's dare. Every time we hail a cab Mark points to me and asks the driver, 'Can he drive?' Most of them, spotting two Westerners at large, rightly refuse and as we hail taxi after taxi a large queue is building down the road.

Eventually we find a cabbie who is prepared to allow me to drive, for rather more baht than we'd usually pay. I climb into the driver's seat, Mark gets in the passenger side and the hapless cabbie sits in the back, no doubt wondering if we will all arrive at the hotel in one piece. Although I've taken a drink or two I seem to know my way back to the hotel quite easily, though Mr Williams attempts to put a spanner in the works by constantly flicking the vehicle out of gear whenever we arrive at junctions and traffic lights. Finally, after much hilarity, we arrive safely and it's only when I'm in my room that I realise just how stupid I've been. If I'd been caught, I'd have been doing a few nights – or maybe longer – in the 'Bangkok Hilton'. Years later I will recount the story to a journalist and will be slaughtered in the press for it. Fair enough, I guess, but I wasn't that drunk – and neither would I have driven through Bangkok sober!

The following day I phone Mandy to tell her what Mark and I have been up to in Bangkok. 'I wish you were that spontaneous when you're with me,' she comments. Sadly, what she says is true. When I get home the last thing I want to do is go out and let my hair down, whereas she's been looking after a baby for a couple of weeks and wouldn't mind an evening off.

By the time the 1998 World Championship has rolled around I've won just the one final – a 9–6 victory over John Parrott in the Thailand Masters. I've made it to three finals, two semis and four quarters. Some players would see this as not a bad season all round, but not me. I can't hide the fact that it's been disappointing, and there is more adverse news when I find out I'm drawn against Jimmy White in the first round of the World Championship. Before the draw, I have an uncanny feeling that this will happen, almost as if fate has directed it. This early fixture feels weird to me and it's definitely weird for Jimmy because this is the first year since turning pro that he's had to qualify for the event – not something that gives a once-great player much confidence. Jimmy and I have had so many epic battles at the Crucible that an early ejection for one of us doesn't seem quite right.

This year, there's something different about Jimmy. Gone are the jokes and the banter. He seems serious, aloof and not his usual warm self. It doesn't add up, until we discover he's been seeing a sports psychologist and has presumably been told that keeping your cards close to your chest is advantageous in a sport like snooker.

I'm never at my best in the first couple of rounds and this, combined with Jimmy's new persona, puts me somewhat on the back foot. We reach in for the customary handshake at the beginning of the match and he deliberately doesn't make eye contact with me. That's unsettling, especially coming from someone like Jimmy. A voice in my head is telling me this is an unusual situation and that it feels uncomfortable, but I try to push this aside and get on with the game.

Quickly, it appears that whoever's been advising Jimmy has done a bloody good job. His game is the strongest I've seen it for years. In the first frame he makes a century and steams through me to go 7–0 ahead. I sit in my chair and can hardly believe this is happening. It's Jimmy White, for Christ's sake! A superb player, undoubtedly, but in the past I've very publicly demonstrated that I can beat him. 'This isn't how it should be,' I think. 'This isn't the way the World Championship plays out.'

Jimmy is putting me under pressure and generally playing with all the hunger and skill that, at this moment, appears to be entirely bypassing me. However, he's not scoring as highly as he might and at 8–1 I pull back three frames in a row. Even that isn't enough to rattle him and at 10–4 the game is over. I'm out in the first round, to the man I've beaten four times in the final. And there is also a question mark looming over my world number one status. At the start of the season it appears to be a dead cert that I will have it for another year, but when John Higgins beats me 9–8 in the final of this season's penultimate event, the British Open, mathematically speaking the door is now open for him to get to the top of the rankings. Although John will have to win the World Championship to do this, my first-round defeat has now made his task much easier. The number-one ranking is so important to me and losing to Jimmy makes me very worried.

The defeat leaves me devastated. Predictably, Jimmy's fans are nothing short of ecstatic. He's exacted revenge for all those years of humiliation and now it's me leaving the floor with my tail between my legs.

After the game I don't linger in Sheffield. There's nothing to stay for so I go home feeling thoroughly miserable and remain that way until the tournament is over. I try to avoid watching any coverage by spending time with Mandy and Blaine, or by playing golf. If I go to the local shop I try to hide my face. I don't want anyone making 'the best man won'-style comments. I couldn't handle it. In my head, I'm thinking, 'This isn't right.

I shouldn't be home so early. What's happening to me? Is my game going to pieces?'

John Higgins eventually wins the title, beating Ken Doherty 18–12 and therefore becoming not only World Champion but world number one. Ian is again delighted that Ken, one of his players, is in the final, but rather less pleased that I'm not the other one. If I were the sporting type, I'd be happy for John; he's a friend and a fellow Scot. John was part of Ian's Cue Masters team for a while but never felt comfortable being number two to me. He understood I would be the priority and decided to leave Cue Masters, opting to be managed by his father. I respected that – and in hindsight it was the right decision. He's a terrific player and thoroughly deserves the win, but though we're mates, I can't bring myself to phone him with my congratulations. The truth is, I'm jealous of him. If I can't win the World Championship or be world number one I don't want anyone else to have these honours.

Somehow, I see losing to Jimmy, plus the fact that John is this year's World Champion and that I no longer have my number one status, as a sign that things happen in threes, and that destiny suggests I will no longer dominate the game. I try to dismiss such thoughts but occasionally doubt creeps in and I wonder how long I might last as the best and most consistent player of the last few years.

Not congratulating John seems petulant and silly in hindsight, but it's part of my winners' mentality. John doesn't quite see it that way, and when I next see him he asks why I haven't been in touch.

'Ach, you know me,' I say, trying to be light-hearted, 'I'm a bad loser.'

It's an honest response, yet it becomes an issue for John. Later, we will be on a flight to a tournament in China and after a few drinks the issue of the unmade call will be brought up again. 'I wouldn't phone anyone to congratulate them,' I tell him. 'Not even if it were my own brother. Sorry, but it's just not me.'

And it isn't. By this stage I might be letting my guard down a touch, but there's a part of me that wants to hang on to my unknowable aloofness like a talisman. It's served me well in the past, that's for sure. Really, though, what would it have cost just to say, 'Nice one, John'?

Top 5 SHOTS OF MY CAREER

1. 1992, World Championship final v Jimmy White. Brown off the spot with cue ball in the jaws of the middle pocket, to go 14–10.
2. 1990, UK Championship final v Steve Davis. Blue with the rest.
3. 1995, World Championship final v Jimmy White. Final black for the 147.
4. 1997, LV Charity Challenge final v Ronnie O'Sullivan. First red potted in maximum made in the final frame.
5. 1991 Masters final v Mike Hallett. Brown played with running side off three cushions for position on the blue.

CHAPTER 17

From my chair on the floor of Bournemouth's International Conference Centre I can just about see movement in the shadows, as more and more figures gather in the seats above me. The familiar faces of people I've been chatting to in the previous few hours are almost pressed together as they whisper to each another. I can't hear them, but I know what they're saying:

'What the hell's going on?'

'Surely he's not going to lose another frame?'

'I've never seen anything like this . . .'

'Do you think it's all over for him?'

And if I were up there, with my fellow players, watching the game unfold down below, I'd be saying the same things too. In fact, sitting here, rooted to the spot, I'm thinking all these questions and more, the main one being, 'How the fuck are you losing to him?'

The occasion is the 1998 UK Championship and I'm in the first round against Marcus Campbell, a Scots player who's been around for a few years and, so far, has had little impact on me. This is only the second match we've contested, the first being a narrow 5–4 win to him in the early part of 1998. Unfortunately for me, there is nothing narrow about this match.

Marcus Campbell is thrashing me all over the table. And that's an understatement. The world's seventy-third best player is tearing my bollocks off very publicly. He wins the first frame, then the second, third, fourth and fifth. Whatever I'm doing, it's not enough. I sit there, with the worst feeling gnawing at the pit of my stomach, and I watch as he plays solidly. His game isn't spectacular in any sense, but it's enough to keep me in my chair. Above me, the rumour mill is going into overdrive. 'What's happened to Hendry?' is the question on everyone's lips. A good question, and one I don't really have an answer for, except for the fact that whatever I do, whatever I try, however much I tell myself that I'm six-times World Champion and was world number one for eight years, I just cannot seem to play like I used to. The natural, innate, unshakeable confidence I have in my ability to play snooker better than anyone else in the world has gone. This is no longer fun. It's torture.

'How are you losing to him?' I ask myself. As I sit rooted to the spot or get to the table only to miss an easy chance, I ask myself the same question over and over and over again. It's the first time I've really listened to such a critical voice and I feel shocked, surprised and sick all at the same time. For some months now I've sensed that something hasn't been right, but I've tried to block out the voice whispering it to me. Now, that whisper has turned into a roar and I can no longer ignore it.

Marcus Campbell looks more surprised than anyone else when, at the close of the first session, he's leading 8–0. He only needs one more frame to win. Agonisingly, this match is played over two afternoons, so I have a whole twenty-four hours to stew over what has happened before we meet again. John Carroll looks sideways at me as we head back to the hotel. I don't want to speak to or see anyone. There are no words of consolation, and although there is tomorrow to contend with, I already know that it's all over. I just want the torture to finish as quickly as possible.

I lie on the bed and stare at the ceiling. In my mind I replay every shot I've taken and they're all horrendous. I imagine Ian giving John Carroll a bollocking over the phone, the essence of which will be relayed to me later. 'What's he playing at? Has he been practising? What was he doing last night? Make sure he stays in tonight.' I wonder what Mandy and Blaine are doing up in faraway Scotland, but I choose not to call her. Having to tell her what's going on, as it's happening, is just too depressing.

The following day I turn up and can barely be bothered to practise. There seem to be even more players occupying the seats above the auditorium than there were the previous day. I put up a cursory scrap, to no avail. Marcus Campbell wins the frame and the match, and I've suffered the worst defeat since the humiliations at the hands of Steve Davis in the far-off 1980s. Back then, of course, I was an untried rookie and needed to learn a few lessons. So what am I going to take away from this little episode? Possibly that I really need some help . . .

After the press conference, at which I admit that I've lost confidence in my game and ungraciously tell journalists that I don't think Marcus Campbell is a 'tournament winner', I want to go straight home but there aren't any flights to Scotland until the next day, which means another twenty-four hours stewing in my room. Hearing of this, Billy Snaddon, one of my regular practice partners, phones me and gently asks me if I'd like to go out.

'Nah, thanks,' I say, 'I'm not really feeling like a night out at the minute.'

'We're going to this club . . . For Your Eyes Only, it's called. It's lap-dancing and that.'

I shake my head. 'I'd rather hang myself, Billy,' I say. Even if I was feeling on top of the world, this wouldn't be my scene.

'Ach, come on,' he says, 'it'll be a laugh. Stop you brooding in there. See you in an hour, yeah?'

I'm not going anywhere until five minutes before Billy phones again. I realise I have to get out of this room, as I'm just lying there looking at the ceiling, so I get changed and wait for Billy. He's pleased I'm tagging along. These places aren't my scene, but I tell myself I might enjoy it once I'm there, plus it might take my mind off what's just happened.

I don't enjoy it. It's a dispiriting experience not made any easier by various players taking the piss out of my snooker misfortune. I spend the evening wondering what I'm doing here, and don't take part in any of the boozy shenanigans involving players, punters and lap dancers. When I arrive home I tell Mandy where I've been. She doesn't seem bothered, but a few weeks later there's a TV programme about lap-dancing clubs and her eyebrows shoot up in astonishment. 'You didn't tell me they did all that there!' she shouts.

'I didn't do a thing,' I reply, thinking back to my total dejection that night.

The horror of the defeat is mitigated somewhat a couple of weeks later when I win the Malta Grand Prix, beating Ken Doherty 7–6. The relief that the Campbell game might have been a blip is, however, short-lived; Tony Drago, who has never previously had a win against me, beats me twice on the trot, in the quarter-final stages of the German Masters and Irish Open events, and that really is unacceptable. Something needs to be done, and quickly. Ian summons me to a meeting in the club and for the first time ever I use the warehouse, not the front door, to gain entrance to his office. I'm too embarrassed to show my face to my fellow players – this is how bad it's become. I sit and listen while Ian tells me I'm not focused, not practising hard enough.

'What's going on, Stephen?' he says.

In response, I shrug my shoulders. I've no idea, only that I seem to have lost my bottle. Ian carries on verbally kicking my arse. And in truth, I need and deserve it, though it doesn't feel that way. I'm a married man with a family of my own, and I'm still being talked to like a teenager.

The upshot of this conversation is that Ian arranges for a guy called Del Hill to come up to Scotland and have a look at what's happening. Del coaches Ronnie O'Sullivan, which sounds good to me as I haven't had a coach in years. At this point, I'd take advice from anyone – if my granny spotted a flaw in my game I'd listen to her.

Del comes up to my house and watches as I practise at the table in the games room. He seems to think that if I change the way I cue to a more downward angle I might see more success. I thank him for his time, knowing full well that the approach won't work for me. Realistically, there is only one person who can come anywhere near to sorting out my difficulties, and without me knowing, John Carroll arranges for him to come and watch me in a match. Enter Frank Callan, for the second time in my career.

If anyone knows my game almost as well as I do, it's Frank. I like him and, more importantly, trust his judgement. Instantly he makes me feel relaxed. Just being in his company reignites the feelings I had about snooker when I was younger, i.e. that I can and will take on anyone, confident I can win. I know that, technically, there isn't much wrong with my game that can't be worked on with a little extra practice. It's the attitude towards it which needs some work.

For all his curmudgeonly approach, Frank is good to be around. We laugh when I remind him of the time he came on a tour with us to Thailand. Blackpool to Bangkok is quite a leap, culturally speaking, especially for a man of the old school like Frank, but fair play to him, he threw himself into his new surroundings. Yet, some old habits die hard. When I called by his room one day, en route to practice, I noticed several pairs of underpants hanging up to dry on a line in the bathroom. I laughed till I cried. 'They'll do laundry for you here, Frank,' I said. 'You don't need to wash them yourself.' In reply he shook his head. He trusted no one with his underwear but himself.

Frank doesn't suggest much other than going back to basics. He notices that I'm unintentionally putting 'side' on the cue ball and immediately I correct this to a central position. He gets me back to practising on my own, hour after hour, just like I did when I first turned pro at sixteen. This is what has been missing – knowing and trusting what I'm capable of. I have allowed a critical voice to develop, and I need to turn that negative voice into a positive one.

Also, there is a clearly defined target to aim for: the elusive record-setting seventh world title. Frank knows I can do it, and he takes every opportunity to remind me of that. Time and again he stresses that only practice will help improve both technique and confidence. My practice routine hasn't slackened, as such, but Ian doesn't drop in on me unannounced as often as he once did, and I have noticed that my tea-breaks are a touch more frequent now than they were.

The news from the table still isn't good. Tony Drago beats me again, this time in the last sixteen of the 1999 Masters, and I lose the Welsh Open final 9–8 to Mark Williams. Mark beats me again in the quarter-final of the Thailand Masters and even my practice partner Billy Snaddon sticks the boot in, winning 6–2 in the semi-final of the China International.

All that said, Frank's down-to-earth advice and his insistence on practice, practice, practice, slowly starts to pay off. I win the 1999 Scottish Open, easily beating Graeme Dott 9–1. In the final of the 1999 Irish Masters I come from 5–0 down to beat Stephen Lee 9–8, a score which includes three century breaks. Out of the jaws of a disastrous season I've now managed to get three final wins under my belt, and while the pressure from all quarters is now on as I head to Sheffield, I'm certainly feeling more optimistic about my chances than I have been all season.

In the first round I'm drawn against Paul Hunter, a very promising young player who's making his World Championship debut. Paul is a real talent and, given what's happened to me over the past season, I'm not looking forward to playing a young guy hungry for success. Predictably, the game is a tough one. Paul makes the running early, forcing me into a real scrap almost to the finish line. The result is 10–8 but Paul has demonstrated he has what it takes to be a winner. In the next few years he will prove his talent, particularly at the Masters, which he wins three times. However, his promise will be cut short by a diagnosis of cancer which, tragically, causes his death in 2006 at the age of just twenty-seven. And snooker is robbed of a very bright star indeed.

Mandy and I attend Paul's funeral in Leeds and it's a very, very sad event. Many of his fellow players are in tears, just sorry that such a talent wasn't allowed to blossom. As a player he had tremendous bottle, playing his best snooker on the biggest occasions, which I identify from my own game. There is no doubt in my mind that had he lived he would've been World Champion one day.

Back in Sheffield, my tournament is very nearly ruined via a break-in at my hotel room. When John, Ian and I return from dinner in a local restaurant I see that someone has been in and relieved me of most of my clothing, including an expensive leather jacket embossed with Ferrari's famous prancing horse,

217

which was given to me by a friend. The thieves seem to have got away with their haul via a sliding door which backs on to the hotel grounds, but what they haven't noticed – or have noticed, but for some reason didn't take – is my cue. There it is, in the corner of the room, still in its case. I breathe the biggest sigh of relief. Everything else is replaceable but had that disappeared . . . well, it doesn't bear thinking about. Now I have some serious clothes shopping to do between matches, but at least they've left me my snooker suit too.

I go on to beat James Wattana and Matthew Stevens, both very handy players, and in the semi-final I face none other than Ronnie O'Sullivan. There is no doubt this will be the biggest test so far of this championship. Ronnie is one of the best front-runners in the game and it's important for anyone playing him to stamp their authority on the match early and keep him on the back foot. In the first three frames I make breaks of 126, 82 and 86 without Ronnie taking a single point and I finish the first session 6–2 up. That would be enough for a lot of players, but I can't afford to take Ronnie lightly and let up for a second, allowing him to gain momentum. He takes the next four frames, throwing in a pair of centuries, and levels the score until I break away to make it 10–7. Again, Ronnie hits back and we scrap it out until, at 13–12, he's ahead for the first time. Now I must give it everything I've got. Finding another gear, I take the final five frames with breaks of 75, 78, 50 and 86 to reach the final.

The win against Ronnie is a huge confidence boost. Finally, I feel I've got a good chunk of the old Stephen Hendry back – the part that says, 'You can do this – this is your time.' There have been moments over the past couple of seasons where I've thought, 'Is there any point going on?' Now, the panic that seemed to have set in has subsided and my problems appear to be nothing more than a temporary blip. Mark Williams, my opponent in the final, knows how high the stakes are. He's well capable of winning this; after all, he's shown good form against me this season. Still, I'm as fired up as I've ever been, in no small part thanks to Frank Callan and his sensible, no-nonsense advice and determination that I stick at it come what may.

I go out into the auditorium determined as ever to quickly put some distance between me and my opponent. Mark is the sort of player who isn't intimidated by anyone. His temperament is one of his biggest strengths and he can make clearances from positions no one else can because of his incredible potting. When he's in, you never feel safe and, as exciting as it is for audiences, I don't want a repeat of the infamous black-ball final at the Masters. I'm feeling strong, but I'm not sure even my nerves could stand another frame like that.

Frank has advised that I slow down and focus more intently on each shot I make. He tells me to decide on the shot I make before I get down to the table. I've probably missed more shots in my career by being down on the table and then changing my mind than any other reason. Now I'm listening to his advice and taking an extra second or two to concentrate. I take the first four frames without too much fuss. Mark responds by winning three frames out of the next four and takes advantage of several errors to close the gap. By the end of the first day we're at 10–8 – not as much room for comfort as I'd like, but still keeping Mark on the back foot.

At 11–9 I feel momentum gathering: 12–9, 13–9, 14–9, 15–9. The gap is widening but I'm careful not to succumb to overexcitement by speeding up and making stupid mistakes. Frank's 'slow and steady' mantra is rattling around my brain as I take a couple more frames, leaving Mark now floundering at 17–9. Just one more frame required. Although he's beginning to look shattered, Mark's not done yet. He wins the next two frames. There's still a big gap but I must go so carefully and be mindful not to look at the winning line too early. I stay in the moment, concentrating on one shot at a time. In the next frame Mark goes forty points ahead and is potting well. I feel I might not get a chance but when I do, I know I will have to give it my all in order to get the match finished as soon as possible. I really don't want to give Mark any more chances to catch up and take us to another final-frame cliffhanger. I begin to make the clearance, walking slowly around the table, breathing deeply, concentrating on every second. Every nerve in my body is focused on putting as much effort into each ball as possible. As the break builds, the finishing line is in sight and my legs are shaking so much they might give way. I get down to business, reminding myself that the Crucible is my arena and that in this final, of all the finals I've ever played in, I owe it to myself – and myself only – to win. Time seems to compress as I play the balls second by second, never daring to lose focus yet willing the end to come swiftly. I catch sight of Mark in his chair, legs crossed, arms spread. He knows it's over, and the applause rippling from each pot I make tells me all I need to know.

I've done it.

A seventh World Championship, a record broken and a season dragged back from a very difficult start. I crack a huge smile in response to the standing ovation and punch the air in celebration. I'm even more delighted that Mandy comes on with Blaine in her arms – I don't do an Alex Higgins and break down in tears while holding my son but it's probably the most outwardly happy I've ever looked at a world final, or any final for that matter.

This is the one. I've achieved something that wouldn't have entered even my wildest dreams in the weeks, months and even years after receiving my life-changing Christmas present. And for this to come after such a terrible run of form makes the victory so much sweeter. I'm aware that over the past season or so, various people have written me off, and for good reason. After that 9–0 horror I've been nervous of going into long-frame matches, the arena in which I've previously been so confident. Following the Marcus Campbell game I've had a thing about making sure I get a frame on the board early, thereby avoiding a panicky feeling about getting my first frame on the scoreboard as quickly as possible. Sportspeople of all types pick up scars as their careers progress, and not necessarily physical ones. The scars that often inflict the most damage are the ones you receive psychologically, which is particularly true for those who play individual sports. A bad defeat, a loss of form, a slip in technique – it all goes in and causes damage. You play the same shot, you get punished for it, you remember that punishment and next time you're in a position where you might play a bad shot you shy away from it, opting for something safer. Then you get punished for playing it safe, and so the vicious circle turns again. At the beginning of your career you have no scars because you have nothing to lose. At the end of it, you emerge feeling like you've been through a giant mincer.

For now, though, I'm on top of the world, even if I'm still number two in the rankings. John Higgins continues to hold on to the top spot. And yes, he has the good grace to offer his congratulations to me after the World Championship.

Naturally, there is extensive press coverage of the win and the events leading up to it. I publicly thank Frank Callan for turning my game around when I needed it most and I acknowledge that I've been through some tough times, to the point where I'd wondered if there was any point going on. Frank, Ian and even Mandy are interviewed about the so-called 'comeback' and they all say they had faith in my ability. There have been times where I've been very unsure that I had the same faith, but here we are. I've lived up to the hopes of those closest to me and I've proved everyone else wrong. The photographs of me, Mandy and Blaine relaxing on the grass in front of our hotel the day after the final speak volumes for the happiness and relief I'm feeling.

Yet, one telling comment I make to the press, which seems insignificant at the time, holds the key to the next stage of my career and, as time goes on, will speak volumes about it. I'm asked what I'd like to do next and I say that I'd like to carry on to an eighth, ninth or even tenth win, though I'm still enjoying letting the seventh sink in. Then I say this:

'I've always felt under pressure. But I will never feel pressure again, not now I've won the seventh title. If I never win anything else, I've achieved everything I've ever dreamed of.'

Subconsciously I've just given myself permission to go easy, to take my foot off the pedal. And in the coming years, that will prove fatal to my game.

Top 5 CAREER PERFORMANCES

1. 1994 UK final v Ken Doherty (I made seven centuries)
2. 1997 Liverpool Victoria Charity Challenge final v Ronnie O'Sullivan (my 147 in the final frame)
3. 1993 World Championship final v Jimmy White (finished a session early)
4. 1991 Benson & Hedges Masters final v Mike Hallett (came back from 8-2 down)
5. 1992 World Championship Final v Jimmy White (winning from 14–8 behind)

CHAPTER 18

November 1999: I'm sitting in a pub in Airdrie following an 'Auld Firm' game – Rangers vs Celtic – I've attended in Glasgow. I'm at the bar with a friend, we're waiting for other people and although I'm trying to relax, I know that these surroundings are not my scene. The atmosphere here is, to put it mildly, heavy, and the pub itself is not the most salubrious I've ever been in.

If you're well known in sport and you're out and about, you're going to get recognised, particularly in a small country like Scotland. Some people have no inhibitions about coming up to you to talk about how well you've done or (if you've lost) how they themselves would've handled themselves if they'd been in your shoes. In the latter situation, my usual tactic is to agree with everything they say. 'You're right,' I'll say, 'I really should've played like that.' Agreeing tends to defuse what could be potentially argumentative situations. But not this time.

A guy comes over looking the worse for wear and clutching a pool cue. 'Hey, Stephen,' he slurs, 'gie's a game. G'wan . . . see how good y'are against me.'

I shake my head. 'No, you're OK, thanks,' I say.

'G'wan, Stephen,' he repeats, 'gie's a game.'

I shake my head, he turns away, then looks back and growls something in our direction. My friend has grown up around here and he's tough. In no uncertain terms, he tells the pool player to clear off. We decide to take ourselves out of the situation by going to the upstairs bar. All is quiet for the next fifteen minutes until the drunk guy comes lumbering up the stairs. He spots us and begins snarling again.

'He's told you already,' my friend says, 'he doesn't want to play. OK?'

'Hey, Stephen,' he says, pointing to my friend, 'what are ye doin' wi' a cunt like him?'

Next second, they're fighting. No doubt there are dozens of other pub scraps breaking out all over the area, but 99 per cent of them will be about football. Unfortunately, this one has me at its epicentre; not a place I want to be at all. I scarper with lightning speed to the nearest exit. Somehow, another large fight has broken out in the main bar. Fists and feet flail, chairs fly, people shout and scream, accompanied by the sound of smashing glasses. I dodge the gunfight at the O.K. Corral and make my escape through a fire exit into the street. I get into the car which brought us to the pub and unashamedly make my escape.

A year later, I will relive the whole scene in court, because my friend has been charged with assault. I appear as a witness for the prosecution because I saw the first punch thrown and, nervous as hell about giving evidence, I don't sleep much the night before. My friend is fined £500 and that's the end of the matter. Rough pubs and seedy nightclubs have never been – and never will be – my thing. Restaurants and hotel bars are my natural habitat now, if I'm not at home. I also consider that only a few years ago, I wouldn't have been allowed anywhere near such a pub – my all-seeing manager would've made sure of that.

Not now. Ian is still around, yet not much for me. In many ways I'm not complaining; I'm no longer a boy. I don't need a father-figure – I'm a father myself. I've proved to Ian repeatedly that the time and effort and expense he's poured into my career has paid off just the way he and I wanted it to. His success with me has attracted other good players to his stable and, while I'm still Cue Masters' top player, there are others snapping at my heels, which is all good for business. For myself, I've done what I set out to do, which is becoming the best snooker player in the world. I'm thirty, happily married, financially comfortable and, as our drunken pool-playing friend proved, have a face that is recognised everywhere. I have it all – but do I still have the hunger which led me here in the first place?

There is the usual post-mortem with Ian on the season just gone but if there is any grand plan being hatched by management for Stephen Hendry, I'm not party to it. 'Just carry on winning' is the general advice. Ideas about 'branding' or monetising my name outside of the usual sponsorship deals are nonexistent, even in this late 90s / early 2000s climate in which sportsmen and women are truly understanding the earning power of themselves as personalities as well as top players. Some are earning as much, if not more, after retirement. In addition, football, golf, motor racing and many other sports are targets for the cult of celebrity and opportunities are building like never before for those willing to take them. In time, snooker players will be granted such chances in reality shows but for now, our game is largely untroubled by notions of fame away from the table. Certainly, snooker has its personalities, but it's still a working man's sport and its practitioners aren't naturally comfortable with the limelight off the table. I include myself in that category.

I take the advice and carry on with my game. The truth is, though, that 'my game' still isn't as it should be. The efforts made with Frank Callan produced a world-beating performance but as we go into the new season it's obvious that something more fundamental is affecting my play – a combination, perhaps, of an attitude born of realising that at this stage I'm less of a winning machine and more of a human being, and a condition that I've yet to put a name to but which I know is physically preventing me from playing as I would like, and as I used to.

Over the past couple of seasons, I've noticed I'm struggling to push the cue through the cue ball properly. I don't shake, and I don't 'twitch' – it isn't quite as physical as that. It's almost like a reluctance on the part of my wrist to allow the cue to accelerate through the ball. When this 'tightness' happens, I butcher the shot. It's a weird phenomenon, and while it isn't happening on every shot – maybe one in ten, or even twenty to begin with – it's enough to freak me out and throw me off my stride temporarily.

When it does happen, it makes me wary of playing a similar shot, should one come up later in the game. For a snooker player, particularly one who plays with aggression and determination, this isn't good news. I don't mention it to anyone, as I don't want any other players finding out and taking the mickey out of me for 'twitching' shots. I wouldn't respond so well to such banter, if indeed it is 'only' banter. Although I've integrated more with the rest of them over the years, I still like to think of myself as 'other' – in a league of his own. Anything that might tarnish or take that away isn't to be welcomed.

As the new season begins and I get off to a flying start, I tell myself that maybe I shouldn't worry about such niggles. I beat Mark Williams 7–5 in the final of the 1999 Champions Cup and a week or so later I reach the final of the British Open in Plymouth. My opponent is Peter Ebdon, a player still disinclined to give an inch, particularly when he's facing me. He makes a great start, taking the first three frames, and I start to panic about falling behind. But there's nothing like a challenge and I win the next four frames to take the lead. And in style, too, because in the seventh frame I make a 147, the sixth of my career in a professional event. I hold my glass of water aloft, acknowledging the crowd's cheers, and basking in the moment.

Peter's natural confidence is unshaken by the 147 and he wins the next frame. Once I'm back in my stride, though, it's full steam ahead and eventually I win 9–5, a score which also boasts a break of 132 to complement the maximum. When I play like this I'm convinced no one can beat me and yet, as the season continues, I find it more and more difficult to capitalise on these two early successes and play consistently well. I'm trying hard and making my way to quarters and semis regularly. Somehow, though, places in ranking finals are becoming more elusive and I'm not entirely confident that I'll be taking home any more trophies this season. Apart from the 2000 World Championship, of course, and as it begins the papers are all talking about 'Hendry the Eighth'. Sure, there seems to be more and more talented players around now capable of winning the championship but what better way to celebrate the new millennium than another victory in my Sheffield-based 'kingdom'?

Is it overconfidence or under-preparation? Is it that I think I have a divine right to the world title? Whatever reasons I have, they don't alter the fact that I go out in the first round to a guy making his debut here. Stuart Bingham, ranked ninety-second in the world, has had to play four qualifying matches just to get to this stage and I've dominated here for more than a decade. I win the first frame and, this being the first round, expect to run away with the game. I'm wrong. I should know that opening rounds can be banana skins. It doesn't matter who you are, you should take nothing for granted, and instead of doing what I think he will do – capitulate – Bingham is hanging on and is never more than a frame behind. Something about his doggedness rattles me and although I take the final three frames of the first session, including a break of 106, it's not enough to throw him off and he replies by taking four in a row. I can only sit and watch, dejected, as Stuart piles on the pressure. At the 10–7 conclusion of the match there is no one more astonished than my opponent and no one more depressed than me. In the press conference I say that I wasn't playing to win; instead, I was trying not to lose, and this isn't something I've ever experienced at the Crucible. This is the second time in three years I've had to go home early, and it's not a good feeling at all.

Once home, and as with the Jimmy White knockout of '98, I avoid the TV as much as possible; as much as he's my good friend off the table, I'm not keen to see Mark Williams holding up the trophy after this year's final. It's the first time he's won it and I should be delighted for him. Instead, it just feels wrong. Quite simply, it hurts, though I'm careful not to sulk. I beat Mark 9–5 the week following the final to win the 2000 Premier League title, but it's no consolation. Mandy understands that I'm feeling gutted after such a defeat, though in our world there is no time to dwell on it and I'm happy she takes that attitude. Home is home – I have very few reminders of my career lining the walls or stuck in display cabinets. All my trophies are in Ian's club and my mum collects the press cuttings. I like the fact that when I come back in through the front door I can leave work behind.

My usual method of getting over the blues associated with a defeat is to get on the practice table as soon as possible. In recent times, though, I've found myself just 'dropping by' for an hour or two or, more frequently, taking a day off. Increasingly, this is extending to a couple of days, particularly if it's summer and there's golf to be had at Gleneagles. When I do go in – and providing I don't feel too embarrassed about whatever defeat

I've had – I'll have a chat with whoever's around, make a cup of tea, watch a bit of sport or news on the TV and, finally, get down to knocking in a few balls. Enthusiasm for the intensive practice routines I carried out so faithfully and regularly at the start of my career and beyond is evidently waning.

The following season is even more disappointing than the previous one. For the first time in many years I don't win a single ranking tournament. I'm still reaching finals, semis and quarters but the focus, intensity and dedication needed to win tournaments is not what it should be. And then there's the recurring problem of the 'tightness' around my cueing action, the psychological effect of which is still causing me to avoid playing certain shots I could previously play with my eyes shut. My confidence is sapped every time this happens. Before I experienced this, I could play every shot in the game. Now, I feel that it is nothing less than a handicap that creates difficulties during matches, with the net result that I'm losing to people I feel shouldn't even be at the same table as me.

It sounds arrogant. It is arrogant, and I'm naming no names because in years to come some of those people will turn into fine, tournament-winning players. But at this point in my career it makes my blood boil to see myself losing time after time to players who are much further down the rankings than me. I sit in my chair as they clear up for the frame and I curse them; their style of playing, their mannerisms, even their clothing. And above all else, I curse myself for no longer possessing the animalistic effortlessness with which I used to sweep away such players with barely a second's thought. Against the top players I appear to be really suffering; in the 2000/01 season Ronnie O'Sullivan beats me on no fewer than six occasions.

The 2001 World Championship is, again, nothing to write home about, though at least this time I make it to the quarter-final. 'At least . . .' just a few short years ago I'd even be annoyed if I'd won a final but played a handful of bad shots. Now I'm almost grateful to have made it through the first couple of rounds without embarrassing myself.

And yet, there are still glimpses, lightning flashes, of the type of play I had. I win the 2001 Malta Grand Prix, beating Mark Williams comprehensively at 7–1 and making a 147 – the eighth of my career – in the third frame. It's still there, the attacking yet poised break-building of old, and looking at the statistics – one final win, four final appearances, four semi-final appearances, a great 147 and prize money in excess of £250,000 – on the face of it I've had a good season. But I know better, and so does everyone else. 'Hendry out to recapture past glories' is a familiar headline this season.

Once again, I need help. I try to describe to Ian where I think the problem lies. His answer is short: 'Just practise more.' It's a fair point, because I'm not practising as I should, and I know it. However, the problem lies deeper than that. I need someone who's been there; who knows how it feels to be sitting in your chair for long periods. The man for the job is Terry Griffiths, the former World Champion and now a highly rated snooker coach.

I've discovered that my cueing problems are being caused by something called the 'yips'. Terry doesn't like the expression but knows what it means. It affects snooker players and golfers, causing the latter to struggle with what should be simple putts. In my case, the inability to accelerate 'through' the ball results in weak shots. There is a debate about whether the yips is a physical or psychological condition, or a mixture of both. Certainly, I can feel a tightness around my wrist which somehow stops me believing that I can play the shot. That, in turn, leaves the 'scar' of a poor shot – one you avoid returning to in the future.

Terry's solution is to change my cue action by shortening it and cutting my backswing in half. Specifically, he wants me to pull the cue back to about half the distance I currently employ before taking a shot, then strike the cue ball faster to avoid the deceleration that is creeping in during the long delivery of the cue. It doesn't sound like a dramatic change but after more than fifteen years of cueing the ball in a way that feels completely natural to me, I must now adapt to a new technique. It's a bit like swapping arms in that it's going to take some getting used to. That said, it gives me something to concentrate on in practice and I'm desperately short of goals at this stage. Terry's patience and persistence inspires me to get back on the practice table. I've become so stale in this respect that anything which will motivate me to put in the hours is welcome. Plus, I like and trust Terry. He knows what he's talking about and knows when to press the right buttons. Equally importantly, he is sympathetic to my struggles but understands when a player must work it out for himself.

As ever, in the intervals during matches, I like to sit in my dressing room and read the paper. I'd rather not be disturbed but I don't mind Terry dropping in, as he is an antidote to my increasing negativity. I'll have a moan to him about all the luck I think my opponent is getting, and he'll counter this by telling me that 'luck' has nothing to do with it – the other guy is just playing solidly, that's all.

'And,' he adds, 'you're three-one up, Stephen. You've a good lead on him. Forget him – build on your own game.'

'Yeah, but did you see that miss I made on the yellow in the third? Stupid, stupid mistake. I shouldn't have let him in.'

'Stephen,' says Terry, in a fatherly way, 'forget the negatives and concentrate on the positives. You made one poor shot. Compare that to the number of great shots you've made so far. You're doing fine – honestly.'

231

Under Terry's guidance the new season starts slowly but surely. It's still semis and quarters up to the 2001 European Open, held in Malta. There I beat Ronnie O'Sullivan and Ken Doherty to reach the final against Joe Perry. It's his first ranking final and he's nervous from the start. After a one-sided match the 9–2 win breaks my ranking tournament drought. Then it's back to the pattern of semis and quarters until the World Championship. Although I'd have liked more titles under my belt by this stage, I can take some small satisfaction that I'm playing reasonably well with a brand-new cue action. I'm still well up there in the rankings and if I can find that little bit of Crucible animal I know lurks within me I might – just might – pull off something spectacular this year. Terry and I discuss the World Championship and he floats the suggestion that, if I win it, I retire immediately after. 'What a way that would be to go out,' he says. I agree that it would be an amazing thing to do, but we decide not to mention it to anyone and see how the tournament plays out.

I squeak past Ken Doherty 13–12 in the quarter-final and am due to face Ronnie O'Sullivan in the semi. On the morning of the match I get an unexpected early knock on my hotel-room door. Slightly annoyed that I'm being disturbed on a match day, I half-open the door to see John Carroll standing outside with a copy of one of the tabloids.

'You'd better read this,' he says, pushing the rolled-up newspaper through the crack. 'Ronnie's had a right go at you.'

I take the paper, flip through the back pages and find the relevant article. As I read, I realise Ronnie's really gone to town this time. He accuses me of being 'unsporting' during our last meeting at the Crucible and says that nothing would give him greater satisfaction than to send me back to my 'sad little life' in Scotland.

I laugh at that bit. To me, it's just verbal sparring and I wonder – quite rightly, as it turns out – whether he's been listening to a certain Sheffield boxer with a penchant for shooting his mouth off. In the last couple of seasons my pal Prince Naseem Hamed has visibly switched his loyalties from me to Ronnie, and the latter has been spotted hanging out with Naz's entourage. So it's not surprising there's a bit of fighting talk, especially given he's the most mercurial player since Alex Higgins.

What does annoy me, however, is that Ronnie claims not to like me. He'll say hello to me, he says, but I'm not his 'cup of tea'. This is news to me; we've always spoken and have what I think are good relations. Ronnie can be up and down, as we know, but I've never felt he's had anything personal against me. Until now.

I put the paper down and head for the shower. 'OK, Ronnie,' I think, 'if that's the way you want it, I'll not bother with you. We'll do the talking at the table.' And with that, I go into the semi-final determined to show him who has the mastery at this venue. It will be the first time I've ever played a match at the Crucible where there is a certain amount of needle involved.

Ronnie finishes the first session 5–3 up. Here and there I catch him smirking whenever I miss an easy shot. However, I'm nowhere near ready to return to my 'sad little life' just yet and I level with him 6–6 before breaking away to make the score 10–7, including two consecutive century breaks. Neither of us are in a mood to concede, and when Ronnie fights back to make it 12–12 I know I must find the magic that seems to exist for me within the maze of corridors around this place. Call it bloody-mindedness or just sheer determination to settle a score – whatever it is, it pushes me to aggressively take five out of the next six frames to send Ronnie home with a 17–13 defeat ringing in his ears. At the end we shake hands, but I don't even crack a smile in his direction and I give a fist-pump to the crowd as he walks out. This has been a grudge match, no doubt about it, but the way it has fired me up leaves me feeling that I've played in a World Championship final and won. Unfortunately for me, the final itself is the following day.

Peter Ebdon, my opponent in the 2002 final, is now more of a complete player. He has shot up the rankings and is considered a potential winner. I know he's one to be wary of and yet I don't think he can possibly beat me over a four-session match. And after the clash with Ronnie, I reckon I'm on a roll strong enough to beat anyone. Big mistake. I go into the final with a feeling of invincibility and although I concentrate on playing my current opponent, and not reliving yesterday's game, I allow Peter to take advantage of the fact that whatever I have left in the tank might not be as much as I need. He goes 4–0 up and leads for most of the match with me hanging on to him, chasing him all the way. We both make great breaks and miss ridiculously easy pots. Nerves are getting a grip of us and as I sit in my chair I grow increasingly frustrated, believing that Peter is somehow harnessing luck – that word again – to get a good run of the balls. It isn't true, of course, but this is becoming my mindset now – focusing on what my opponent is or isn't doing instead of keeping my cool and concentrating on my own game.

From 10–12 down I win four frames on the trot, but the pressure is enormous as the frames fall away. At 16–16 we can both see the winning line. I desperately want it to be my night. I'm convinced that an eighth win will really put my career back on track and justify all Terry's efforts to improve my cue action. Peter goes 17–16 ahead but in the next frame he misses a simple black off the spot and I jump in to clear up and level the score. Then, in the decider, he plays a bad safety shot early on and gives me a tricky red to go for. I must attempt it because it's a chance to win the championship. I take on the risky red and miss it. I'm now on the back foot and, as predicted, Peter makes a couple of solid breaks and wins frame, final and championship.

Losing the match and the championship really, really hurts. To this day, when I think of that final I get a sickening, uneasy feeling. The 9–0 defeat by Marcus Campbell was bad enough but, in a way, I can cope with a very uncharacteristic whitewash better than I can an 'almost did it' result, especially at the Crucible. And in May 2002, as I head homewards in a state of total dejection, I'm not to know that the match which should have been mine marks the last time I will ever appear in a World Championship final.

Top 5 FAVOURITE SHOTS TO PLAY

1. Blue into middle pocket to split the pack
2. Brown off the spot with check side off two cushions for position on blue
3. Potting the pink and taking white off middle knuckle to come back to the black
4. A long straight red to get position on the black
5. Black off spot with top spin off three cushions to get position on the yellow

CHAPTER 19

In the usual sharp reversal of fortune which is ever-present in the world of individual sports, the opening to the 2002/03 season begins with a 6–4 win against Peter Ebdon followed by a 6–3 defeat at the hands of Ronnie O'Sullivan, in the respective quarter- and semi-final matches of the 2002 Scottish Masters, played in Glasgow. Although the past season hasn't been great, Mandy, Blaine and I have had a lovely time in Dubai, which is becoming our regular go-to holiday spot, and I've played a lot of golf. In all honesty I'm enjoying my time off more than I've ever done, and I'm in no great hurry to return to the practice table. I've tried to put the feeling that my game isn't what it was out of my mind, at least temporarily, and Mandy is always quick to snap me out of too much brooding, but as I head into the new season I'm not as enthusiastic or optimistic about it as I should be.

It's not a great approach. Instead of going all out to win, and at least dying with honour during the attempt, my game remains cautious. I do nothing of note in the LG and British Open events and I'm comfortably knocked out at the quarter-final stage of the UK Championship by Mark Williams, who steamrollers me 9–2.

The frustrations are obvious, reflecting an ongoing situation at home in which attempts at achieving something seem to be thwarted, no matter how much we try. Since he was born, Mandy and I have been keen to provide Blaine with a brother or sister. An addition to the family, we feel, would be great for us all – but not to put too fine a point on it, it's just not happening. We've had three tries with IVF and, as anyone who's been through this knows, the disappointment and heartbreak increase with each 'not pregnant' result.

Then, in the early part of 2003, we finally receive some good news. Mandy is expecting, and although it's early days and we necessarily keep quiet about it, we're thrilled that at last we have something to celebrate.

This happier turn of events coincides with better news for me. I make it into the final of the 2003 Welsh Open at the Cardiff International Arena and, although I'm up against Mark Williams, I really tap into some of the old magic. Mark takes the first frame, but after equalising I find great form and I'm in the lead until the end, which finishes at 9–5 and includes a very healthy total of four century breaks. The confidence and renewed energy which comes with such a decisive win propels me into the next tournament, the Masters, which I've always enjoyed playing.

In the quarter-final I'm drawn against Jimmy White. As ever, the London-centric crowd are willing him on, even though Jimmy's glory days are behind him now. And as usual, I come in for a bit of sledging from the sidelines, not all of it light-hearted. I take little notice and get on with the job in hand. Jimmy plays well and we're evenly matched until I light the touchpaper in the eighth frame and build a break that is heading nicely towards a 147 and a prize of a new Honda sports car in a fetching shade of canary yellow. I'm within three balls of the maximum when I play a bad positional shot on the blue, leading to a missed pink; a 'gimme' that in most other circumstances I'd expect to pot. Of course, in this situation the pressure is intense and in despair I slide my cue along the table and slump over the baize. The crowd applauds the attempt and I bite my lip in response, reflecting that the Stephen Hendry of old would never have made such a cock-up. Even so, I make a century break to finish off Jimmy 6–4 but, as I tell the press afterwards, 'That car was in the garage . . .'

I face down Ken Doherty in the semi-final, a 6–3 win which includes the acquisition of this tournament's high-break prize after I take the second frame with 144 total clearance. Unfortunately, the fun ends when Mark Williams pays me back for the Welsh Open and beats me 10–4 in the final. This is the last ever Masters to be sponsored by Benson & Hedges. The new millennium has brought in an end to tobacco sponsorship of major events, and in a few short years the Conference Centre itself will disappear to make way for the new Wembley Stadium. All we will have of this electric event, with its big, boisterous crowds, are fond memories.

The rest of the season, up until the World Championship, is a mixed bag. In the 2003 European Championship I face the 'Class of 92' – Higgins, Williams and O'Sullivan – in the quarter-final, semi-final and final respectively. They are all fine players: Ronnie is the most naturally talented and has the best cue-ball control; John is the best match player and if I was to bet my house on someone clearing up to pinch a frame, it would be him; Mark has without doubt the best temperament. Against me, John and Mark go down fairly easily but Ronnie is a tougher nut to crack and after an opening break of 140 he flies for the rest of the match, eventually winning 9–6. I'm still avoiding him, and I sense his unease as we pass each other around the table. He keeps approaching John Carroll, telling him that he does actually like me, but I take no notice and, apart from the customary handshake, blank him completely.

It's very unlike me to hold a grudge; however, I feel there is little point in speaking to someone who says he doesn't like you. That's personal. I'll admit freely that I hate losing and I don't like seeing anyone win apart from me, but it's only professional rivalry and away from the table I don't like to be thought of as anything less than polite and respectful. For the time being, the silence continues.

I don't get further than the quarter-final of the World Championship, despite having the honour of being the first player ever to make one hundred century breaks at the Crucible, which I achieve in the first round against Gary Wilkinson. Mark Williams makes short work of the hopes I still have for an eighth title in a tough game that ends 13–7, but any disappointment I might have is dwarfed by a phone call from Mandy. She is in tears, and when I ask what's wrong her reply shocks me to the core.

'It's the baby,' she says. 'We've lost it. I thought something was wrong, I had a test and it's dead inside me.'

I leave for home immediately. As I drive through the night I'm numb with pain and sorrow. I think of the much-wanted second child for us and a sibling for Blaine. Instead of looking forward to celebrating a new life, we will be planning a funeral.

I don't know how we get through the three days before Mandy will deliver the baby. We are heartbroken, and I wander round the house in a state of shock. The day comes, and she goes into hospital to give birth. It's a boy. We call him Joseph and we arrange to have a funeral for him in the small church close to our house. I carry the small coffin in my arms, barely able to believe that we've gone from the joy of anticipation to this, and he is laid to rest in the churchyard.

Word is already out that Mandy is pregnant and so the management company are in touch, suggesting that I release a statement to the press. Although this is horrendous, to me it makes sense. It'll head off any awkward questions and (hopefully) gain us some privacy. The last thing we need now is reporters knocking on the door. Mandy finds the decision to release a statement almost inexplicable.

Although I explain that it's to keep the press away, she doesn't feel we need to say anything. I understand this. People with normal lives don't have to do this stuff at just about the worst time possible. But I haven't lived a normal life since I was a teenager . . .

Putting out the statement does keep the press at a distance, though people we know still offer their condolences, reminding us of what's happened. Slowly, Mandy and I try to heal ourselves, and the awful experience we've been through brings us closer. We take walks on the nearby beach with our dogs, not really talking, just slowly going through all that has happened and trying to process it. When I feel ready, I head back to the practice table and pick up my routine. Snooker, for all its ups and downs, is my sanctuary and always has been. Whenever I've felt depressed, disappointed or caught up in some kind of crisis, the table has always been there for me, comforting and unchanging. When I get down and pot balls, I'm able to block out to a large extent whatever's going on, good or bad, and concentrate on the moment. And so I return to the world I know best.

August goes by and soon it's time to return to work. Before the new season starts I'm due to play tournaments in Hong Kong and Thailand. Everything goes well and, as ever, I enjoy spending time in the Far East, a place I've come to regard as a second home.

One of the most important pieces of luggage I take on any work-related flight is, of course, my cue. In all the years I've been playing I've never considered changing it; it's come in for some stick, and 'stick' is how it's often jokingly referred to by other players. Yet it's worked for me. It's a one-piece which I carry in a wooden, leather-bound case that is much more expensive than the cue it houses. Before 9/11 snooker players could carry their cues on board and hand them to a steward, who would lock them away safely. Since the terrible events in New York, increased security means that cues must be checked in with suitcases. Once this is done, they are taken by hand to the aircraft's hold.

We all understand and comply with this, so when I check in my cue at Bangkok Airport I think nothing more about it, assuming without question that it will be safe. My flight takes me to Glasgow Airport with a change at Heathrow, but when John Carroll (who still accompanies me everywhere) and I arrive in England we're met by an airport employee with a somewhat tense look on his face.

'Mr Hendry,' he says, 'we've got a little bit of bad news for you. There's been some damage to one of your items of luggage.'

A sense of dread creeps up the back of my neck. 'Is it a long case?' I ask hesitantly.

'Well, yes, it is, I'm afraid,' replies the airport guy.

'Is it badly damaged?'

'Errm, we don't really know at the moment,' he says. 'It's just been reported as "damaged". I'm afraid you'll have to wait until you get to the carousel at Glasgow Airport. You'll be able to check its condition there.'

Over the next hour or so, I'm almost biting my nails to the bone wondering what might have happened to my cue. Maybe the damage is restricted to the case only – a snapped hinge or something. I'm hoping against hope that whatever happened is minimal, but I doubt it.

At Glasgow Airport John and I stand at the carousel, waiting anxiously for our luggage. The minutes feel like hours. And then I see it, emerging through the rubber flaps and bouncing slightly on the carousel track. Even at twenty yards I can see that both case and cue are broken. Snapped almost clean in two, the whole thing now resembling some form of shepherd's crook. The cue comes to where I'm standing, and I pick it up, the broken end dangling down forlornly.

I could weep. Instead, I laugh.

'Well,' I say to a stunned-looking John Carroll, 'that's my career over.'

John can barely speak. He knows I've had this cue for as long as I've been playing professionally and beyond. He knows it was only cheap and not even straight. And, like me, he knows what it symbolises – perhaps the most successful career in the history of snooker. It's like Harry Potter's wand breaking. And it's odd that it's happened now, when serious doubts have crept into my mind about the quality of my game.

I try not to think that way and instead look at a practical solution. It isn't insured, despite its history, because you can only insure cues for their face value, and this is worth all of forty quid. And anyway, I tell myself, wood breaks all the time. Even delicate things made of wood can be repaired. Only one man I know is up to this task. When the initial shock subsides, I phone Lawrie Annandale immediately and he tells me to bring the cue over the following day.

Lawrie doesn't pull punches. After examining the cue and the area of breakage, down at the butt end, he delivers his verdict.

'It's a shite cue, Stephen,' he says, 'though I don't need to tell you that. If I replace this bit with a nice piece of wood the whole thing is gonna be unbalanced.'

This is bad news. Essentially, an unbalanced cue is an unplayable one. You may as well have a game of snooker with a broom handle, as the result won't be much different. Even so, I plead with Lawrie to at least have a try.

He does, and in a few days I go back to test the results. Sadly for me, Lawrie is right. It looks fine enough, but the bottom end – made of maple like the rest of the cue, but a much better quality of wood – is dragging the whole thing down. It's useless; not even fit to practise with. I'm devastated, but there is nothing anyone can do. I will need to obtain another cue, and as all cues are slightly different in their own way, I'm not going to get one that is a 100 per cent replica of my cheap yet trusty old Rex Williams model.

The season is upon us and I can't hang around. Unlike a tennis player who arrives on court with six rackets and has no problem using all of them equally well, I can't just turn up to a tournament with a flight case full of cues and hope that by swapping them around I'll somehow create the magic. I need to find something I'm comfortable with, and stick with it.

John Parris is the go-to cuemaker for most, if not all, the professional players so I arrange an emergency appointment with him. I give him measurements based on my dear departed bit of wood and he makes three cues for me to try. Immediately, I notice how much better quality they are, and how differently they react compared to the Rex Williams, and I pick the one I feel most comfortable with. Several sessions of intensive practice follow and I'm delighted to discover that I can actually pot balls and play well with the new cue.

As we know, though, practising is one thing. Playing in a major event, and on TV, is quite another. My game has been shaky for some time now and anything that increases the jitters isn't to be welcomed. I go out embarrassingly early in the LG Cup and the talk around the players' lounge is that Hendry is not the same player with the new cue. As ever, I try to ignore popular opinion and concentrate on making the best of a challenging new set of circumstances. It's a new cue, that's all. Common sense says that if you're a talented player you can adapt to another cue, albeit that they are like extensions of your arm. Trouble is, talented players of all sports are prone to a lot of very strange psychological trickery, resulting in the mind telling them all sorts of fairy stories. Unfortunately, this applies to me too, and if I make a miss in a pressure situation I immediately blame the cue for 'not feeling right' in my hand.

The facts, however, appear to tell a more positive story. The 2003 British Open, played in Brighton, sees some of my best performances for a while. I take out Joe Perry 5–0 in the last sixteen and in the quarter-final I come from 3–1 down against John Higgins to win 5–4. Next it's Matthew Stevens, who I beat 6–3, and I'm into the final against Ronnie. I'm still very cool towards him and I hope he knows I've put aside all talk about not playing as well with a new cue. Certainly, I go into the final with a new-found optimism and the energy that flows from this manifests itself in a very high-scoring first session. Ronnie builds a 5–3 lead and he's looking dangerous but I jump in after the interval, taking three frames in succession to secure the lead. From then on, it's pretty much plain sailing all the way and at 9–6 I take the title, to my complete delight. The whole tournament has seen a consistency from me that has been elusive for too long. New cue or old, I've proved I'm nowhere near finished yet.

After the final, a sheepish Ronnie comes up to me and apologises for the 'sad little life' outburst. He explains he was put up to it by Prince Naseem's entourage – just as I thought

– and says he considered it a good idea at the time. I accept his apology, telling him there are no hard feelings. I was never going to make the first move, but am pleased now that the intensity between us – off the table, at least – is over.

Top

5 CELEBRITY CHEFS

1. **Anthony Bourdain**
2. **Rick Stein**
3. **David Chang**
4. **Jamie Oliver**
5. **Giorgio Locatelli**

CHAPTER 20

I put down the phone after the short conversation with John Carroll and stand for a moment, shocked. John has had a phone call from Lee Doyle, Ian's son. There is terrible news. Ian's wife, Irene, has died suddenly while on holiday in Spain. She is only sixty-six and appears to have had a brain haemorrhage. She has shown no previous signs of ill-health and often tagged along when Ian was attending matches regularly. She and Ian lived a good life and they were a happy couple. I know how devastated he will be.

As it turns out, Ian's grief is so deep that he feels unable to continue working at the same level, which will allow Lee Doyle to have much more responsibility for the day-to-day management of the business. Ian hasn't said officially that he's stepping down, but he isn't the visible presence he once was. Irene's loss has taken away his appetite for the various battles he has had with snooker's governing body, the WPBSA; for many years Ian has wanted snooker to be run differently, and many of his own players have shared his concerns. But these run-ins have often been long and complicated, and as I've already said he's not the most popular figure on the circuit.

But for all Ian's faults he is passionate about snooker and he – along with my parents – has been my guiding light in this game. There would be no 'Stephen Hendry, World Champion' without Ian Doyle encouraging, cajoling, financing and sometimes bullying me into huge success. And in my wake came a whole stable of talented players, winning trophies and making great reputations for themselves as ambassadors of the game. There are times – many times – that Ian has almost driven me insane, and he hasn't endeared himself to my family, particularly Mandy. Yet I owe a hell of a lot to him, and the fact that he practically disappears from my life from now on has a significant effect on my game. In simple terms, the regular boot up the arse that Ian's unique style of management centred around is no longer happening, and I will come to realise – too late – that I need such motivation to get me going. As the new century begins and the seasons pass my success rate will plummet, along with my confidence and my physical and mental ability to win matches. This period in my career, resulting in my retirement from the game in May 2012, will be scarred with disappointment, despair and depression (albeit of the undiagnosed kind). As they say in football, if you don't want to know the score, look away now . . .

As I proved in the 2003 British Open, I can still put in performances that enable me to push aside the nagging worries I'm having about my game. I go 4–0 up against Matthew Stevens in the final of the 2003 UK Championship and although he makes a strong comeback and eventually beats me 10–8, I certainly haven't disgraced myself. My good form there doesn't last though. The rest of the season is a mixture of quarter-finals and 'last sixteens', including the Masters, at which I lose to Jimmy 6–4. As we go into the final frame, some wag from the crowd shouts, 'Taxi for Hendry!' Cruel, but in the circumstances, fair.

In March's 2004 Premier League final I do achieve a

comprehensive 9–6 win over John Higgins, with ten fifty-plus breaks, and drive home from the venue in Wales satisfied with what I see as a possible return to form.

As ever, I hold out hope for the Crucible and the World Championship, though I have a very close shave in the last sixteen against Barry Pinches, winning 13–12. I make it as far as the semi-final, but facing me is Ronnie O'Sullivan and, for the first time ever in this event, I go into a later-stage match not really believing I can win. Of course, I can beat Ronnie when I'm feeling on top and in control, but such feelings are becoming rarer and there's something about his talent and energy, and the fact he's on a roll, that I just can't seem to compete against. His time has come, and he knows it. My time is passing, and I too know it. In the pre-match press conference I acknowledge the fact that if Ronnie gets three or four frames under his belt he can be unstoppable, and that I will 'have to take my chances and play to my capabilities'. I add that while I'm capable of 'steamrollering' him, he's capable of doing just that to me. It doesn't sound much like fighting talk from me and, in truth, I have given myself a way out of this semi-final by talking up Ronnie and excusing the fact that if he breaks away early I might not catch him. I'm not scared of playing him by any means and he knows this, but neither is he stupid.

From the off, I feel he can read the signs that I'm not 100 per cent up for this. Like me, he's an intuitive player and we're both very capable of knowing when an opponent is showing weakness, subconsciously or not. As the first frame begins he knows – not to put too fine a point on it – that I'm playing shit. He wins the first frame with a break of eighty-five and, while I pick up the next one, from here on he marches ahead, winning the next five frames easily. Here and there I pick up a frame, but Ronnie puts in a commanding performance and slaughters me 17–4, with one full session to spare. I'm embarrassed, humiliated and furious with myself for playing so badly. I've not been the favourite to win this event and although I've tried to ignore what the papers have been saying as the tournament has progressed, it's hard not to be influenced by the voices all around the Crucible who say that this year belongs to Ronnie. When I was winning, year after year I would hear those same voices talking about me, and it all added to my belief that yes, I am the best in the world. Now, the voices that whisper about another's success are convincing me that I'm nowhere near as invincible as I used to be. I tell myself that it's nonsense and that I can still play at the highest level of snooker – but I also know that I'm not playing at anywhere near my best, and every time I lose I see the evidence all around.

I drive home with the sinking feeling that increasingly accompanies me on journeys back to Auchterarder. I reflect on the match, and the fact that if Ian had been there I'd have received a between-sessions dressing down that might just have achieved the desired effect and seen me back out there to win, or at least not to lose so dramatically. But he wasn't there, and so the motivation was missing. Now I will take the rest of the summer off, forget about snooker, play some golf and spend time with Mandy and Blaine. The good news is that after the tragedy we suffered in 2003, she is expecting again. This time there is no IVF or even any planning. It just happens, and it feels like it is meant to be after what we've been through. In August 2004 a healthy baby boy is delivered, and we couldn't be more delighted. In keeping with our habit of picking slightly unusual names for our children, we call him Carter. There's an eight-year gap between our sons, of course, but we're not going to let that bother us. We feel incredibly lucky just to have been able to give Blaine a brother.

So I go into the season as a proud new parent, albeit one less and less confident about his ability to do his day job as he should. Terry Griffiths is still helping me, encouraging me to see that, on my day, I can still play well. Away from the table, we talk, and Terry tapes our conversations. He's got into motivational psychology and he asks me to listen to the tapes we've made, picking out where I express negativity and seeing if I can change such a viewpoint into a more positive outlook. I see what he's getting at – by changing your mindset you can change your whole approach. Yet the evidence for my general negativity appears to be everywhere. I'm still suffering from the yips, I can't play certain shots (or I shy away from playing them), I can't dominate matches and I'm finding it very hard to win anything. To my mind, trying to think the thought that 'I can win' and get back to who I was in the 1990s simply doesn't translate to what's happening in real life. I listen to this stuff and try to pick up on the bits Terry is highlighting, but none of it really strikes a chord. Still, I don't give up because to accept that everything is 100 per cent bad and that there is no chance of ever winning again is too terrible to contemplate. I have a family to feed and bills to pay. No matter what, I need to keep playing.

In January 2005 I arrive in Malta for the Malta Cup. The first three matches see me win 5–1 each time. With the shot of confidence this gives me I go into the semi-final against Matthew Stevens, the talented Welsh player who's also something of an under-achiever. I establish a comfortable early lead and though Matthew plays catch-up it's not enough. A score of 6–3 sees me into the final against Graeme Dott, a young Scotsman who has shown significant form. This time, I'm too strong for Graeme and win the match 9–7. Finally, I have some silverware to take home. I don't know it, of course, but this will be my last ever ranking win and if I can't see clearly into the future the rest of the season might provide some pointers. In short, there is no good news and even when I get to my next final – the 2005 China Open – I throw away the game after initially being 4–1 up. My opponent is Ding Junhui, a young player who's taking snooker by storm, and when I let him in he demolishes me 9–5. The Chinese can't believe it, and to this day it's often assumed that I somehow let him win so that he would be a huge star in his own country.

Unfortunately, the truth is more mundane; during the match I take my eye off the ball and as he wins frames I somehow lose the concentration needed to make a comeback, or to stop it from happening at all. This situation is becoming more noticeable as time passes.

'I make one bad shot which becomes another bad shot, then I make three in a row,' I tell Terry. 'Before I know it, my head's gone and it's game over.'

'Look at it this way, Stephen,' he says. 'In the nineties, when you were winning, did you ever make any bad shots then?'

'Of course I did,' I reply.

'And did you take any notice of them?'

'Sometimes I was furious. I'd beat myself up over them,' I reply. 'But mostly I was winning then, wasn't I?'

'Not just that,' Terry says. 'It's also because you were determined to follow one bad shot with a good shot, to cancel out the bad one. You can do that again if you try.'

I try, but I can't. My mind – or my ego – is telling me that I've made a bad shot, that I'm going to make another and when I do I won't be able to get back into the match. And – surprise, surprise – that's what keeps happening. The ego is an extremely powerful thing and if it's telling you one thing, it's very hard to ignore it and try to concentrate on something else. Of course I make good shots, get chances and build decent breaks; if I didn't,

I wouldn't even be entering any of these matches, never mind getting into quarters, semis and finals. However, it's like looking at an optical illusion – your eyes see one thing but your ego tells you that it's another. Increasingly, my mind is telling me I'm a loser and nothing seems to be able to shift that voice. A quarter-final defeat in the 2005 World Championship to Matthew Stevens also reinforces my despondency.

The 2005/06 season is the first in which I win nothing at all though, in a twist of fate, I find myself world number one for the first time since 1999. Terry's help has, at least, made me a consistent player in that I'm reaching lots of finals and semi-finals. His patience while teaching me new techniques that give me a bit of inspiration has paid off and it's good to know I'm top of the rankings again. But to me, the word 'consistent' means 'boring'. It isn't really a compliment. I just want to get back to winning tournaments but, however much I try, I can't shake off the effects of the yips and the subsequent psychological blockage which goes with the condition. At this stage, I will consider anything I hope will bring back even a slice of the magic that seemed to be all around me in the 1990s. So when Chris Henry, Peter Ebdon's coach and sports psychologist, suggests a new cue might do the trick, I jump at the chance of finding out whether he might be right.

Chris is involved in a Belgium-based company called Acuerate, which has developed a cue you don't have to 'allow' for when you're playing a shot with a bit of side. Chris talks up its benefits and I'm very easily persuaded to give one of these new cues a try. The way my game is going it seems silly not to give his idea a chance, and when I make a 147 on the very first day I practice with it, I truly believe it is the answer to my prayers. I'm looking for anything that can give me the inspiration and confidence that used to come so naturally, so when the 2006

World Championship comes around in the spring of that year, I leave my John Parris cue at home and arrive at the Crucible with the Acuerate.

When I announce to the pre-tournament press conference that I'll be trying out a brand-new cue in a live situation the other players look at me like I've lost my mind. 'How could anyone play at the World Championship with an untested cue?' is the general response. They must be rubbing their hands with glee. But I've made a maximum break with it, and at this stage all I'm looking for is some inspiration.

They're right, of course. In the first round I'm pegged against Nigel Bond – a player I used to take winning against for granted – and he beats me 10–9, the match being won on the final black ball. At one stage Nigel is leading 7–3 and despite me making a half-decent fightback it simply isn't enough. I feel like a fish out of water using this new cue. In practice it seemed OK; now, on the Crucible's slick tables, complete with new cloths, it feels all over the place. I'm missing by miles and piling on the bad shots, one after another. I haven't spent anywhere near enough time with this cue to play it in a nineteen-frame match and the cue ball isn't going where I expect it to. I feel very stupid indeed for not listening to the advice given to me by the players at the club. In hindsight, the 10–9 defeat doesn't seem such a bad result given how terribly I feel I've played.

It isn't just the cue, of course, though not getting used to it before a major event was a poor decision of mine. On my day, I should be able to play with any cue and still pot balls. It's my attitude which needs fixing. I believe I'm no longer a winner, and I can't snap out of this mindset. The spark that has propelled me forward since the age of thirteen seems to have gone, and the new season brings little joy. I reach but one final (the 2006 UK Championship, held in York) and lose that 10–6 to Peter Ebdon, despite having been 3–1 ahead after four frames. This tournament is memorable mainly for the extraordinary circumstances in which I defeat Ronnie O'Sullivan in the quarter-final. I'm 4–1 up in a best of seventeen and playing confidently in the sixth frame when Ronnie gets down on the table and, after poor positioning on a red, misses the shot. Then he strides up to me, shakes my hand and says he's had enough, before leaving the auditorium. There is a gasp from the audience, followed by a low murmur of disapproval. 'I can't believe he's going to concede the match,' says a stunned Clive Everton from the commentary box. I stare at the referee in bewilderment. I can't believe he's going to concede either.

But that's exactly what he does, without explanation, and by default I'm the winner. I go back to my dressing room, still puzzled by Ronnie's actions, and tournament director Michael Ganley drops in to see if I'm OK.

'I'm fine,' I say. 'I've won the match and I've also got the night off!'

In the immediate post-match interview I refuse to criticise Ronnie for his actions and say I had no idea that this might be coming. Ronnie is Ronnie, he has his challenges, and while I'm delighted to be in the semi-final, I do feel for him. That said, in the evening I go out into York for dinner and I spot Ronnie walking up the street with a few mates, like he doesn't have a care in the world. It's all very bizarre, but Ronnie is his own man. The following day he apologises, saying he's 'had a bad day at the office'. Increasingly, I know how that feels.

By now, I seem to have accepted that constant defeat is part and parcel of my current existence as a snooker player. Terry Griffiths is concerned enough to introduce me to Veronica Leigh, who he knows has been helping Ian through his bereavement. It's hard to describe what Veronica does, other than she's an expert in human behaviour and aims to deal with negativity while improving performance. We meet and have a couple of conversations; her approach is very new to me but while I can't say it's totally within my comfort zone, I am at least prepared to listen to her.

In a nutshell, Veronica tells me that I must play for the love of the game. This is a very interesting departure because, predominantly, I've always played to win. Don't get me wrong; when it's being played beautifully and stylishly there is no bigger fan of snooker than me. But beautiful isn't enough – as I've said before, my enjoyment comes from winning, and when that is taken away there is no enjoyment. The idea of just turning up and playing for the love of it, or even just for fun, is something I havn't done since the age of thirteen. And yet, I notice this in other players who've experienced a decline in their success. At this stage Steve Davis is still playing competitively (and in fact, will not retire until 2016) but despite not winning very much at all, he still enjoys the atmosphere around tournaments and seems untroubled by the fact that other players are enjoying far more success than he is. I wish I had that kind of acceptance, but I don't. I'm still fighting the fact that I'm no longer the best snooker player in the world.

Veronica says I need to be able to win 'for me' as opposed to performing according to Ian's way of doing things. Ian isn't around much now, so I need to learn a whole new way of motivating myself while ignoring the voice – the ego, as she describes it – telling me constantly that I'm no good.

'You're going into matches and playing badly because that just confirms how bad a player you think you've become,' she says. 'This gives you the perfect opportunity to beat yourself up, over and over again.'

She's right. That is exactly what's happening. I might have a good first frame, then I'll make a mistake in the second and think, 'Ah! Here it is again. The shit shot. I'm rubbish, and I know it.' Never mind how well I played in the first frame – the mistake has overridden everything else. So, according to Veronica, controlling the ego is key to solving my difficulties.

I understand what she's saying. I stopped enjoying the game for its own sake a long time back. The focus on winning has dominated everything and while that's paid off in terms of success, I'm now finding decline and failure (as I see it) very hard to deal with.

Some weeks after our first conversations I head to Malta for the 2007 Malta Cup. Having just been beaten 6–2 by Ding Junhui in the 2007 Masters semi-final, I'm not expecting much from this tournament. Yet in the first round I beat Robert Milkins 5–1 and then face Neil Robertson, who I beat 5–0, racking up four century breaks in the process. After the match I go back to my hotel room, lie on the bed and, from nowhere, just burst into tears. The fact that I've played so well, and that such performances seem so rare now, prompts an outpouring of emotion, the like of which I've never experienced. Veronica's words echo around my mind as I sit there alone: 'You have to stop beating yourself up and play for the love of snooker . . .' Yet I realise that I no longer love snooker.

Top
5 TV SHOWS

1. **Curb Your Enthusiasm**
2. **The Wire**
3. **The Sopranos**
4. **Entourage**
5. **Peaky Blinders**

CHAPTER 21

I tell Veronica about the tearful episode in Malta and she sees it as something of a breakthrough. She wants me to go deeper, exploring my past, right back to childhood, investigating my motivations for what I do and how I do it, and what I need psychologically to make me a winner. I understand what it is she wants to do, and how it might benefit me, but I just can't go there. The whole delving-deep thing feels unsettling and scary. I'm not sure what will happen and what it might lead to. To make it effective I feel that you must 100 per cent buy in to such an approach, surrendering yourself to it, and I'm too resistant and self-protective to go into all that. I just want to get back to playing good snooker that I can be proud of.

In 2007 Chris Henry becomes my coach and introduces me to the positive-thinking techniques he's used to make Peter Ebdon so successful. He also drills me in the use of the Acuerate cue, which I'm still using despite the previous year's World Championship debacle. He films me striking the cue ball and notices that again I'm not hitting it right in the middle. As every snooker player knows, hitting the cue ball even a millimetre off-centre can translate to missing a pot by a mile, so Chris really nails me down on this and I respond well to his advice. His practice drills are taxing and unlike any I've ever played before. For example, he gives me one which involves only the black and pink balls on their spots. The routine is to pot the pink into a corner pocket, followed by a black, and after the black to get position on the pink for the middle pockets. Alternately, you're playing pink-black-corner, then pink-black-middle. As you play you're counting the points (one point for every pair of pink-blacks potted) and the aim is to score as many as possible. At first this feels very difficult, but once there are a few points on the board you find you're getting into the flow of things and your concentration focuses naturally – which, of course, is exactly what I need.

Although Chris lives in Belgium and is therefore not around to breathe down my neck when I'm practising, I do what I'm instructed and I find that I'm racking up the points each time I try the routine. My record is 103 points chalked up in a three-hour session – the equivalent of 206 balls potted. That is a lot of snooker.

Chris is tackling the psychological side of his programme by giving me a bunch of CDs, which I listen to in the car. They tend to feature American guys talking about the power of positive thinking and, while they're quite interesting to listen to, I don't feel that what they're saying is making much impact. He gets me to watch videos of me during my glory years in the hope that by seeing how I used to play some of the old magic will return. But all this does is make me more despondent about the current state of my game, compared to how it was. Chris also tries to teach me to meditate and visualise what winning looks like, and when I'm in my dressing room we attempt these routines, including breathing exercises, to see if they make a difference. But I can't get into it, and all the while I'm thinking that when I was in my prime, all I needed as preparation for a major final was a copy of the day's newspaper and a bit of peace and quiet. It seemed so easy back then. Why is it so difficult now?

I enjoy following Chris's practice routines but, by and large, I can't seem to translate them into victories. There are flashes of good snooker, but the stats speak for themselves; there are no final appearances from me in the 2007/08 season. For me, this is beyond terrible and had this been just a few short years previously, I'd have been called into Ian's office and absolutely carpeted. In fact, we wouldn't have even been near such a situation; the Alex Ferguson-style 'hairdryer treatment' would've happened at a much earlier stage in the season and after that I'd have been going all out to show Ian that I was made of sterner stuff. Back then, when I was on the table his voice would be in my head, urging me on and threatening me with the wagging finger should I be caught slacking.

'You're playing shite, Stephen.'

'You're a bloody disgrace, Stephen.'

'How could you let him beat you, Stephen!?'

'Get out there and get at him, Stephen!'

Now, the only voice I hear is mine, constantly telling me how badly I'm doing. And when I do see him, all Ian offers is sympathy. There are no finger-wagging debriefs or verbal pastings now. He seems indifferent to what's going on. For so long I've resented his bollockings and general control-freakery, but I realise that no matter how much he annoys me, I need him to kick my arse on a regular basis.

Yet sometimes – just sometimes – the magic happens once more. At the World Championship I make a textbook comeback against Mark Allen in the first round to win 10–9. The young guy from Northern Ireland outplays me almost the entire match and my ego is screaming at me to give in, sit in my chair and let him have his moment of glory. But I'm not beaten yet and I win a solid four frames to get myself back in the game, which goes to a deciding frame. Mark sends the cue ball into the middle pocket after slotting a long red, and I jump in. Now is the moment to try out a new technique Chris has taught me, whereby I imagine I'm commentating on my own game. So I'm telling myself that 'I'm going to pot this red and line up the cue ball on the black . . .' while taking each shot step-by-step and thinking myself through it. Following Mark's mistake I make a break of seventy-two and win the match.

I'm delighted, and I believe that with my new-found technique for shutting out the critical voice, I might just be able to go on and win this thing. For the second time in three years I make it to the semi-final against Ronnie – who then comprehensively dashes any hopes I have of even reaching the final. In the first frame I make a very encouraging break of 140 and win the subsequent two frames but, really, this is the only form I'll show for the rest of the match. After this initial shock Ronnie gets back on it and destroys me. He wins the second session 8–0 and although I have a late surge to reclaim three frames, I have no hope of catching him. If I could play the way I used to, I wouldn't need any meditation, visualisation or positive thinking in the world to beat Ronnie, and yet I make no criticism of Chris Henry – or Terry Griffiths, for that matter – for trying his best with me. The sports psychology approach did wonders for Peter Ebdon and has worked for many other players since, Ronnie included. The truth is, I'm just not in the right state of mind for it. You have to buy into it 100 per cent for it to work. In the past it's just been me, my talent, hours of practice and Ian's bollockings that have worked together to create success. It's simplistic to say that snooker is a purely working-class sport and that you must put in the hours in a smoky snooker club to make the grade – but there is some truth in the cliché, and anything different can be looked down on. I don't deny that the motivational approach is a good thing; it just doesn't work for me. All I want to do is get back to playing naturally, the way I used to. Trying to force myself into a 'natural' state through psychology or motivational stuff feels fake.

Slowly but surely, I am sliding down the rankings. I've dropped to number eight this season. For twenty years I have only been out of the top four twice, and even falling to the bottom of the top ten seems a huge drop. From being the best I'm now definitely one of the rest; no longer part of the elite. When I was number one I wouldn't have a clue who might be at number eight. On my way to winning tournaments I wouldn't have even considered them a threat. Now I'm not even considered one of the best players in the world anymore, and it's not a good feeling at all.

Despite the occasional blip, like a rise in the rankings during the 2008/09 season, my whole approach now is based on trying not to lose, as opposed to going out there to win. Although I still don't keep an eye on my financial affairs I'm aware (or, rather, made aware) that the amount of prize money I'm taking home is dropping year on year. I can hardly plead poverty, but I have financial commitments like anyone else. I start to see tournaments as more of a means of keeping an income coming in than winning trophies. I look at the prize money split and think to myself, 'If I can get through the first couple of rounds, I can earn this amount for the quarter-final and that amount for the semi . . . if I make it there at all.' I rarely consider making a final now, never mind winning the thing.

I try not to bring such difficulties home, but struggles at work, whatever your occupation, aren't always easy to hide. The way I'm thinking now is that I'm essentially playing for money, and that has never sat at all comfortably with me. I don't play my best snooker under such circumstances and there is pressure from the start – pressure to win and get into the next round for a bigger slice of the pie. This isn't the kind of pressure I thrive on, the pressure to maintain a certain standard of living despite a year-on-year drop in earnings. I'm proud of what I've achieved and what has resulted from it in terms of our home and the things we enjoy doing as a family. Such pride makes it very difficult to contemplate making cutbacks, but the truth is that if we keep spending the money I earn at the rate we are, we're going to end up in trouble.

Mandy is understanding about the pressure I'm under. Equally, she has never been keen on me bringing my frustrations home and isn't going to put up with increased moodiness now. I know I'm becoming more difficult. Not horrendously so, but there is a marked difference in my temperament now, compared to the way I was during the glory years. I know I don't give the kids the attention they deserve and when weekends come around I'm not keen to do much family stuff. The irony is that when I was winning I was barely at home to do the 'dad' things, and now I'm losing (and consequently at home more often) I don't want to spend much time with them, simply because I feel too bloody miserable about my career. I make excuses that I need to practice, and head down to Stirling alone – but when I get there I become distracted and don't put in the hours needed to make a significant difference.

It should be clear that I'm suffering from a kind of depression – all the classic signs and symptoms are present – but at the time I don't see it that way and it's never diagnosed. I don't seek help, perhaps because I'd see it as yet another sign of weakness. As a participant in an individual sport like snooker, the worst thing you can hear about yourself is that you've 'gone'. Not disappeared off the face of the earth, but no longer what you were in terms of your game. I'm hearing this a lot now – 'Hendry's gone – he's finished' – and it's crucifying me. People might say, 'Ah, come on, don't worry, it's only a game, worse things happen,' but to a professional sportsman that's nonsense, especially if you've had as much success as me. Being told you're 'gone', and knowing it to be true, is devastating.

Matters aren't helped by the introduction, by Barry Hearn, of the Championship League in 2008. Barry is keen to expand snooker's range of tournaments, but this is something beyond many players' understanding of what professional snooker should be. It's a group event, held at a golf club in Essex, and there is no audience. The whole thing is filmed live to betting shops. For every frame you win you earn £100, and £200 for every match. There are groups and play-offs, and you can earn around £40,000 if you keep yourself in the tournament until the end.

I don't like the sound of this way of playing and I choose not to enter the first event. When I do eventually play in it I realise my instincts are right. I hate it – absolutely loathe it. When we're not playing, we're kept in a kind of holding area where there is banter and joking around, but no audience means no atmosphere and I've always been at my best in front of a decent-sized crowd. And I'm by no means the only player to think this way. In a couple of years the Championship League will be joined by the Players Tour Championship and, again, I'll find myself playing in cubicles with no one watching and no atmosphere. I'll be in a cubicle in the Sheffield Sports Institute, playing a young kid whose parents are the only audience. They clap every time he makes a good shot, which annoys the shit out of me, and while they're excited for their son's big day – as my mum and dad would have been all those years ago – I can't share their enthusiasm. 'What am I doing here?' I think. 'Is this what snooker has been reduced to for me?' I don't want to be here; I want to be down the road at the Crucible, or at the Wembley Conference Centre. I know the idea is to give lower-ranked players the chance to compete in more tournaments, as it's only £100 to enter, but the set-up doesn't inspire me at all. I enter reluctantly, knowing I must do so to keep up the ranking points, and I drive to Sheffield and back in a day, not even bothering to stay over. Not that there is much good news for me at the major events . . . I lose to Stephen Lee in the first round of the UK Championship in December 2008, playing terribly. The frames are scrappy and dispiriting, and although I'd rather forget such a performance it comes back to haunt me when, much later on, the Gambling Commission visits me amid allegations that Stephen Lee had bet on himself to lose the first frame in this particular match. I'm honest with the investigators; I tell them that I didn't notice anything untoward happening, assuming we were both playing as badly as each other. For this and other match-fixing charges, Stephen Lee will eventually be banned from professional snooker for twelve years.

The World Championship comes and goes, and I barely make a dent in it. I scrape through the first round of the 2010 event, just about beating a Chinese player who'd only turned professional the year previously. In the next round I'm slaughtered 13–5 by Mark Selby, who almost repeats the feat at the World Championship the following year, beating me 13–4 in the last sixteen.

The story of these seasons can be summed up in one phrase: 'Going through the motions'. I don't practise properly, I play badly, I win a couple of early matches (if I'm lucky) against untried or poor players and I almost automatically lose to anyone who's any good. In the 2010 UK Championship Jimmy White and I are fixtured in the first round and I beat him 9–8 but the snooker we both play is unbelievably poor. In seventeen frames we make only nine fifty-plus breaks between us. At the end of the match we shake hands and I say, 'That was embarrassing, wasn't it?' Jimmy is also finding it hard to play well and he's even further down the rankings than me. After all the great matches we had in the 1990s, to be reduced to this kind of performance, and in the first round, is nothing less than tragic.

Tragic too is the death of Alex Higgins in July 2010. Difficult though he could be (and often was), in my opinion Alex dragged snooker out of a dull place and into the TV age. He was the first player to put showmanship into the game at a time when it was dominated by older players who plodded around the table, slowly considering every possible permutation of a shot. I attend his funeral in Belfast and I'm shocked that so few of the new generation of players bother to turn up. His amazing talent on the table, as well as his antics off it, will be what he is remembered for, and it should never be forgotten that he was a genius of a player who made snooker what it is now. At least thousands of local people turn out in Belfast to give him a decent send-off.

During the funeral I think about one of the last conversations I had with him. Although his playing days were finished and he was obviously ill, he turned up to an Irish Masters event that I was competing in. Later, in the hotel bar, he spied me with his laser eyes and came over to sit by me. You'd never know what to expect when Alex collared you in this way, but this time he was quite mellow and chatty.

'I'm gonna start playing again, you know,' he said.

'Oh yeah?' I replied cautiously, unsure where this was leading.

'Yeah, and you know what? I'm gonna get a caravan so that I can come up to your house and we can practise together. I'll park it in your garden. Or maybe I could live in your house? Either way, we can get some good practice in. What d'you reckon?'

I was stuck for words, and mumbled some kind of encouraging reply, all the while hoping that Alex didn't really mean this. 'It'll never happen,' I said to myself, '. . . but what if it does?' I pictured Mandy's expression at the sight of Alex's caravan entering the drive and I tried to put that thought right out of my head. Needless to say, he didn't follow up on his threat.

Back to the present, and by this stage I feel that I'd rather not turn up for tournaments at all than play so badly. Any chance of winning has gone and with it the enjoyment of playing snooker for a living. Having been professional since leaving school I have no qualifications to do anything else and I've no idea how else I'll earn any money. This is the only proper job I've ever had. However, there seems little option other than to consider retirement from the game. Having only just turned forty it seems somewhat premature, but I don't think I can spend much longer putting up with such humiliation, match after match, tournament after tournament, season after season.

I think about it long and hard and discuss it with Mandy. As ever, she's very black-and-white about it.

'What's the point of doing it,' she says, 'if you don't enjoy it? Just pack it in and see what happens next.'

Therein lies the problem. I can't visualise what might lie ahead for me, career-wise. There has never been any management plan for me post-snooker and it's not something I've ever given any thought to personally. Despite all the gloom I still believe there is a faint hope that, somehow, I might be able to turn things around and achieve the success that seems to have eluded me for so long. I could be deluding myself, but I feel that I haven't 'gone' just yet and after much thought I decide to give myself one more season – and give it my all.

Top
5 CUISINES
1. Chinese
2. Italian
3. British
4. Indian
5. Japanese

CHAPTER 22

The 2011/2012 season sees me playing in no fewer than twenty-two events, ranging from the hated PTC to the World Championship, taking in tournaments in Australia, China, Brazil, Belgium and Ireland, as well as around the UK.

As ever, I enjoy the trip to China for the 2011 Shanghai Masters, though the snooker I play is disastrous. It's doubly disappointing, because the Chinese audience, aware of my past glories, have taken me to their hearts. There is pressure to be worthy of this level of support but this time I cannot rise to expectations. Embarrassingly, I lose 5–1 to Robert Milkins in a match that I may as well have not bothered turning up for. Feeling as dreadful as it's possible to feel, I walk back to the hotel in a daze. Some Chinese fans have been waiting patiently for me in the lobby and as I approach they thrust out programmes and pictures for me to sign. Normally I have no problem doing this but this time something tells me I need to get the ritual over as quickly as possible. Autographs done, I press the elevator button and make my way to my room. Once inside, I shut the door, lie on the bed and burst into tears.

I've never cried in defeat before. I've been disappointed, angry, annoyed, moody and everything else, but I've never shed tears at being beaten. Now, the mixture of shame and depression completely gets to me and I just can't help myself. I wonder what the hell I've become in the last few years, and what has brought me to this sorry state of affairs? The tears seem to last for ages and afterwards I feel better than I have done for a while. When I calm down I try to look at things objectively. I can no longer play like I used to, no matter how hard I try to resolve the various issues plaguing me, but I just can't go on sinking further and further down.

The Brazil trip is a hell of a schlep. I fly from Edinburgh to Frankfurt, then change planes for São Paulo before taking another flight to Florianopolis, a holiday resort in the south of the country where the Brazil Masters is being held. It's out of season, so the place is a ghost town and my hotel room so bad that I ask to change it immediately. The food, though, is amazing, and at least the crowd that turns up to watch those of us who make the journey, including Steve Davis, Mark Selby, Graeme Dott and Peter Ebdon among others, is enthusiastic and supportive. Against the odds I make it to the semi-final and before the event I have a practice session against Ali Carter. On the practice table I demonstrate the flair I seem unable to show in matches. Ali looks surprised.

'What are you doing potting all these shots?' he says, shocked.

I manage a rueful smile. 'I did used to be quite good at this game, you know,' I reply.

'Yeah, but the players back then couldn't even make a fifteen break against you when you missed,' he says. I'm a bit stung by that, so in our subsequent quarter-final match I enjoy beating him 4–0.

Even so, something needs to change, and I have to see beyond the black clouds to a future that isn't so bleak as currently appears. Luckily, there is an opportunity on the horizon and it shows itself in China. A while back, my management company was approached by a Chinese billiard-table manufacturer called JOY, wondering if I might like to promote a local form of pool called Chinese eight-ball. This is a mish-mash of English eight-ball and American nine-ball pool and the story goes that in the 1970s someone in China wanted to make an American nine-ball table but based its dimensions on English eight-ball, complete with smaller pockets. The bigger American balls were used anyway, so by accident the Chinese invented their own form of pool. At the time we were approached the game was seen as rather downmarket. However, the owner of the company, a guy called Qiao Bing, who goes by the name of 'Ken', is passionate about Chinese eight-ball and aims to make it as popular as snooker became in the West during the 1980s.

I don't do anything about this initial approach but, a while later, he asks again and this time I'm more receptive. After the misery of the Shanghai event I'm due to make a return visit to China to play in an exhibition match, so I agree to meet Ken during this visit and see what the possibilities for me might be.

After the exhibition in Shenzhen, Ken and I fly to Baotou, an industrial city in northern China, so that I can see the game in action. Although snooker is my sport, I'm intrigued by his enthusiasm for Chinese eight-ball and his determination to bring it upmarket. Ken explains how the game came about and how it's currently seen as something only played in the Chinese equivalent of working men's clubs, and by people you wouldn't want to bump into on a dark night. The parallels with snooker's image in the UK before TV dragged it out of the darkness are obvious, and Ken is keen that someone who has helped to change that image can be an ambassador for Chinese eight-ball. He admits he's thought about approaching Steve Davis but says he'd rather have me because of my status as the 'King' of snooker in China. It is now that I tell Ken I'm considering retirement, but swear him to secrecy. At this stage only Mandy and I know my plans.

I ask Ken what being an ambassador involves. He tells me that I would need to visit China regularly – fifteen appearances a year – promoting Chinese eight-ball right across the country as the 'face' of the game and playing exhibition matches against local players. The travel side is no problem; after getting over my initial worries about what food I'd be eating I've loved coming to China over the years. The buzz of the place is indescribable, and every visit has been a mind-blowing experience. So the travel poses no difficulties. Ken and I discuss a fee, and he offers me a sum which will tie me into a ten-year contract, with options every three years should either of us want a break. I request that the contract should include a clause that I will always fly to China business class and stay in international hotels wherever possible. There will be a lot of travelling involved and I feel I've earned the right to be comfortable. If I'm not comfortable I won't enjoy it and that's the last thing any of us need. Ken agrees to this without argument.

What Ken is offering is a way out of the sheer torture I'm going through with my snooker. Despite my determination to give the 2011/2012 season my all, it's clear that my time at the table is coming rapidly to a close. I can't play shots properly any more, I'm losing to guys I used to beat comfortably in my prime and my confidence is such that I don't even want to get past the last-sixteen stage, because doing so will take me off the outside tables and on to the match tables. I just can't face the embarrassment of the spotlight any longer.

When I arrive home from China I discuss the options with Mandy. I'm likely to be away from home just as much – if not more – than at present. She's not entirely happy about that, as the boys are growing up and would like to see more of their dad, particularly if he retires. Being at home is what retirement means to Mandy. However, she understands that I need to keep working, and if a lifeline is being thrown, even from as far away as China, then I should take it. She knows how much I'm hating my present situation. Again, she poses the question: 'If you're not enjoying it, why are you doing it?'

As for my management company . . . well, 'management' is not something I've experienced for a while. The company itself, having failed to take over the management of all snooker tournaments (which Barry Hearn has by now successfully done) has branched into other sports. Ian has all but retired, I'm no longer playing to anywhere near the standard I was in the golden years and so the relationship between us has dwindled to a point where I don't even go down to Stirling to practice. Some years previously Ian sold the lease of his snooker club to a guy called Jim Hendry (no relation) and when Jim came out of the lease after three years or so I decided to create a snooker room with a full-sized table in my garage. If I have the inclination, this is where I now practise. Ian and I aren't on bad terms; it's just that our lives have gone in different directions and so our professional relationship ends with less of a bang and more of a whimper.

In truth, I don't need to think too hard about Ken's offer. I can handle the travelling; in fact, I'm really looking forward to it. I've always enjoyed sitting in the lounge at Heathrow with a glass of wine and thinking about what experiences I'll be having over the next few days. Unlike many snooker players, being away from home in foreign countries has never been any bother to me. And so the decision is made: after the 2012 World Championship I will announce my retirement from the game that has taken me from a toy table in a cramped bedroom to the very top of the tree in terms of success. I will miss snooker, but I won't miss the kind of snooker I'm currently playing. To put down my cue, even for a while, and think about something else will be nothing short of a relief.

At the 2011 UK Championship in York I reach the dizzy heights of the last thirty-two before being put out of the competition by Stephen Maguire. As ever, I go straight home, only to be contacted a couple of days later from someone at IMG, the company which produces snooker coverage for the BBC. Would I like to have a go at commentating? It won't be a big thing, I'm assured, just a guest slot in the semi and final events. Well, in for a penny . . . so I get the train back to York wondering what might await me in the commentary box. I know many players have successfully crossed over into commentating but I'm not certain I have the patter or banter to carry it off.

The day I'm due on-air for a spell of commentary on the evening session Dennis Taylor and I go out for lunch – a Chinese meal in York – and we share a bottle of wine. I wouldn't have dreamed of doing this before playing in a match, but I figure that a little Dutch courage might help on this occasion. And, by and large, adding my opinion to the views on the match seems to go reasonably well, though I'm surprised at how difficult it is, as opposed to how it looks. I think I know about snooker – I should do by now – but I find that I can't always predict which shots players will attempt, particularly those players less familiar to me than the likes of John Higgins, Ronnie O'Sullivan or Mark Williams. I feel I'm calling everything wrong, but it seems that I haven't done too badly because a producer asks me if I ever fancy doing a bit more to give her a shout. Little does she know that, in a few months' time, I'm more than likely to take her up on the kind offer.

I tell my parents my plans. They're understanding, and see the reasons why, but they're still shocked, my dad in particular. 'But you're still young,' he says. 'Surely you've got a few years left in you? Look at Steve Davis . . .'

Yes, Steve is still playing. But he's not winning anything. As he himself says, he treats it as a day out. If he wins, great; if he doesn't, he goes home and simply forgets about it. That seems to suit him just fine, but I can't be that way. If I'm not winning, I don't see the point in continuing – and I can't put in the hours to recapture the form that might put me within sight of a tournament final. Also, snooker seems to have changed so much that I sometimes don't recognise the game I loved and watched avidly as an obsessed thirteen-year-old. In early 2012 I play at a 'Snooker Shoot-Out' competition at the Blackpool Tower Ballroom – a one-frame event which is more like a game-show than a snooker tournament. There is a countdown clock and the audience is encouraged to shout out its encouragement, or otherwise. When I come out, I'm greeted by a member of the audience who shouts, 'I fucked your sister-in-law!' referring to the fact that Mandy's family are from Blackpool. Classy . . . Needless to say, the whole thing is yet more torture.

And if I need 100 per cent cast-iron proof, the very fact that I'll have to qualify for this year's World Championship is all the evidence I need.

This is the first time I've had to qualify since 1989 and that itself is a humiliating feeling. I hate having to go through this, but my attitude is to win the match quickly and get it over with. It doesn't matter whether I play well or not, as long as I win. The thought of losing and having to retire without making it to the Crucible doesn't bear thinking about, and I'm determined not to let that happen. I'm up against Chinese player Yu Delu and it's not pretty snooker by any means, but I win 10–6 and I'm delighted and relieved to have made it to the Crucible.

The match is played over two afternoons and on the second afternoon, following my victory, I drive straight over to Preston, where I play in an exhibition match with Jimmy White. That done, I head off to Manchester Airport and take a flight to China for the first of my contracted appearances promoting Chinese eight-ball. I fly home with a day to spare before my first-round match against Stuart Bingham. In the old days, the idea of me flying anywhere between World Championship matches would be unthinkable; now, my priorities have changed and, instead of practising and resting, I'm playing pool in China.

Stuart is the guy who famously knocked me out in the first round of the 2000 World Championship and I do not want to go out again so early, especially this year. I hope against hope that I can pull off a miracle, take the championship and retire immediately after the most amazing comeback in the history of the game. It's a fantasy, of course, but meanwhile, in the seventh frame of this match, I seem to be doing something that I haven't done at the Crucible for a long time – building a break that might just turn into a maximum.

After a nervy start from both of us, the audience must think they're watching a version of me from twenty years ago. Like the Hendry of old, I stride around the table with a determination and confidence not seen for a long time. In my heart, I know that I'm not building such an amazing break like I used to be able to – in fact, I probably only hit around half a dozen shots the way I want – but those watching don't recognise that. Play stops on the next table as the audience start to applaud each shot and no one, least of all me, believes this is happening. With expectation building I get down into the zone, focus and concentrate. And when the final black goes down in the corner pocket there is a huge cheer from the crowd. I've done it – my third maximum at the World Championship and my eleventh in competition. I pump my fist and smile broadly, knowing that this will be the last time I will ever do this at the Crucible.

Stuart has been nervous from the start – despite my form, no one wants to be drawn against me in the first round – and although he has a three-frame resurgence towards the end, it's nowhere near enough to inspire the confidence he needs to pull this around. At 10–4 we're done and up next is an unbelievably tough match against John Higgins, the defending World Champion. Given my form, you wouldn't put money on me, but this is the Crucible after all; if I can pull off a shock defeat anywhere, it's here. Neither of us plays well, but in the second session I find rhythm and win seven frames out of eight, finishing on a sixty-four break to defeat John 13–4.

In the post-match press conference there are excited questions about the elusive eighth – can I really do it, after all this poor form? I try to play down all the buzz but inside I feel elated at the prospect of going into the quarter-final against Stephen Maguire. He goes 3–0 up, and when in the fourth frame I have the chance of clearing up, I line up on *that* pink that a few years ago I'd have been able to pot with my eyes shut. I know I must hit it properly, and I also know that my cue action is such that I'm not going to be able to.

'I'm going to miss this,' I think. 'I'm going to miss it and fuck up . . .'

All the fear and dread rushes in and, of course, I butcher it. After this, any chance I think I have of winning is gone. In the interval which follows, my coach Chris Henry can't believe that I think I cannot win. 'But Maguire still has to win nine frames,' he says incredulously. 'You're nowhere near finished!'

Oh yes I am. I've been in situations where I was five frames down and pulled it back to win, but I know I can never play like that again. Only pride stops me from doing a Ronnie and going back out after the break to shake Stephen Maguire's hand and concede the game. 'It'll be less embarrassing,' I think. But it's not how I want to end my career.

And then Maguire is leading 7–1 after the first session, and all the despair and depression and disappointment come flooding back as I sit in my chair, watching my opponent pile on the pressure and showing me no mercy – just as I've done to so many others in the past – destroying any hope I might have had of going home from Sheffield on the most incredible high. It's the final nail in the coffin of my career at the snooker table.

Top

5 DISHES
1. **Beijing duck**
2. **Jamón ibérico**
3. **Steak and chips**
4. **Green beans with spicy pork and chilli (Chinese)**
5. **Haggis, neeps and tatties**

CHAPTER 23

'**S**o,' asks the interviewer, 'you've just said you'll "miss it". You said your "last match". Is this it, then?'

Finally, the hints I've just dropped into the first couple of minutes of the post-match press conference are picked up on.

'Yes,' I reply. 'I'm now officially retired from tournament snooker. The decision was made about three months ago and I didn't tell many people . . . it was quite an easy decision. There were a few reasons . . . the schedule didn't help, the fact that I'm not playing the snooker I want to didn't help, the fact that I don't enjoy practice doesn't help. I want to do other things; there's a lot coming up in China which I've signed up for and I can't do that and play snooker. So the time is right for me . . . and if I'd won here, it would have been an even better way to go out.'

I elaborate a little more, telling the journalists that my game hasn't been right for ten years, and that I've been 'ground down and down'. They know that, of course; they've seen the difficulties unfold as the years have passed, though I don't go into details about the technical problems with my cue action. I say a little more about the work I'll be doing in China and

I conclude the question-and-answer by saying that 'I think I've had a decent career'.

When news gets out there is shock and surprise which, itself, is a surprise to me. Barry Hearn thinks I'm going out too early, as does Stephen Maguire, my most recent opponent. Peter Ebdon also thinks I'm too young to give up now. Jimmy White hopes I enjoy retirement and looks forward to playing me in the upcoming 'Legends' matches. Terry Griffiths, shrewd as ever, says he thinks I should've retired a while back, and if anyone's able to make this call it's him, as my former coach. He's probably right; I guess I've been hoping for the miracle that's never come. I know that sitting on the sidelines will never be the same as getting on the table at the Crucible and becoming World Champion, and even though I've experienced that seven times I'll still never quite get over the fact that I'll never do it again. Even if the ability is lacking, the drive to win is still strong.

Again, I'm asked by IMG to contribute a bit of punditry on the 2012 final and I enter the auditorium to a surprise celebration in my honour. I'm very touched by this, though as I say, I'd rather be walking down the steps with a cue in my hand than a microphone. Many kind words are spoken and although I don't cry, as is perhaps expected these days, I am genuinely moved by what is said about me. Snooker has given me an amazing life; not a normal life, not the life I'd have had if I'd just learned a trade and stayed in Kirkliston. I've experienced many different cultures and been lucky enough to play a game I love against the best in the world. I've had some real highs and lows and it's hard to see how anything else I do will match up to those years. The answer is that it won't, but now I must make the best of what is on offer.

With that in mind I throw myself headfirst into my new role

in China. In the calendar year following retirement I make no fewer than twenty-six appearances in twenty-six different cities, such is the demand for me over there. I'm away almost every month, for ten days at a time, visiting three or four cities to promote Chinese eight-ball and play in exhibition matches. And the buzz is incredible. Because the Chinese refer to me as the 'King of Snooker' (sometimes I even get promoted to 'Emperor') often I'm asked, quite seriously, if I live in a castle, like other kings and emperors. When I admit that I don't, there is genuine disappointment.

I'm known as 'Hengdeli' (the Chinese translation of my surname) and recognised almost everywhere I go, even in the most far-flung areas of the country. If I'm stopped and asked for a picture, the attention this generates prompts a large, curious crowd to gather. Ken and Shaun (my Chinese PA and interpreter) feel it necessary to assign me a security detail, and these guys don't mess around if it is felt the crowd is becoming too big or too pushy. Sometimes they're even posted outside my hotel room. I've never needed or even thought about having security in my life. It's certainly a far cry from nipping down to the local Co-op in Auchterarder.

Each appearance comprises a lunch with local dignitaries, a visit to an eight-ball club, an exhibition match and a meet-and-greet with a sponsor, very often a car dealership. In the first couple of years I visit, the sponsor is very often Geely, the Chinese car manufacturers who make a taxi brand called 'Englon', which can be seen all over London. Quite often I'm picked up at airports all over China by one of these cabs.

Of all these, I must admit that my least favourite part is the exhibition. I'm not the world's most enthusiastic pool player, it must be said. I see the difference between snooker and pool as like that between chess and draughts. I've never had the will to get particularly good at pool but of course, being the King of Snooker, the Chinese expect me to perform just as well at the pool table.

Unfortunately, this pressure to perform at pool is having the same effect on me as my last years of snooker, i.e. I don't win as many games as I probably should and I'm not keen on practising. Anyone who knows Chinese people well understands that they're honest to the point of bluntness, and Ken asks me straight out why I'm not winning more, and would I like them to send a pool table over to my house in Scotland, so I can practise?

'No thanks,' I reply. I tell them with equal honesty that my snooker has suffered because of the pressure I've put upon myself to maintain my position, and I don't want to go through all that again. I don't mind playing the occasional match, I say, but I don't want to put in the hours on the practice table needed to be Emperor of Pool. At first, Ken and Shaun have some difficulty with this; they seem to want me to take on a whole new career as a pool player and I just don't want that. Eventually they will come to understand this and actually my ambassador role off the table seems to be enough because the eight-ball game is now going through a real resurgence.

When I do play, however, the atmosphere is often electric, which might have something to do with the fact that I'm playing in front of big crowds, sometimes as large as 5,000 people. These are bigger (and much noisier) audiences than I've ever experienced and even in my reluctant state I must admit that performing to massive crowds is a real thrill. On one such occasion I win the match 7–6 and, after the final shot, an overenthusiastic fan runs towards me. He doesn't mean to do me harm but is grabbed by Shaun before he reaches me. In the chaos we are forced to find shelter in a small room and wait until the buzzed-up crowd has dispersed.

As time goes on I visit more and more places, witnessing the incredible gulf between cities and rural areas, and the poor and the rich. When I first came to China in 1987 I hated the place. I was eighteen and naive, and I couldn't believe how dull and grey it seemed. There seemed to be nothing to do, nowhere to go, and when I wasn't playing I spent most of my time listening to my Walkman and sulking about the lack of a McDonald's.

By now, though, I'm much more open to new experiences, particularly in the food arena. I love the fact that Chinese food bears little or no resemblance to what we'd expect in a Chinese restaurant in London, Birmingham or Edinburgh. I attend formal dinners, sometimes with around thirty or forty people, and it almost always begins with a range of teas – depending on the region of China we're in – before a procession of cold plates is brought to the table. I'm up for trying almost anything but tend to balk a bit at offal. And tofu, which I hate and consider to be the devil's work! Otherwise, I'm happy to go with whatever. I particularly love the famous Peking Duck, and the Chinese seem to employ every part of the bird in their cooking except for the beak. As in most places, the Chinese are always keen for you to try food you've never experienced but they're not particularly offended if you're not keen. Even so, if I don't like the look of a dish I employ an old trick that Terry Griffiths taught me, which is to marshal the item around the plate with the chopsticks, so it looks like you're at least having a good time. Nine times out of ten, it works!

Much harder to refuse is alcohol. Drinking regular toasts is obligatory (ganbei! is the local word for 'cheers', used with much frequency during a meal) and this is almost always centred around lethal rice wine, known as baijiu, which is necked down in one go. I don't like this, so I ask for red wine instead, and I'm often served some exceptionally high-quality French wines at eye-watering prices. There are some top Chinese wines around too; since I've been coming to China the quality of their wine has improved dramatically, but more often than not my fellow diners stick to *baijiu*. When they do drink red they often water it down and I have had the heartbreaking experience of seeing £2,000 bottles of Chateau Lafite Rothschild being cut with Sprite, and a slice of lemon added. Because drinking and toasting is ingrained in Chinese business culture, to refuse is to appear rude and I've been pissed more times than I care to recall. Now, I try to keep the measure in the glass as small as possible, wherever possible, and especially at lunch. This tends to be early – around 11am – and invariably drinks will be served with it. Dinner is at 5pm and I do think that such early eating is possibly linked to the fact that you don't see much obesity in China. They don't stuff themselves full of food late at night before heading straight for bed. Neither do they do desserts, and while there can be many courses over the progress of a typical meal, rice and noodles are only served at the very end, as it is believed they spoil the flavour of the main courses. As I've mentioned, some of my favourite dishes are the simplest; I love the way they cook meat, fish and vegetables, or create salads consisting of peppers, tomatoes, lettuce, cucumbers and raw peanuts, complete with a delicious dressing. I eat very healthily there – more so than I do in the UK – I never seem to put on any weight while I'm in China.

Seeing extremes of poverty and wealth across China is always food for thought. Yet people from all strands of society seem to have an enthusiasm for life, and at all ages. Shaun is shocked by how we treat older people in the West; in China, he says, the elderly are revered and almost always come to live with their relatives. The idea of putting them in old people's homes fills him with horror. He's also surprised at our benefits system in the UK and finds it hard to believe that people are paid for 'doing nothing', as he puts it. I explain that the benefits system is no bed of roses, but that's how it is.

I've now visited around sixty cities, and while there is still a language barrier, I've made friends right across China. At the start of my contract with JOY I make efforts to learn Mandarin and take lessons with a student from Edinburgh University. After the first lesson I'm given a pile of books to study from and immediately it reminds me of my schooldays – and that I didn't enjoy studying then, never mind now. I do make efforts to keep up but it's incredibly difficult, with every letter and every word having a variety of different tones. It's confusing, to say the least. To illustrate the point, the Mandarin word for 'pen' is *bi* – which is very close to the word for female genitals. So if I'm signing autographs and I need Shaun to provide me with a *bi*, very often he grimaces and tells me I'm pronouncing the word incorrectly. All in all, it's safer for me to stick mainly to English and let Shaun do the translating. That said, if I'm at the dinner table and I listen to my fellow guests talking I can recognise words here and there and get the sense of what the conversation is about, especially if I hear the word 'Hengdeli'. Then I know they're talking about me! Every trip I pick up new words but, as a whole, the language is too difficult for me to learn in any fluent way.

I still worry about the quality of the hotels I'm booked to stay in. The Chinese-branded ones are better than they were, but you can still experience freezing conditions in the rooms (I'm always concerned when I see reception staff wearing ultra-thermal winter coats) or beds that are rock-hard. I think the Chinese either have very severe back problems, or no back problems at all! The one consistently good element is the food in hotel restaurants – even if the place is far from luxurious you can guarantee the food is immaculately prepared and served. This applies even in regions like the grasslands of Inner Mongolia, where you still see yurt-dwelling people on horseback as their regular form of transport. The spicy barbecued lamb they serve whole and roasted on a spit is to die for. They give you a plastic glove and a knife, and you simply hack away at it.

One thing I've only ever tried in China – and which I will never, ever share with the rest of the world, for reasons that will become obvious – is karaoke. I can't sing to save my life, but karaoke is huge in China and after a meal the party very often continues in a karaoke bar, known as a KTV. These places are often very plush indeed – five-star standard. The rooms will feature a selection of wines and whiskies, and I've even seen full-sized snooker tables in them. It's a bit rude to refuse to sing, so, after a few drinks on board, I can just about be persuaded to give it a go. I will pick a song I think is quite easy and because they can't speak much English and maybe have a different sense of musicality than we do in the West, my dinner guests will applaud enthusiastically at whatever I do, however badly I do it. It makes you feel you're an amazing singer – at least until the effect of the red wine wears off.

My go-to song is 'Easy Like Sunday Morning' by Lionel Richie and the Commodores; the version I learn is the cover by Faith No More, and somehow I can make my way through this song without too much hideousness. Hopefully I'm more than a match for Ken Doherty, whose karaoke speciality is Boyzone's back catalogue, but I do remember one occasion when Shaun got out his phone as I was singing, and I made him delete all evidence of my crime against music! Interestingly, just as we might have snacks in karaoke bars in the form of nuts and crisps, so the Chinese have their own snacks – spicy ducks' tongues. Believe me, they taste much better than they sound.

My favourite Chinese city is Shanghai. I love the sights, the skyline and the buzz that only a city of 25 million people can generate. It's just an incredible place to be. Beijing is in many ways more sober and serious than Shanghai, and not quite as relaxed and cosmopolitan, though being there is also endlessly fascinating. When I'm there I often walk around the city, taking in the sights, visiting markets and generally just people-watching.

I think back to when I first visited China, and how reluctant I was to see any sights. For a long time, I refused to even see the Great Wall – 'What's the big deal?' I'd say. 'It's only a wall . . .' Then, rather than take a two-hour drive to see this amazing sight, I'd opt to stay in my room or practice instead. It's just out of ignorance and laziness, and when I do finally visit it, I realise just what an incredible experience I've been missing out on. I recall seeing many Chinese fathers there with their baby sons – it's said in China that only when you visit the Great Wall do you become a real man.

I've also seen the Terracotta Army but I have to confess that it wasn't for long. Years back, Steve Davis, John Higgins and I took a bus trip to Xi'an, where they're displayed, but on the way we got deeply into a game called Lie Dice, which is similar to poker except played with dice, and we were so engrossed that when we arrived at the museum where the warriors are kept we nipped out, took a couple of quick pictures and got back to the game. Again, it was a result of ignorance on our part – we're snooker players and we prefer anything we can compete in above tourist attractions.

Since then, I've also visited the Benxi water caves, which was an incredible and eerie journey by boat through flooded caves, seeing all the stalagmites and stalactites, with bats flying everywhere. What also strikes me about China is its sheer size – I've had journeys between cities which involve a three-hour drive, followed by a five-hour train journey and then two hours by plane. And that is a regular occurrence.

My eight-ball matches are limited to playing occasional games against fans or local dignitaries. As I said to Ken and Shaun, I'm not into anything serious or formal. As far as Chinese eight-ball goes, I'm proud of what I've achieved for the game in China. From being a game with a very downmarket image, the lowest of the low, it's become one of the biggest billiard sports in the country. There are tournaments and qualifiers across China now, with substantial prize money, including two tournaments where the pot for first prize is more than £150,000, which might even tempt some snooker players to come over and try their hand. As Ken appreciates, it wouldn't be where it is today without my involvement and I love being in one of the most interesting and diverse countries on this planet. Every time I go there I have a new experience to remember.

Top
5 STRANGEST CHINESE DISHES
1. **Bear Claw**
2. **Anteater**
3. **Wolf**
4. **Pigs' Anus Kebab**
5. **Chicken Soup with Bulls' Penis Pieces**

CHAPTER 24

Alongside the numerous appearances in China, I'm also contracted to play in a series of exhibition matches called 'Snooker Legends', organised by promoter Jason Francis and featuring the likes of Jimmy White, Tony Knowles, Dennis Taylor, John Parrott, John Virgo and Steve Davis, among others. In fact, almost all the players of my generation become involved in this series at one time or another.

These events are a way of playing snooker in front of audiences without the pressure of ranking or other professional tournaments. We're there for a good time and to reminisce about our careers and the game itself. Although I'm now retired, I don't want to lose touch with these guys and the game itself. I have said that I 'want to spend more time at home', which is what Mandy and I had agreed and planned for. However, when I am at home there are times when I think, 'Is this it? Am I just going through the motions here? Where's the buzz?'

It's selfish, I know. I've had an amazing career. I should be grateful for what I've had – and have – while looking forward to slowing down, taking it easy, resting on my laurels, etc. But if you retire at forty-three you're unlikely to approach 'slowing down' with much enthusiasm, particularly if you've been in sport. I retired because I felt I had to, not because I particularly wanted to. As a sportsperson you still crave the excitement and energy that comes from a pressured situation. When it's no longer there, you begin to see just how big the gap left by the absence of the 'buzz' is and you wonder how it might be filled. Yet, when something new and exciting comes along for me, it is completely unexpected and not from a direction I could ever have anticipated.

At this point, Mandy and I have a very good marriage. There are ups and downs, of course, just as in every marriage – over the years she has coped well with my life on the road and has been a superb mum to our boys. For me, there has never been anyone else; snooker players aren't rock stars (though one or two might have acted that way in the past) and while there are opportunities to misbehave if you're in the public eye, as a professional sportsman that side of life has never been of interest to me. The nearest I've ever come to it is when I find a name and number scrawled on a piece of paper and tucked away in my cue case, courtesy of an air stewardess who stows the case for me. I just laugh, take no notice and throw the note away.

The Legends events are always convivial and great fun, and after the matches players and staff gather in hotel bars to socialise and wind down from the day's play. It is at one of these that I notice a young blonde-haired woman who is working for Jason's company selling merchandise and helping to set up before each event. She's attractive and we smile at each other, but I think nothing of it. Gradually, we start to say 'hi' and share a bit of small talk. Like me, she seems shy. Players and staff tend to socialise in one big group after each event so we see each other frequently on the tour, though at this stage we're not singling each other out. I would never be one to go striding over to any woman who caught my eye – after all, I'm the person who got to know my wife's parents before I plucked up the courage to talk to her.

As time goes on, we find ourselves chatting more often. The woman's name is Lauren and it's becoming clear that we have a connection. The Legends event goes from place to place and with it the same crew of support staff. Over a period of a few months Lauren and I become friendly.

After a while we realise we're falling in love. That much is obvious, and very unsettling indeed for me. I am married to the woman I've been with for almost thirty years. We have two amazing boys and a great lifestyle. Lauren is single and twenty years younger than me. I've no wish to hurt Mandy even though I know that, either way, she is going to get hurt. I also know that I have no desire, or even the capability, to sneak around behind anyone's back. Yet I can't help the way I'm feeling and I'm beginning to wonder whether my marriage is over. It's a very confusing and troubling sensation.

At home, I become increasingly quiet and in time Mandy notices. She asks me what is wrong. I tell her I'm fine, and that it's nothing. But I'm not fine. I've fallen in love with someone else and I haven't the faintest idea what to do about such feelings. Mandy tells me she thinks I'm not as loving towards her. When you've been together as long as we have, you can spot even the smallest differences in demeanour.

Lauren and I become closer, and there comes a point where I can't hide my feelings any longer. One afternoon Mandy and I are driving back from a shopping trip in Aberdeen and again, she asks me what's wrong. She assumes it's money-related. I tell her it isn't. Then she tells me to stop the car, saying that we're not going an inch further until I tell her what's going on.

So I do. I tell her that I have feelings for someone else. She is completely shocked and devastated. It's the last thing she expected me to say. She knows me well enough to know that other women have never been my thing at all. We drive home in a fog of bewilderment, but we don't tell the children. There are tears and conversations late into the evening. Mandy tells me she wants me to move out until we've sorted it. After thirty happy years together we now find ourselves in a position we'd never have imagined.

I move out for a short while, staying with friends and family, while Mandy and I attempt to patch up our marriage. We agree to give it another go. I'm riddled with guilt about the whole thing, but I'm also in love with someone else. Even so, my attitude is that trying to make our marriage work is the right thing to do for the family. In the summer of 2013 we take a holiday to Portugal and, although we try to have a good time, the issue of our marriage is never far from the surface. When it arises, and there are more tears and recriminations, I realise that this is the way it will be from now on. Mandy can never wholly trust me again, and I completely understand why that is.

When we return, we both start seeing Veronica, the woman who tried to help me with my attitude towards my failing career. We have faith that, somehow, talking this out will bring us back together. Veronica is wise and generous with her advice. And honest too. She says that, deep down, I know my marriage is over. Mandy thinks Veronica has taken my side but, in truth, there are no 'sides'. Veronica has just made a clear assessment of the situation. I hadn't been looking for anyone else, but I've met someone else and it's turned my life upside down. After retiring I had wondered how I might fit into what could be described as a 'normal' life. Since turning pro at sixteen, and even for a couple of years before that, I've done what I've wanted to do and the domestic world of being at home and doing all the things associated with that hasn't been a big part of my existence. So there are a few factors at work here.

Our attempt to patch things up fails and there is acknowledgement that the marriage is over. Again, I move out, but before I do, Mandy tells me that I must inform the boys. This is the hardest thing I have ever done and will probably ever have to do. The parallels with the way my brother Keith and I were told about my parents' marriage split are obvious. I try to be as gentle as possible, telling them I have feelings for someone else. But however you try to explain things to children, there is going to be upset and hurt. Carter bursts into tears; Blaine becomes very quiet, just like I did when I found out about my parents splitting up. It's horrible, and I feel like the worst person in the world. Before I leave I tell a couple of male friends about what's happened. They can't believe I've admitted it. 'You could have a bit of fun on the side and just not say anything,' they tell me. 'It would've petered out and no one would've been the wiser.'

I know I can't be this way. The pressure would be too great for me, and I couldn't live with the guilt. Besides, the feelings I have for Lauren aren't going to just disappear overnight. They're too strong, and she feels the same way. I tell Mandy that I will be leaving not just Auchterarder but Scotland altogether. I need some time and space to get my head together, and make sure that what I'm doing is the right thing. The company now looking after my financial affairs has offered me the use of a flat in Liverpool for two months.

So with my belongings in black plastic bags and placed in the back of my car, I head off to Liverpool in January 2014. I don't know the city at all and I have no friends or contacts there. The flat I'm renting is on the waterfront, close to the Malmaison Hotel. It's OK, but also sparsely furnished and anonymous. I don't want anyone to know what I'm doing in Liverpool, and why I'm there, so when I go out to buy food I keep my head down and my hoodie up. Inevitably, I am recognised and asked what I'm up to in the city. I reply that I'm just playing a few exhibition matches in the area and try to end the conversation as quickly as possible.

For two months I'm a virtual recluse. I just sit and think about what's happened, and whether I've done the right thing. I know that I have – I also know it's the hardest decision of my life and that it will have all sorts of repercussions. I worry about the relationship I will have with my boys in the future, and if they will ever come to terms with the fact that I'm no longer physically close to them. I hope they will understand one day that such things happen, and not just to them. In their school and university they will know other young people going through the same thing and, while this doesn't make it right, Blaine and Carter aren't alone.

While I'm away I realise the marriage is over, and if I was still unsure this is spelled out to me in no uncertain terms when I make a brief visit to Scotland to see the boys. Mandy is barely speaking to me but does manage to ask whether I've checked my mail recently. I haven't – there is a communal letterbox with the numbers of the flats on each individual box, but mine is broken and unusable. What I don't know is that the postman has been putting my mail on the top of the box. I tell Mandy my mailbox is broken.

'Well, you'd better check around it then,' she says. 'And you'll need a lawyer. I've served divorce papers on you.'

When I go home I check the top of the box and, sure enough, there is the letter from Mandy's solicitors. Seeing this in black and white is particularly depressing, but now I know there is no turning back. It will be the start of a painful, drawn-out and very difficult period.

I'm able to rent the flat for two months, which takes me to the end of March. This fits in well with a contracted ten-day visit to China, so I drive to Manchester Airport and leave the car in the car park with all my belongings once again stuffed into the back of it. When I come back to the UK to play a Legends exhibition match, I have nowhere to call home. I try not to entertain the thought that, technically, I'm homeless.

As if I don't have enough on my mind, I'm tipped off at the Legends exhibition match that the press have got hold of the news that I've left my wife for another woman. Having been in the public eye for so long I know the score, understanding that while it will be messy and embarrassing for a few days, today's news is tomorrow's fish-and-chip paper. And to be honest, I'm surprised the story hasn't broken sooner. Lauren, though, has never had an experience of press attention so I call her to let her know what's coming.

The night before the *Sun* publishes, the story appears on their website. 'Hendry dumps wife for Noddy blonde' is the headline, referring to Lauren's career in children's theatre, during which she had a part in the stage show of the kids' TV series *Noddy in Toyland*. There is also an unflattering photo of her in costume, but without the head, which she worries will land her in trouble as she's not supposed to be pictured without the full costume on. When reporters contact me, I 'decline to comment' as I find that doing so usually makes things worse. Neither Lauren nor I are sure where the story has come from, though we suspect someone she knows has tipped off the *Sun*. No matter. It's out now and although I get the inevitable bout of ribbing from my fellow Legends at least I don't have to hide any longer. It's much worse for Mandy, of course, because she's still living in Auchterarder. It's a small place and everyone will talk.

I have to decide about where I'm going to live. Financially speaking, I haven't ended my career in the best possible shape and there are debts, as well as what is to come by way of a divorce settlement to Mandy. Lauren and I want to be together at some stage, so the best policy is to relocate to her home area and stay in a hotel until a property is found. I move into the Crowne Plaza by Heathrow Airport as it's convenient for the ongoing trips to China. Lauren and I agree that I should find a flat by myself at first. I can't afford a huge amount of rent, but I want to find somewhere I'm comfortable in. After occupying two different places I eventually find a flat close to the village of Sunningdale. It's small, but comfortably furnished, and I'm happy here.

The three years between my leaving and the divorce itself is the most stressful of my life. It's a weird situation to be in, a seven-times World Champion driving around in his car piled up with his possessions and virtually homeless, but at least now I have a roof over my head. Work keeps me going and Lauren understands that I'm in a difficult situation. Following the divorce, the legal bill comes to a hefty six-figure sum and a couple of investment properties have to be sold to pay it. Mandy will continue to live in the house in Scotland with the boys. I have ongoing tax commitments and, although I have the China contract and regular commentating work, my earnings are nothing compared to what they were during the glory years.

That matters in some ways, but in many other ways it doesn't matter at all. I am happy where I am in my life, both professionally and personally.

Top

5 **FIVE ACTORS**
1) Tom Hardy
2) Leonardo DiCaprio
3) Robert De Niro
4) Paul Giamatti
5) Gary Oldman

CHAPTER 25

The last few years of my life, overall, have been quiet. I feel I haven't done much since the roller coaster of the divorce, but perhaps that's as well. The visits to China are still ongoing, around ten or more each year, and when I can I take part in the snooker Legends events, though quite often with trepidation. I like seeing the guys again and sharing the banter, but I'm less enthusiastic when it comes to actually playing. I still feel I'm embarrassing myself by not being able to play the way I'd like to and, even if the audience doesn't see it, I know it's there.

As far as professional snooker goes, these days I'm confined to the commentary box. Largely I enjoy it, though there are sometimes long, dull matches during which it's hard to find something positive to say. Even after all these years, my tolerance of safety play is still quite limited! I like watching the players whose style most resembles my own – attacking, break-building, going for everything, taking risks. I guess I'm quite a critical commentator – maybe that's because I played to the highest standard and sometimes find it hard to comment on players who don't play the way I played. Joe Perry calls me 'the pantomime villain' because I can be scathing about individual performances, but I just say what I see and don't bullshit. If it's a good shot, I say that. If it's bad shot, I say that too. I think I'm qualified to have strong opinions about snooker. I've had players come up to me before matches and say, 'Oh, are you commentating on me today? Are you going to be nice about me?'

'Play well,' I reply, 'and you won't get a hard time!'

My fellow commentators are great to be around. In terms of analysing the game, Neal Foulds and Alan McManus are the best. Steve Davis and John Parrott are fantastic in front of the camera and Dennis Taylor and John Virgo are superb when matches are reaching an exciting stage. Both can really transmit that sense of excitement to the viewers at home. Hazel Irvine is a terrific professional; I've known her for the best part of thirty years and get on very well with her. When we're live in the studio her timing is impeccable, even when the director is talking into her earpiece, counting down to when we're off-air, and she's summing up or concluding an interview. I don't know how she does it, but she's bang on time, every time.

If we have a night off we'll go for dinner, usually in the company of some of the current players. I always wish I was among the latter bunch and I'll admit I do feel more than pangs of envy when I see them having success in the big tournaments. It still hurts that they're playing the snooker I could play and I'm just commentating on it. In that respect – having the success I've had – I haven't coped so well with retirement. That said, I wasn't coping well during the years leading up to retirement and I'm hoping this feeling will fade as the years go by.

I can't overstate the part the yips played in bringing my career to a close. I think the word yips trivialises it; it is completely debilitating, like a cancer spreading through your game and just destroying it. For me, it was the constant deceleration on shots I was playing; it's like being a painter and trying to paint without using the colour red, or a writer trying to write without using the letter 's'. It took away a major part of what I could do as a player and to this day there are shots I can't play properly because I'm not hitting the ball correctly. I do still practise – though not anywhere near the extent I once did – and occasionally everything seems to fall into place. Then I play an exhibition match and it all falls apart again. I always loved playing in front of big audiences; now I'm jittery if one person is in the room watching me. For me, it's a psychological difficulty that has translated into a physical one and although I'd love to play more snooker I really don't think there is a way back for me now. I practise for an hour and try new things every time just to interrupt my ego, the voice in my head that says, 'You can't play this shot.' Even though I say to myself that I was seven-times World Champion, therefore how can I *not* play this shot, I will still have trouble with it. It's completely mental – quite literally.

I did speak about this with Veronica. She wanted me to work on interrupting my ego – the voice that tells me, in a nutshell, that I'm shit. It's known as 'dynamic meditation' and it does work but you must commit to really throwing yourself into it, and I couldn't. I can't let go to that extent, and my own fear, weakness, reluctance and laziness got in the way. I just couldn't go deep enough to make real changes. I wish I could because I'm certain it could help me, but I'm just not that sort of guy. That said, Veronica and I are still in touch and maybe one day I'll find the courage to go deeper. Veronica's daughter Mia got me into yoga, which I began in Liverpool when I was alone in the flat. I had a DVD of a teacher of Ashtanga yoga called David Swenson which I followed, and found myself getting fitter, slimmer and more flexible than I've ever been, which is great after years spent bending over a snooker table.

Whether there is a way back into snooker for me remains to be seen. If I put the practice in, six hours a day, seven days a week, then maybe. Am I prepared to do that? Probably not. Practising on your own for so many hours is lonely, and I think I'm past that stage. All I would like to do is play to a good standard, and in an environment that feels less like huge pressure and fear and more like fun. In fact, if snooker tournaments were more like poker events I'd be playing in them all.

Ever since I turned pro I've always enjoyed a game of cards between or after matches. Ian was never keen on me having a game of pontoon or three-card brag, thinking it would somehow take my focus away from the snooker, but in truth I've always had a touch of the gambler in me, no doubt inherited from my dad, though I'm not one for the horses like he was. When I practised at Broxburn I would always put a few quid into the fruit machines; if I won, it would invariably all go back in.

So when the current fad for poker started in the early 2000s I was immediately interested. I would watch it on the TV in the players' lounges and as the internet developed the game found a new home online. I remember being at a snooker tournament and seeing Steve Davis playing poker on his laptop. Intrigued, I had a go myself and found it to be a great way of passing what can be lengthy periods of time stuck in hotel rooms between matches. In fact, I recognised that it was becoming too much when I'd find myself playing until 3am on the day of a match which started at 10am.

I wasn't the only one. Quite a few of the players formed poker schools at the tournaments or they'd play online, not for big money because nobody was that good, but with a reasonable degree of success. Snooker players have something of an advantage in poker in that they can get straight back in to the action when something has gone wrong. For example, in snooker if you're fifty points up and you miss, letting your opponent clear up, then you just have to forget that frame and get on with the next one. It's the same in poker; if you've had a bad hand or lost money you need to control your emotions, clear your mind immediately and get on with the next hand.

My enthusiasm for poker is such that Betfred, who sponsored me some years back, paid for me to take part twice in the World Series event in Las Vegas. I came nowhere, not surprisingly, but it was great fun. Some years later, out of the blue I was made the offer of an appearance at the PokerStars Festival in London. I accepted, enjoyed it immensely and in 2017 I was asked to be an ambassador for PokerStars. This has led to tournaments in London, Marbella and Dublin (where I came 56th out of 544 after two days of play, earning 2,700 euros and getting a bigger buzz out of it than any of the snooker I've played for the previous ten years!).

So it's good fun and because I'm not the world's best player I don't need to take it too seriously – that's important to me. More involvement in the game would be great and as time goes by, I'd like to become known as a player who knows a bit about the game and is OK at it.

I mentioned in the last chapter that the whole celebrity thing has pretty much passed me by. My comfort zone is quite small, and I can't see myself stepping out of it to dance on ice or do the tango for the entertainment of millions of TV viewers. That said, I've been told many times that I've not made 'enough' of my name and my track record in sport. When Lauren and I are watching some reality-TV show she'll often say, 'Oh, you could do that . . .' and while I don't want to embarrass myself in the jungle – or anywhere else for that matter – I am aware that maybe I could do something unrelated to snooker in this area. For me, the barrier is one of self-esteem. I had 100 per cent of this during my best years in snooker, but away from the table I was shy and unconfident in all other aspects of life.

Recently I read a magazine interview with Graham Coxon, the guitarist from Blur, who was talking about his low self-esteem and saying that if you believe you're not worth much and you think nothing good will happen to you, then it won't. And this really resonated with me, because I've often felt that off the table I'm not worth much, and therefore why would anyone be interested in me? Which is why I've not put myself 'out there' – because I don't believe much will happen if I do. Recently, I was telling a friend that I was finding it hard to book a table at a popular London restaurant and they said, 'Why don't you ring them up and tell them who you are?' And in all honesty, it has never once occurred to me to do this – I'm just not that kind of person. Yet I'd like to hope that, in time, people might see me as more than just a snooker player.

With that in mind, I accept an offer in 2017 to appear on *Celebrity MasterChef*. I love food and cooking and have an ambition to open a deli or small restaurant one day. Anyone who follows me on Twitter knows that I regularly post pictures of dishes I've eaten, mostly in China, and this is how the people at *MasterChef* become interested in me as a contestant. Anyway, I agree and, very nervous, am transported to a studio in east London to take part in the first of three trials: an 'invention' test, a stint working in a restaurant and the opportunity to cook a familiar dish. I'm a keen fan of cooking shows, including this one, so I hope that I'll fare reasonably well under pressure. When I arrive I'm relieved to find that the other contestants – Jim Moir (better known as comedian Vic Reeves), newsreader Julia Somerville, tennis player Henri Leconte and TV presenter Angellica Bell – are as nervous as me. The first task is to open a box and cook whatever is inside within an hour. At that moment it feels like I'm about to open proceedings at the World Championship. There is a sudden lurch of nerves but once I start I'm fine. I cook a fillet of spiced lamb with accompanying potatoes, peas and a sauce, and I finish around twenty minutes early. I wander around the set, seeing what everyone else is up to, and then I have the idea of cooking a fried egg and topping off my dish with it. I reckon everything tastes better with a fried egg or a bit of bacon on top!

The next round is a kitchen experience. I've watched a lot of chefs at work in my time, but never quite appreciated just how hard and stressful it is. But I've always wanted to give it a go, so I'm quickly shown how to cook a cod dish and sent off to my station. I don't think I've ever experienced anything so manic – all the yelling and shouting, and food being rushed here and there. At one point I have seven pieces of cod on the go; three pieces to be ready in three minutes, two in two minutes and another two in one minute. The chef is constantly shouting, 'How long for the cod?' and I'm feeling a touch flustered. Luckily, there is a sous chef around to lend a hand if necessary. It's a bit like a snooker match – intense at the time but thrilling to look back on. And it gives me a whole new respect for chefs and kitchen staff who put in so many hours doing this stuff. I don't think I'll ever complain about a restaurant dish again.

The final task is cooking a dish you're familiar with. I do a beef carpaccio starter, very similar to one I've seen Jamie Oliver do, followed by halibut that I've watched James Martin do on TV – I'm obsessed with cooking shows. At home I'm used to cooking this dish with a glass of wine in my hand and just generally chilling over it, but in the studio the clock is ticking, and I feel very much under pressure. The judges eat everything cold, because they can't eat all the hot food at once, but I cook as though I'm at home and everything needs to be ready at once. I should've paced myself more evenly, with the result that I finish too early. I don't cook the wine out of the sauce and the fish itself isn't properly cooked.

As they taste it, I know I've blown it, and usually I can cook these dishes with my eyes shut. My mistake is that I cook dishes done by TV chefs and I think that has gone against me. Had I thought it out, I'd have done a great steak and chips with a béarnaise sauce, which is something I know I can cook consistently well, even under pressure. Anyway, out I go, and I'm devastated. I still haven't watched the show itself – it's too embarrassing. I can't believe I messed up so much – it's like losing a big snooker match. Even so, the one nice thing that comes out of it is when a couple of the other contestants say to me, 'We can't believe you're like this. You're so chatty and sociable!' I guess I haven't exactly given off much of a warm impression over the years, so it's pleasing that people see through the 'iceman' thing to who I really am. I was more comfortable in that environment than I thought I would be, and with a bit of luck I might get the chance to take part in another cookery show one day.

And I confess – I did have an interview for *Strictly Come Dancing*! I really wasn't sure at all but my new management persuaded me to at least talk to them, so I went along. Let's not beat around the bush – after talking to them they didn't want me, which I was very relieved about. It's a huge commitment between August and December each year and you really have to put everything into it. Also, it's far, far out of my comfort zone. It's a great show, but I'm not comfortable in that showbiz world and I couldn't bring out the level of emotion required to be a contestant on there.

That said, at some stage I will have to leave my self-protective shell if I want to broaden my employment horizons. I'd love to do something cooking-related again, and it would be great to tie this in with my travels in China. Perhaps presenting to camera in a non-snooker-related setting would be something very different and interesting for me.

Top
5
SPORTS I LIKE
WATCHING ON TV
1. Golf
2. Football
3. Poker
4. Formula One
5. Cricket

EPILOGUE

April 2018: It's that time of year again and I'm packing my suitcase and heading to the World Championship in Sheffield. Preparing for the event now doesn't give me the same buzz as it once did – I still wish I was packing my cue along with my clothes – but even so I look forward to arriving at the Crucible, walking through the backstage area, down the steps and on to the floor of the arena. To this day, just being back there gives me goose bumps.

I enjoy the atmosphere around the building and socialising in the Champions Lounge, where players past and present gather to swap stories, share jokes and talk snooker. And the atmosphere here is like no other; when the likes of Ronnie O'Sullivan gets on the table the same hush and sense of excited anticipation descends on the audience as it has always done.

Although I'm there, I miss not 'being there' – in my natural home at the table, going up through each stage to the quarters, semis and final. And winning the event, of course. I'm known as the 'King of the Crucible', of course, and I always laugh when I hear the joke that my pipe and slippers are waiting for me underneath one of the tables. As I've said, I'm a bit envious of those still doing what I did. If I'm commentating on the final of the World Championship I tend to go straight home afterwards rather than hang around; although I'm pleased for whoever wins, it still hurts to see someone else lift the trophy. If I could still play the way I used to I'd be tempted to give it another go. But I can't, so I won't. Besides, I'd have to qualify now and with the greatest respect, I can't get inspired by playing three matches at a local leisure centre before heading to the Crucible. If the qualifiers were to be played at the Crucible itself then maybe I'd think again, but as it stands I don't have to make that decision. And I get to play there on the Legends tour, so it's still special to walk down the steps towards the table holding a cue, even if the stakes are nowhere near as high.

I'm often asked if I think I was the best snooker player ever, or, if not, who do I think was, or is? I usually say that, on my day, I could beat anyone then, and if I still had the same form I could beat anyone now. As a commentator I watch players all the time and some of them are brilliant, but no one is playing any differently to me at my peak and my records speak for themselves. A while back I watched a documentary about Tiger Woods and at one stage he was asked if he thought he was better than Jack Nicklaus. He said, 'As long as you're still in the conversation about who's the best player ever you know you've done something right.' I couldn't put it better.

Certainly, the game has changed a lot since I started playing. There have been ups and downs – from the wall-to-wall TV coverage in the 80s to the end of tobacco sponsorship and an uncertain future after that – but now it is in great shape, thanks to Barry Hearn's involvement. There are twice as many tournaments to play in as there were when I was around and the prize money this season totals some £20 million. So snooker today is in a very healthy state.

Also, there are more players around now playing to a high standard, particularly down the rankings where the standard has improved hugely since my playing days. However, players generally don't seem to want to dominate the game in the way Steve Davis and I did back in the day. They're different animals and I guess it's just about what you want from being a snooker professional. I was driven by the idea of winning more and more trophies. Rightly or wrongly, keeping winning was all I wanted to do, which is why it was so hard when I stopped winning and started losing. Also, I forget how good I was. People rave about certain players in tournaments now and sometimes I think, 'Was I as good as he is?' Then I see something on YouTube from one of my past performances and I say to myself, 'Yes, you were pretty good at this game.' And against some amazing players – Ronnie, John Higgins, Mark Williams – who are still in excellent form today.

I had a massive amount of success very quickly and it's arguable that such a high trajectory can't be sustained – in other words, what goes up must come down. The old football cliché that it's a game of two halves rings true for my career. The first half was all about dominating and taking winning for granted. The second half was marked by a downward spiral, from something that came to me so easily to a point where it became incredibly hard. The sensation of losing is so much more intense than that of winning. I took winning for granted, whereas I took losing very badly.

I've been very lucky to have experienced a career like the one I've had. Yet I'm not a big believer in luck – I think you make your own, in whatever field you're in. That said, I had an innate talent for playing snooker which may never have emerged had I not been given that little table for Christmas, aged twelve. So that was lucky, I guess, and I owe a huge amount of thanks to my mum and dad for making that call. There was also an element of luck involved in Ian Doyle coming into my life. If I hadn't played his son he may never have heard of me, and I might have been on the amateur circuit for ever.

After that, the luck stopped and, under Ian, the hard work began. Without any doubt, he instilled the work ethic into me that made me a champion. Results came quickly, and for that I owe him a great deal. In short, he got me off my arse in a way that no one else could've done. My dad always believed that my natural talent was enough, but he was wrong. I had to put in eight hours a day, seven days a week, to get anywhere. Ian also stopped me having to worry about anything other than my snooker, giving my career a solid footing.

I realise that he's not been portrayed as a saint in these pages but, overall, I look back at my time with Ian with fondness. There were many times I hated his guts and would moan about him to Mandy or John, calling him all the names under the sun, but as I've said, essentially it was me and him against the world for a long time. When I turned pro at sixteen, received wisdom was that I'd soon be destroyed, and the defeats I suffered seemed to indicate that. But he talked me up and had faith in me, and he pushed me towards all those titles. He took over my life, sometimes for the good – sometimes not. He treated me like his son, bollocking me in a manner he'd never employ on the other players who came into his stable later. But I wasn't his son; sometimes I just wanted to be my own person and was jealous of other players who had a far less authoritarian management.

I wonder now whether a less controlling regime might have worked out better for the second half of my career. By then I was a man with my own family and Ian couldn't control me as tightly as he did before. In a way I rebelled against him – the boot up the arse no longer worked – and perhaps that rebellion led to an increased complacency on my part. If the regime had been more relaxed from the start I might have been able to carry on playing tournaments for longer, not having crammed all the successes into a few short years. It says a lot about my attitude towards the game – that it was my job to win, and win well – that I never had and still don't have much snooker-related memorabilia around the house. I didn't care for the trophies themselves; they were props, something to have a photo with, and I never kept any at home. They were all displayed in Ian's snooker club. When I arrived home after a tournament the last thing I wanted was to be reminded of snooker, even in the years I was winning. I've kept two things as mementoes; the first is a casting of my hands, a copy of which is displayed outside Wembley Stadium as a reminder that I won six Masters tournaments at the now-demolished Wembley Conference Centre. Although I've not seen them in situ, I'm told they're in between the concrete hands of Kylie Minogue and Madonna. Not a bad place to be!

I've also kept the monkey . . . In 2012 I met the artist Damien Hirst, snooker fan and a friend of Ronnie O' Sullivan. We went out for dinner, and Damien promised that if I beat John Higgins in that year's World Championship, he'd give me a monkey in a glass box. It's not a sentence you hear every day, and although I did beat John that year, I heard no more about Damien's strange offer until the following year, when I was commentating for the BBC at the Crucible and Damien came again. He'd parked his car outside the venue and asked me to come out to see what he had for me. When he lifted his boot lid, inside was a large Perspex box containing a marmoset monkey, pickled in formaldehyde, dressed as a snooker player and sitting on a chair, cue in paw. Quite a gift! I drove home very carefully indeed, terrified of spilling the formaldehyde everywhere. However, the monkey and I arrived safely and he still sits at the side of my sofa, horrifying and intriguing guests in equal measure.

I'd like to think I changed the game of snooker in some ways. People say the shot in which I pot the blue and smash the reds open at the same time is something I invented. Sorry to say that I didn't! It had been done before, but I think I played it a lot sooner in the frame than anyone else. I certainly brought an aggression to the game and a style of going for everything, no matter how risky. Sometimes I'd miss but when I didn't the results were spectacular. My ability to win frames in one visit after potting a red was always good and at this, statistically, I was always streets ahead of others.

Some might say that my lack of emotion at the table counted against me, in that I was never the people's choice. I know that, and there have been many times I've wished it could've been different. I remember once queuing up at an airport security gate, just minding my own business, and I heard someone say, 'He's just as miserable off the telly as he is on it.' As if they expected me to come singing and dancing through security! Really, I just carried on where Steve Davis left off, showing no emotion, giving no advantage, just turning up to win. From him, I learned the art of giving nothing away. That said, I could never have been as cold as him in his prime. I'd always acknowledge the other players; I'd have found it impossible to walk past someone I knew and not say hello, as Steve could. I think players are generally more sociable now than then. There was always banter, but usually after the game. Now it's before, during and after. I couldn't do that at the beginning, and when I did do it, in the second half of my career, I think my game lost something because of it. Ian would be horrified now at the amount of socialising that goes on. I wasn't allowed anywhere with anyone when I was under his command, and today I still can't believe it when I see players chatting just before they go out to play a match. I'd have been told to stay away from my opponent and not make any conversation.

When you're playing snooker competitively from the age of thirteen and you become professional at sixteen, it's not easy to have what passes for a 'normal' life. I was always at the mercy of some schedule or other taking me here, there and everywhere. I'm not complaining; it's what I wanted to do, I did it and it led to so many new experiences along with the success. Although they separated when I was young my parents were never less than totally supportive of everything I did. They believed in me 100 per cent and never said, 'Don't you think you should be doing this or that instead of playing snooker?' They believed in my talent and put in the hours driving me around, ironing my shirts and generally looking after me until Ian took over. I'm still close to my mum, although having left Scotland now, I don't see as much of her as I did. But we talk on the phone and actually, since my divorce, we're closer now than we've ever been.

Sadly, my dad died in 2017. He was suffering from Alzheimer's and was diagnosed with cancer just a few months before his death. He and I had been somewhat estranged since my marriage broke up. For whatever reason I found it difficult to talk to him about what was going on in my life at that time and we drifted apart, eventually hardly speaking at all. I was devastated about this because he was my dad and he was always at my side when I was travelling to matches all over Scotland, trying to make a name for myself. At his funeral I carried his coffin and, although I was very upset, I felt more numb than anything else. We hardly spoke for two years, but in all honesty we never had that kind of father-son relationship that involves the big conversations. We were both quite reserved people that way.

Not having a normal life often excluded me from doing normal stuff and if I have regrets about this it's around my own sons. My drive was such that my usual reaction to doing most things was, 'I can't, I have to practise.' The work ethic instilled in me was such that I'd feel guilty if I even took a day off and in hindsight perhaps I could've been more flexible in this sense, especially when I became a dad. I always thought that snooker came first. Or, maybe more accurately, that *I* came first. Yet it would have been hard to achieve what I did without that attitude.

That said, I'm very proud of Blaine and Carter and the way they've turned out. They're amazing, polite and well-mannered boys, and that pleases me because I was brought up to say 'please' and 'thank you' and to show respect for other people. At the time of writing Blaine is at university studying business, while Carter is still at school. They're different in personality – Blaine is more like me, while Carter takes after Mandy – and they're very much their own people, which I admire about them.

Blaine showed an early natural talent for snooker and, when he was eight, he joined the junior league at the club I practised at in Stirling. I didn't want to pressure him in any way, although occasionally he'd ask me for advice and I'd show him something. Then he'd say, 'That's not how we've been taught to do it at the club.'

'Well,' I'd reply, smiling, 'I might not know much about much but one thing your dad has some idea about is snooker!'

He improved quickly and while I had the feeling that he might not make a career in the game, he knew enough to look after himself on the table. He started playing in Scottish junior and amateur tournaments and won a few matches. My dad took pride in accompanying him, just as he'd done with me, and although I did go along occasionally, I didn't want to get in the way and become the focus of attention. Blaine took some stick over the fact he was my son, but I told him to ignore it and focus on his game which, to his credit, he did.

When the club closed Blaine would practise in the snooker room I'd built at home. He'd knock a few balls around, then come to find me and ask if I wanted a game. A lot of the time I'd say 'no' and, looking back, I feel bad about that. By that time, I was deep into the losing years and not playing well, and the last thing I wanted to see when I was at home was that snooker table. But it upsets me now to know he was in there playing on his own. I should've swallowed my misery and gone and joined him. As he became a teenager he started to live the life I never lived; having mates, seeing girls, going to the pictures and just hanging out generally. He played less and less snooker as he embraced his teen years and now does what I could never do – play the game for fun.

Carter is an extrovert and a real performer. As soon as he could stand he was dancing and singing and now he loves plays and the theatre. He's quite grown-up for his age and will say things that make you think, 'Where did that come from?' He's a right little character and I do regret that he never saw my own performances when they were good. Blaine was aware of my successes but would also be devastated when I lost and would notice how I was feeling about it when I got home.

There is no doubt they were affected by the divorce – Carter more than Blaine, I think. When I see them or speak to them they seem fine, but it's hard to know how they're really feeling. Mandy is a very good mother to them and I know they're happy at home but I'm sorry I don't see them as often as I'd like as they grow up. I hated having to tell them that we were splitting up, and why. It's something that will live with me forever and you always hope it won't happen to you. I hope that in the future I'll be able to have a closer relationship with them both. It'd be great if one day they might have careers that enable them to travel and see some of the places that I've seen. I'd really love them to have those sort of opportunities, and for their minds to be broadened as a result.

As for me – well, after an amazing career that has provided me with so many incredible moments, I'm in a very happy place both personally and professionally. I'm really looking forward to seeing what the rest of my life brings in terms of new career opportunities and horizons. I have ideas around snooker academies in my name, and maybe some form of higher-level coaching on the finer points of the game. I'm keen to expand my interests in cooking and travel and, as I've mentioned, perhaps combine them into a TV presenting role. I'm very proud of the work I've done, and still do, to promote Chinese eight-ball in its home country and I'd like to take that further, possibly by doing more snooker-related events in China. Although I'm not playing competitively now, and still miss the buzz that playing at the very highest level brings, I'm coming to terms with the fact that I will find satisfaction in different areas of my life and work. Even today, I am still happiest when it's just me and the table; just me on my own, potting balls and making breaks. It's where I'm most comfortable. In some way, shape or form I'll always have a cue in my hand. It's what I was born to do.

ACKNOWLEDGEMENTS

For the support and belief I received during my career in snooker I would like to thank my parents, Gordon and Irene, my brother, Keith, and all my family. Thanks to Ian Doyle for his vision and drive, and to Mandy and the boys, Blaine and Carter, for their support. I would also like to thank Veronica Leigh for her support and advice.

For bringing this book together, I'd like to thank Jane Aspinall and all the team at Bonnier Publishing. I would also like to thank Tom Henry for his editorial help.

PICTURE CREDITS

INDEX